THE POMPING FOLK
IN THE NINETEENTH-CENTURY THEATRE

Also by J. C. Trewin

THEATRE HISTORY AND CRITICISM
- The Shakespeare Memorial Theatre (with M. C. Day)
- The English Theatre
- We'll Hear a Play
- Drama, 1945–1950
- The Theatre Since 1900
- A Play To-night
- The Stratford Festival (with T. C. Kemp)
- Dramatists of To-day
- Edith Evans
- Mr Macready: A Nineteenth-Century Tragedian and His Theatre
- Sybil Thorndike
- Paul Scofield
- The Night Has Been Unruly
- The Gay Twenties (with Raymond Mander and Joe Mitchenson)
- Alec Clunes
- Benson and the Bensonians
- The Turbulent Thirties (with Raymond Mander and Joe Mitchenson)
- John Neville
- Theatre Programme (editor)
- The Birmingham Repertory Theatre: 1913–1963
- Shakespeare on the English Stage: 1900–1964
- Drama in Britain: 1951–1965
- The Drama Bedside Book (with H. F. Rubinstein)
- The Journal of W. C. Macready (edited)

AUTOBIOGRAPHY
- Up From The Lizard
- Down To The Lion

BELLES-LETTRES
- London–Bodmin (with H. J. Willmott)
- Lamb's Tales (completed: Nonesuch)

HISTORY
- Printer to the House (with E. M. King)
- The Story of Stratford-upon-Avon
- The Story of Bath

ECCENTRICITY
- An Evening at The Larches (with Harry Hearson, Ronald Searle)

PLAYS
- A Sword for a Prince: Plays for a Young Company
- Plays of the Year (32 vols.) (editor)

ALSO EDITED
- The West Country Book
- The Critic (Sheridan)
- A Year in the Country (Beach Thomas)
- Sir Walter Scott: A Prose Anthology
- Shakespeare's Country
- Footprints of Former Men in Far Cornwall (Hawker)
- *etc.*

THE POMPING FOLK

IN THE NINETEENTH-CENTURY THEATRE

Edited, with an Introduction, by
J. C. TREWIN

LONDON
J. M. DENT & SONS LTD

© Introduction and editing, J. C. Trewin, 1968
All rights reserved
Made in Great Britain
at the
Aldine Press · Letchworth · Herts
for
J. M. DENT & SONS LTD
Aldine House · Bedford Street · London
First published 1968

SBN: 460 03820 6

for
WENDY
who is used, by now, to the ways of
the Pomping Folk

CONTENTS

(The books mentioned were published in London, unless otherwise stated)

		page
	Introduction	xi
I	A CHICHESTER FESTIVAL Lord William Pitt Lennox *Plays, Players, and Playhouses at Home and Abroad:* 1881	1
II	MR COOKE William Dunlap *The Life of George Fred. Cooke:* 1813	11
III	THE SEAPORT STAGES Henry Whitfeld *Plymouth and Devonport: in Times of War and Peace:* Plymouth, 1900	20
IV	AFTER THE FIRE James Boaden *Memoirs of the Life of John Philip Kemble:* 1825	24
V	ACTING WITH THE SIDDONS William Charles Macready *Reminiscences*, edited by Sir Frederick Pollock: 1875	28
VI	HARLEQUIN KEAN 'Barry Cornwall' (Bryan Waller Procter) *The Life of Edmund Kean:* 1835	33
VII	STROLLING Edward Stirling *Old Drury Lane: Fifty Years' Recollections of Author, Actor and Manager:* 1881	37
VIII	COMEDIAN OFF-STAGE Julian Charles Young *A Memoir of Charles Mayne Young, with Extracts from the Journal of J. C. Young:* 1871	49

CONTENTS

IX	A GUINEA A WEEK *Fifty Years of Green-Room Gossip; or, Recollections of an Actor:* 1865 (reprinted 1881)	W. Donaldson	56
X	AMATEUR NIGHTS *Sketches by Boz:* 1836	Charles Dickens	61
XI	RESPECTABLE ACTORS *Recollections and Reflections:* 1872	James Robinson Planché	66
XII	DOLPHIN AND FOTHERINGAY *Pendennis:* 1849	W. M. Thackeray	70
XIII	A PINT OF PORTER *The Stage: Both Before and Behind the Curtain:* 1840	Alfred Bunn	82
XIV	GREEN-ROOM *Dramatic Reminiscences:* 1860	George Vandenhoff	85
XV	MANNERISM *Players and Playwrights I Have Known:* 1888 George Vandenhoff: *Dramatic Reminiscences:* 1860	John Coleman	90
XVI	PALACE BY THE LAKE *The Lady of Lyons:* 1838	Sir E. Lytton Bulwer	94
XVII	IMOGEN AND PAULINE *On Some of Shakespeare's Female Characters:* Edinburgh and London, 1885	Helena Faucit, Lady Martin	98
XVIII	A FORGOTTEN HAMLET *The Stage: Both Before and Behind the Curtain:* 1840	Alfred Bunn	104
XIX	LOLA MONTEZ OBLIGES *Thirty-Five Years of a Dramatic Author's Life:* 1859	Edward Fitzball	109
XX	THE ECCENTRIC MR KNOWLES *Recollections and Reflections:* 1872	James Robinson Planché	113
XXI	MEMS. BY BUNN *The Stage: Both Before and Behind the Curtain:* 1840	Alfred Bunn	116

CONTENTS

XXII	FROM THE THEATRE ROYAL *Fifty Years of an Actor's Life:* 1904	John Coleman	120
XXIII	FANNY KEMBLE ON TOUR *Records of Later Life:* 1882	Fanny Kemble	127
XXIV	IN THOSE DAYS *Edmund Yates: His Recollections and Experiences:* 1884	Edmund Yates	133
XXV	ACTING WITH MACREADY *Records of Later Life:* 1882	Fanny Kemble	138
XXVI	THE CURATE'S DAUGHTER *Rambles Beyond Railways:* 1851	Wilkie Collins	141
XXVII	LIZZIE ANN *The Drama of Yesterday and To-day:* 1899	Clement Scott	149
XXVIII	RETURN OF POST *The Life and Theatrical Times of Charles Kean, F.S.A.:* 1859	John William Cole	153
XXIX	THE DUST HOLE *The London Stage: Its History and Traditions:* 1889	H. Barton Baker	160
XXX	PIGMY INDIGNATION *The Players:* February 1860	Wilfrid Wisgast, M.A.	166
XXXI	THE YOUNG SOLDENE *My Theatrical and Musical Recollections:* 1897	Emily Soldene	170
XXXII	SWORD AND DAGGER *The Wheel of Life:* new edition, 1898	Clement Scott	176
XXXIII	DUNDREARY *Edward Askew Sothern: A Memoir:* 1889	T. Edgar Pemberton	180
XXXIV	CRITICISM *The Life and Theatrical Times of Charles Kean, F.S.A.:* 1859	John William Cole	187
XXXV	PERIOD PIECE *The Players:* May 1861	Tom Taylor	191
XXXVI	SWEETHEARTING *A Memoir of Charles Mayne Young, with Extracts from the Journal of J. C. Young:* 1871	Julian Charles Young	196

CONTENTS

XXXVII	A FRENCH JULIET	Henry Morley	198
	The Journal of a London Playgoer, 1851–1866: 1891		
XXXVIII	AN ITALIAN LEAR	Joseph Knight	202
	Theatrical Notes: 1893		
XXXIX	WRITING THE PLAY	Freeman Wills	205
	W. G. Wills: Dramatist and Painter: 1898		
XL	DOWN ALONG	Dutton Cook	209
	Nights at the Play: 1883		
XLI	STRATFORD, 1879	Sir Theodore Martin	213
	Helena Faucit, Lady Martin: 1900 (and other sources)		
XLII	ONE NIGHT ONLY	Clement Scott	217
	The Drama of Yesterday and To-day: 1899		
XLIII	AN ACTOR CALLS ON TENNYSON	Frank Archer	221
	An Actor's Notebooks: 1912		
XLIV	'CARELESS, IMMORAL AUTHORS'	Clement Scott	228
	The Drama of Yesterday and Today: 1899		
	Last Words		**230**

INTRODUCTION

I

DURING the eighteen-seventies my mother, who was the fourth of six sisters—a brother, Courtenay, came midway—lived on a hidden Southern Cornish farm beyond the oak-shelved, heron-graced shores of Helford River, and a few bowshots from the hamlet of St Anthony-in-Meneage. With three others of the family she walked through sinuous, tangled lanes to school in the larger village of Manaccan. A labourer who watched them as they hurried past in the mornings would say, a little teasily: 'You do blaze through like the pomping folk.' When angrier, he would have still more to add about the pomping folk; from what I heard of him (and he could quote at will the most alarming fragments of the Book of Revelation) he was, without knowing, a figure thoroughly theatrical. But then Cornish people, in spite of the surviving Puritan view of the stage, have always been innately dramatic. I cannot think that any of them would have responded to *Othello* quite as naïvely as Julian Charles Young's Warwickshire coachman did ('It ran upon sweethearting'). Though Henry Irving was Somerset-born, I have long suspected that he owed what we are told was his haunted quality to those imagination-kindling years, as Johnnie Brodribb, with his Penberthy aunt and uncle at Halsetown behind St Ives.

The Manaccan villager would have packed Irving in with the rest of the pomping folk, for neither he nor his neighbours could have classified and selected. A player was just a player. In any event, nobody strolled, or pomped, in this corner of Cornwall among the riparian hamlets and branch-charmed valleys. All their lives my mother and her sisters spoke of pomping when they meant any kind of acting, or, loosely, flamboyant display. Certainly, too, I heard the word used sternly in my own youth, far from any playhouse, at The Lizard, a dozen miles southward from Helford River, and beyond the emphatic plateau of Goonhilly. Invariably I thought of actors as pomping folk; I use this now for all who had their hour upon the stage, not simply for the occasional strollers in their temporary booth. The grumbler of Manaccan and Pinero's Sir William Gower (*Trelawny of the 'Wells'*) would have understood each other, though Sir William's term was 'gypsies'. (He melted at last in remembering that 'splendid gypsy', Edmund Kean: I believe myself that Macready must have been the greater all-round actor of the two, but that is irrelevant.)

Borrowing from a dimming world, the river-threaded remoteness of nearly a century ago, I have sought to give a composite portrait of the Pomping Folk, from Tragedian to the pond-life of General Utility. There are the people of the barns and gaffs and canvas theatres, as in Wilkie Collins's description of the Sans Pareil at Redruth, fifteen years or so before my mother was born; the people, too, of more urban companies, Crummles-fashion, even if I have not depended upon such familiars as Vincent himself, Mrs Crummles, who was 'the original Blood-drinker', Mr Lenville and Mr Folair, Miss Snevellicci, and the infant Phenomenon. (The work of Edward Stirling and John Coleman shows the Crummles company as it might have been in life.)

Then there are the metropolitan players on tour—Fanny Kemble, with faithful maid—and the Bohemians of London, for the theatre, in spite of such an influence as Macready, was based upon the very sea-coast of Bohemia. Other personages also. From many sources the pomping folk return in their primary colours and their varieties of plumage—from the outer circuits where they toiled between the towns, walking sometimes to save the fare, and from London both before and after 1843 when the 'Patent' houses, the Theatres Royal of Drury Lane and Covent Garden, shed their preposterous monopoly.

During the first half of the century an actor on, say, the Nottingham circuit could be put up for Hamlet at a week's notice, and told: 'If your professional pack don't contain the article, I can't help it.' Actors had to have many parts in reserve. With the lights of London as a mirage far ahead, they would move with 'professional pack' from one cluttered dressing-room to the next, among the same litter, the cracked, mottled make-up dish, the cardboard helmet, the dagger; in their nostrils a reek of pomatum, a hint of orange-peel, the smeech of a candle carelessly snuffed. This was also the time of the formal dignity of the Covent Garden Green-Room, and of the pomp of leading players who, though at the crest of their profession, were still (to the snobbish) gypsies, rogues, vagabonds. Towards the end of the century the profession was establishing itself. Irving had been knighted (1895); Frank Benson—and we can discount the belittling legends—ruled a touring university of the stage; the old circuits and the stock system had vanished, and touring companies were out from London in regiments: as the railways had developed, so had the mobility of the pomping folk. It was far from the night when G. F. Cooke, as remembered (more or less) by the ageing Lord William Pitt Lennox, came to appear with the local troupe at Chichester: an example of the habit, long-enduring, by which a great man travelled round from one set of minnows to another, acting for an appropriate fee in the kind of interminable programmes then expected.

Here are the pomping folk, and here are their plays. It was a sad period for the drama. Apart from Shakespeare, often garbled, a few other classical pieces, and a multitude of stock melodramas and comedies (observe that dreadful line of Tom Taylor, 'Where truncheon-like my fan I used to wield'), companies in the first half of the century had to search in a current drama that was merely arid: pompous plays for the pomping folk: clotted prose, or tushery (frequently in iambics) that reminds us of Dryden's 'dwarfish thought dressed up in gigantic words, repetition in abundance, looseness of expression, and loose hyperboles'. Again and again there recur the names of Lytton (*The Lady of Lyons*, written when he was Bulwer, became a standby), and of the copious Sheridan Knowles, particularly *The Hunchback*:

> *How know you me for Master Walter? By*
> *My hunchback, eh?*
> *Heav'n made me, sir, as well as them and you.*
> *'Sdeath! I demand of you, unhand me, sir!*

Walter is revealed during the last few minutes as the real Earl of Rochdale; but the strong theatrical figure is Julia, his daughter, a part that all young actresses coveted. Fanny Kemble created it; the author himself was the first Hunchback (Covent Garden, 1832), and Charles Kemble the first Sir Thomas Clifford, another showy part.

Macready, though he toiled to help the dramatists of his period, found nothing that would live. Bulwer Lytton, at the farewell banquet (1851) did his best: 'Who does not recall the rough-and-ready vigour of Tell, the simple grandeur of Virginius, or the exquisite sweetness and dignity and pathos with which he [Macready] invested the self-sacrifice of Ion? * And who does not feel that, but for him, these great plays might never have obtained their hold upon the stage, or ranked among those masterpieces which this age will leave to posterity?' Posterity has not been grateful. In the sixties, with the coming of T. W. Robertson, and, later, with the new drama, the sky lightened; but that story belongs to the pomping folk of the twentieth century.

II

We begin now with George Frederick Cooke, first at Chichester, and then confiding to his diary. Next, a local historian's view of two south-western seaport stages. We may remember Q's impression of the Theatre Royal at Plymouth in *The Mayor of Troy* when, ante-dating both the erection of the theatre and the craze for nautical drama, he arranged for his visiting Mayor (Major Solomon Hymen) to be press-ganged during the performance of *Love Between Decks; or, The Triumph of Constancy*. (Text by Q; Orlando B. Sturge, as Tom Taffrail, crying: 'Hear me, kyind Heaven! for Heaven is at least my witness that beneath the tar-stained shirt of a British sailor there may beat the heart of a Man!')

From Plymouth we go to the London scene on the morning after the 1808 fire at Covent Garden, with John Philip Kemble ('Black Jack') trying to shave; to Newcastle and the young Macready acting with Sarah Siddons four years before his own London adventure; to a Harlequin exploit of Kean at Exeter, according to 'Barry Cornwall's' first popular *Life*; to provincial pomping in the eighteen-thirties and forties; to the eccentricities of the metropolitan comedian, Charles Mathews; to the other end of the scale, an old stroller on life at a guinea a week; to Dickens on

---

* These plays were by Knowles (*Virginius* and *William Tell*) and T. N. Talfourd (*Ion*).

stage-struck amateurs, Planché on 'respectable actors', and Thackeray (in the novel of *Pendennis*) on the Fotheringay and 'Mr Dolphin'. The name disguises the figure of Alfred 'Poet' Bunn, showman of Drury Lane (and of Covent Garden), who was Macready's rancorous foe. John Vandenhoff describes the etiquette of the Green-Room; John Coleman speaks of the influence recognizable in every period, of a major actor upon his juniors; two passages, one from the play itself, and another from a book by Helen Faucit, who created Pauline, evoke the show-piece of *The Lady of Lyons*. There is Bunn again, upon an amateur tragedian as persistent as the better-known 'Romeo' Coates; and the name of Edward Fitzball—who had a single meeting with Lola Montez—may remind us of Dickens's Theatrical Young Gentleman: 'He looks upon Mr Fitz-Ball as the principal dramatic genius and poet of the day.'

So to the wayward Sheridan Knowles; to Bunn once more, in his own journal; and to Coleman pomping with the Robertsons, Fanny Kemble pomping in luxury, Edmund Yates recalling himself as a young playgoer, Fanny Kemble in Macready's clutches (they had strong opinions of each other), and Wilkie Collins taking a long, ironical glance at *The Curate's Daughter* in the canvas booth of the Sans Pareil: I doubt whether news of this special 'blaze' travelled from Redruth to Manaccan. We trace the story of 'Lizzie Ann', who was Adelaide Neilson. Charles Kean, as actor-manager, and Douglas Jerrold, as haughty dramatist, correspond with growing acerbity. We visit the 'Dust Hole' (its portico still stands) in the years before the teacup-and-saucer sequence of Robertson, and read—from a transient stage journal—a leading article that puts Wilfrid Wisgast, M.A., on a level with Pott and Slurk.

Emily Soldene summons the early 'halls'; Clement Scott, most prolific theatre journalist of his time, talks of stage fights ('that's two of his weapons'); and the name of Dundreary brings from the darkness a pair of whiskers, an eye-glass, and a long frock-coat. John William Cole exposes the wrong kind of drama criticism; a *pièce d'occasion* by Tom Taylor reminds us of a project that was never developed; Julian Charles Young's coachman tells him what really happened in *Othello*; three celebrated critics review a French Juliet (Colas), an Italian Lear (Rossi), and a popular melodrama, Cornish style: clearly we were desperate creatures down along. Freeman Wills remembers W. G. Wills (who now remembers either of the brothers?); the Stratford Festivals begin on a drenched April night in 1879, after a flicker of temperament by Barry Sullivan; Clement Scott observes a one-night run ('They pulled the carpet deliberately from under the feet of the author and his companions'); an actor, visiting Tennyson in 1885, is vastly impressed by the privilege ('He passed me an ivory pepper-mill with the query, "Have you seen this dodge?"'); and we end with a word from 1899 upon the vagaries of the Censorship.

III

It has been a long journey: one in which I have not tried to be inclusive. Many famous events and people are off-stage: the Robertson plays, for example; Irving at the Lyceum. Often I have gone to sources seldom explored now; in places I have silently cut or condensed. One familiar voice still insists on being heard, so here for a moment only is Vincent Crummles (*Nicholas Nickleby* *):

> 'Does no other profession occur to you, which a young man of your figure and address could take up easily, and see the world to advantage in?' asked the manager.
> 'No,' said Nicholas, shaking his head.
> 'Why, then, I'll tell you one,' said Mr Crummles, throwing his pipe into the fire, and raising his voice. 'The stage.'
> 'The stage!' cried Nicholas, in a voice almost as loud.
> 'The theatrical profession,' said Mr Vincent Crummles. 'I am in the theatrical profession myself, my wife is in the theatrical profession, my children are in the theatrical profession. I had a dog that lived and died in it from a puppy; and my chaise-pony goes on in "Timour the Tartar". I'll bring you out, and your friend, too. Say the word. I want a novelty.'

He will have it: a new dramatist, a new show-piece, the insertion of a real pump and two washing-tubs (bought cheap at a sale). 'They will look very well on the bills in separate lines, "Real pump! Splendid tubs! Great attraction!"....'

* Dickens's novel appeared in monthly instalments during 1838-39.

Off goes Crummles, satisfied; Nicholas more dubiously. As they go, the pomping folk fade with them, the great attractions vanish, candle-light wavers, gas-light dims. Stentorian voices, the roll of the thunder-sheet, distant clapping, a cry from *The Lady of Lyons*, '*Mille diables!* I should like to see her married to a strolling player!': all dwindle and die. We are left, from a mid-Victorian April, with the sound of a slow Cornish voice as the girls whisk by between the brambled hedges: 'You, Annie James!... You do blaze through like the pomping folk.'

J. C. T.

Hampstead, 1967.

AUTHOR'S NOTE

I am most grateful to my wife, Wendy; to Elvira Niggeman, Herbert van Thal, Ivor Brown (who looks at 'pomp' and 'pomping' in *Chosen Words*), and the resolute ghost of Wilfrid Wisgast, M.A.

I
A Chichester Festival

LORD WILLIAM PITT LENNOX (1799–1881) was the fourth son of the fourth Duke of Richmond and Lennox, whose estate was at Goodwood, Sussex, and whose Duchess gave the ball in Brussels on the night before Waterloo. William was nearly ten years old when he saw George Frederick Cooke playing Shylock and Sir Archy MacSarcasm (in Macklin's farce, *Love à la Mode*) at the old Chichester theatre. Though he did not record this reminiscence until the end of his life—he died, aged eighty-one, in the year when his *Plays, Players, and Playhouses at Home and Abroad* was published—it is a plausible impression of a strange figure.

Cooke, born in 1756, was an actor of bold, coarse authority, particularly in such parts as Shylock, Iago, Sir Archy, and Richard III. A man with a square, hook-nosed face, wide mouth, and eyes set far apart, he glowers at us from British theatre history as if expecting trouble. In life he had plenty of it; quarrelsome and intemperate, he seems to loom across the stage of his period, a glass permanently in his hand. Again and again, in London and elsewhere, he failed to appear when announced, or had—among angry heckling—to apologize for inability to proceed: 'Ladies and gentlemen—my old complaint— my old complaint!'

At Covent Garden during June 1810, as Falstaff in *Henry IV, Part I*, he spoke his last words in the London theatre, 'I'll purge, and leave sack, and live cleanly as a nobleman should do.' That autumn he was in New York, and in America he remained until his death (of dropsy) on 26 September 1812. During the following year William Dunlap published a biography which, I imagine from internal evidence, Lord William Pitt Lennox had beside him when writing *Plays, Players, and Playhouses*. (But the date of the Chichester performance was 27 May 1809, not 21 July.)

THE FIRST dramatic performance that I attended was at Chichester, early in the present century. My father being in Ireland, Goodwood House was shut up, and myself and my brother Frederick were at a farmhouse at Stoke, preparing for Westminster School. When passing a barn, my attention was attracted by the following posting bill:

THEATRE, CHICHESTER,
Friday, July 21st, 180–
MR GEORGE FREDERICK COOKE,
The Celebrated Tragedian
Will have the honour of appearing in two of
his most favourite characters,
Shylock in 'The Merchant of Venice'
and Sir Archy MacSarcasm in 'Love à la Mode',
For further particulars see small bills.

As we stopped for a few minutes to arrange the harness, I descended from the vehicle and read the announcement over and over again. I had heard of the delights of a theatre from many a young companion; I had seen characters and scenes descriptive of the gorgeousness of 'Bluebeard', the 'Blood Red Knight', and 'Lodoiska', had laughed over the tricks and transformations in 'Mother Goose', had peeped through a glass at a fair when 'Obi, or Three-fingered Jack' and 'Harlequin Magic' were performed, all for the small sum of one penny; but a regular play I had never attended.

I was recalled to real life by the approach of my tutor, who appeared in the highest spirits, caused, as I was afterwards informed, at the thought of seeing this truly eminent tragedian.

'Why, what are you studying, my boy, so intently?' he inquired.

'A playbill,' I meekly responded.

'What, Cooke, the great actor, coming to Chichester to act two of his best characters! That would be a treat indeed.'

We proceeded on our way; during the whole of the drive I could think of nothing but the play, and my joy knew no bounds when my tutor promised to take us to the theatre on the following Friday.

Upon reaching Chichester, we secured five front seats in the boxes, and then proceeded to the house of Captain Humphreys, to invite him and his wife to accompany us to the play. This the worthy militiaman's wife cheerfully assented to, inviting us to dine with them at four o'clock on the evening of the performance. I will not attempt to describe my state of restlessness during the time that intervened.

Ths house was crowded to the roof, and the discordant sounds that issued from the occupiers of the gallery perfectly astounded me. The good old green curtain (deemed plebeian in the present day) was down, and a man in a carpenter's dress was lighting six tallow candles that were stuck into wet clay, and partly screened by dirty tin shades. The front of the boxes, the ceiling, and the proscenium were somewhat tarnished, and the figures of Thalia and Melpomene were a little worn and rather out of proportion. The musicians were perched up in a small division in the centre of the orchestra—a regular bandbox, as a wit in the gallery called it, the rest of the seats having been thrown into the pit. The stage doors had been removed, and two small private boxes erected in their stead; these were reserved for the officers of a cavalry regiment stationed at the barracks. The pit was full almost to suffocation, and there was not much room to spare in the boxes.

A somewhat boisterous appeal from the gallery for music, and the orchestra, reduced to a squeaking fiddle and a spasmodic clarionet, performed two of Haydn's symphonies and an overture in an almost incredible space of time. At last, after a great deal of yelling, shouting, hallooing, cat-calling, during which the roaring of lions, warbling of cats and screech-owls, with a mixture of the howling of dogs, was judiciously imitated, the curtain rose and disclosed a scene in Venice as unlike the view of that fairy city 'of wealth the mart', which I had been accustomed to see at Richmond House, my father's London residence, from the pencil of Canaletto, as the Adriatic Bucentaur is to a Thames sand-barge.

Three personages now appeared, looking more like Venetian bravoes than the honest merchant and his two friends, and I became thoroughly engrossed with the plot of the play; it is true that the interest was not a little marred by the imperfect manner in which the trio delivered themselves of their respective speeches. The scene was followed by one between Portia and Nerissa, Portia flaunting about in a bright, cherry-coloured cotton velvet, elaborately ornamented with tinsel, spangles, and imitation gold lace, while her waiting woman appeared in a very faded satin dress such as no English Abigail would condescend to wear. Unquestionably, the costumes of both mistress and maid gave the spectator a poor opinion of the wealth and taste of the Belmont heiress.

No sooner had these two ladies left the stage than a breathless silence ensued, which was almost instantaneously followed by shouts that rent the air. Shylock appeared; the applause increased. After a time he commenced, 'Three thousand ducats—well. For three months—well. Antonio shall be bound—well.' These words were uttered in such a tone and given with such an expression that my whole feeling was with the actor. I could think of nothing else; I listened, I gazed, I watched every movement, every muscle. Not a word, not a look, escaped me; and although, perhaps, the opinion of so youthful a critic may be deemed presumptuous, and some allowance must be made for the excitement attending a first play, I have never had any reason for changing the impression thus early formed that Cooke as Shylock stood unrivalled.

During the time that he was off the stage I was all impatient for his return; the drolleries of Launcelot Gobbo, his practical joke with his 'sand' or rather 'high gravel' blind father were lost upon me. Nor could the melodious strains of the pretty Jessica, represented by a dark-eyed maid of Judah, captivate my senses. This young syren was the *prima donna* of the company; her dress, if such a term can be applied to the very scanty apparel that unadorned her person, consisted of a short tunic and a very scant pair of Turkish trousers.

With a thorough contempt for time, place and action, Miss Woolf, as the Hebrew Melodist was called, had stipulated for the introduction of two popular ballads, and, to the surprise of the Shakespearean audience, where the usurer's daughter soliloquises,

> O Lorenzo,
> If thou keep promise, I shall end this strife,
> Become a Christian, and thy loving wife

she proceeded as follows: 'But should you prove faithless, then will the hapless Jessica know no peace of mind; all will be dull and dreary; for in the words of the popular ballad, "What would be this dull town to me if Lorenzo was not here?"' At this introduction, the band struck up 'Robin Adair.' The other occasion for this unclassical interpolation was equally inappropriate; for, when Jessica's lover asked, 'How cheer'st thou?' she replied:

'Happy and content as the inmate of the lowly cot by Afton's crystal stream. How lovely it glides and winds among the green trees:

> How wanton thy waters her snowy feet lave,
> As gathering sweet flow'rets she stems the clear wave.'

At this cue the leader, tapping his rosined bow against the tin candlestick, played the opening bars of 'Mary of Afton Water', another favourite melody of the day.

The fourth act had commenced. Shylock, with balance in hand, was gloating over his Christian victim, and was preparing to take the pound of flesh, when an event occurred that nearly paralysed the audience. In whetting his knife, to cut the forfeiture from the bankrupt's breast, the blade slipped, and nearly severed the actor's thumb; in a second the stage was deluged with blood. A cry for surgical aid was raised by those who witnessed the accident from the side-boxes and front row of the pit; but to those who, like myself, were at a little distance, and were totally unacquainted with the plot of the play, the effect was terrible. I watched the agonized look, the writhing expression of the suffering man as he attempted to staunch the blood, and was about to reward his truly living personification with a round of applause when the curtain dropped, and the manager came forward to request the indulgence of the audience until the medical practitioner could decide whether Mr Cooke would be enabled to go through the remainder of the performance.

The cause of the accident was soon buzzed about throughout the house, but did not reach my ears. The great George Frederick Cooke was no teetotaller, and, having dined rather freely at 'The Swan', had got a little elevated. A few glasses of whisky-punch, and brandy and water during the first three acts, had produced a strong effect, and by the time he had arrived at the trial scene the 'potations pottle deep' began to tell.

The manager again made his appearance to claim further indulgence, as the medical man had not yet made his report. During the necessary delay the majority consoled themselves by refreshing the inward man with all the delicacies the house could furnish—adulterated porter, mixed ale, flavourless ginger-beer, sour cider, stale cakes, unripe apples and acrid plums. To me the suspense was most painful, for I could not help entertaining a fear that the performance would terminate, or that some other farce would be substituted for the one announced. After a few minutes of watchful anxiety the manager relieved the minds of the audience by reading the following bulletin:

> 'I, the undersigned, certify that the injury Mr Cooke has met with is not likely to be attended with serious circumstances, and that no fear of tetanus need be entertained. The wound, though inflamed and painful, has been brought into a state of apposition, and maintained in that position by adhesive plaster and bandage. (*Signed*) GILBERT FORBES, M.D.'

The manager continued: 'Ladies and gentlemen, under these gratifying circumstances, Mr Cooke, ever anxious to fulfil his duty towards his kind patrons, will have the honour of re-commencing the fourth act of *The Merchant of Venice* and trusts that he will be able, with your indulgence, to go through the part of Sir Archy MacSarcasm.'

The address was received with shouts of applause, and the trial scene proceeded. There was no diminution of the actor's vigour, and the curtain fell amidst cheers from all parts of the house. I had now but one wish ungratified, and that was to go behind the scenes to see and converse with the great tragedian, and this was soon brought about. The heat had been so intense throughout the evening that I gladly availed myself of my tutor's proposition to get a little fresh air. As we stood under the small portico of the theatre, enjoying a slight southerly breeze, the manager addressed us, expressing a hope that he might announce a performance under the immediate patronage of myself and my brother.

'I fear', responded Mr Taylor, 'that the Duke would scarcely approve of such a step, but if you like to say "under distinguished patronage", we will make up a party and attend the performance.'

'A thousand thanks, sir. Perhaps you would like to see Mr Cooke; if so, it will afford me much pleasure to take you behind the scenes; we are rather cramped for room.'

'It will afford me much gratification,' replied our dominie. Following the manager up a rather perpendicular ladder, we reached the box over the stage-door, then used as the stars' *sanctum sanctorum* in which the cash-taker at the doors, after the receipts were taken, temporarily placed the amount; here, too, the checks were counted, the playbills filed, and here all sudden changes of dress took place, subjecting too often the hurried actor or actress to the chance of breaking their limbs in their hasty descent. Here, too, the manager's wife, the leading tragedienne and Portia of the night, was enabled, through a small aperture which opened on the first circle, to count the house, so as to ascertain whether her numbers tallied with the return. Whenever a star visited Chichester, this box was given up to the newcomer as a dressing-room. We were then ushered into the presence of the suffering man.

The apartment was about five feet in breadth and ten in depth; the floor was covered with a coarse, showy-looking drugget; the walls were distempered a bright amber colour; a wooden chandelier, with four tallow dips, hung from the ceiling; a looking-glass, from which a considerable quantity of the mineral fluid had escaped, a deal table, and a few rickety chairs, formed the remaining furniture. From pegs in the wall hung the Jew's gaberdine, his hat, wig, beard and stick. An embroidered coat and waistcoat and a powdered peruke, were in the hands of the dresser and coiffeur, ready to be put on. The great man himself was seated in a state theatrical chair, covered with purple velvet and gold tinsel, by the side of the small table, upon which were sundry decanters and wine-glasses, hot water, lemon, and sugar; and a bottle of brandy had just been brought in from a neighbouring public-house.

While another bandage was being applied by Mr Forbes, who

had followed us into the room, I had a good opportunity of scanning the physiognomy of the great tragedian. The most prominent features of his countenance were a broad, long, hooked nose, dark eyes full of fire and expression, a strongly-marked and flexible brow, a high forehead, a mouth capable of delineating the worst passions of our nature. Cooke's manner was polished and refined until maddened with the inevitable spirit of wine; and, as at the time I saw him he had partly recovered from his excess, nothing could surpass his urbanity.

'Sit down, Mr Taylor; take a chair, my boy. A capital bowl of punch,' said the actor, as he filled three tumblers with this most potent beverage. 'So I hear you like my Shylock. I was rather wild in the trial scene; but wait for the farce, I'll give it them in my best style.'

With all the enthusiasm of youth, I launched forth into a criticism upon his unrivalled performance.

'Another glass, my boy?' I modestly declined, and he proceeded: 'If you come up to London, send your name into me at the stage-door—you must see me in Richard the Third.' Bowl after bowl was now vanishing, and the strength of the punch was evidently operating upon the principal toper.

'The audience are getting impatient,' said the manager. 'Would you kindly finish dressing?'

'Impatient?' responded the tragedian, raising his voice from the low tone in which he had been speaking to its sharp, emphatic key. 'Tell the Chichester people that George Frederick Cooke will not be dictated to by them; I that have acted before royalty will not stoop to these Sussex rustics.'

The manager did all in his power to soothe the ruffled temper of the star.

'Fill your glass, my friend, I drink to your health,' continued the histrionic hero of the night.

'Thank you, Mr Cooke,' responded the manager; 'but pray consider the audience, the lateness of the hour, and your kind friends, the British public.'

'All right, my boy. Go and tell them that I'll soon astonish their weak minds.'

A sound of hissing and cat-calling was now heard, and the wretched manager, anticipating a riot, again urged Cooke to prepare himself for the performance.

'It shall be done—I will arraign them straight,' he replied, and was rising from his chair when the entrance of the prompter gave another current to his thoughts.

'Sim, my dear boy, a glass of punch?'

The prompter was all gratitude; before, however, he sipped the liquor, he ventured to make one more appeal urging the danger a further delay might cause.

'Avaunt!' cried Cooke in his sharpest and shrillest tone. 'One word more, and I'll walk out of the theatre. Let the money be returned to the disontented crew; I'll none of it.'

Fortunately for the manager's interest, a simple remark made by a stripling produced more effect. 'Is Sir Archy as good a part as Shylock?' I inquired with boyish curiosity.

'I forgot; you shall see, and judge for yourself.' So, starting up, he finished dressing, and with a chuckle said, in a strong Scotch dialect 'Vary well, vary weel, hear what Sir Archy has to say.'

We lost no time in returning to the box; and when the curtain drew up for the farce, the actor had so far recovered his senses, that, being perfectly 'up' in the part, as it is technically called, he went through it with the most consummate ability. At the conclusion of the performance I crossed the stage and shook hands with the great man.

'I shall expect to see you in London, my boy,' said he. 'You must not judge of me by my Shylock of tonight. Come to Covent Garden, and you shall see it to perfection.'

'I hope I shall,' I responded.

Alas, that expectation was never realized. I passed the Christmas holidays in London. On the 28th of December Cooke was announced for Shylock at Covent Garden Theatre, with the following cast: Bassanio, Charles Kemble; Gratiano, Farley; Shylock, Cooke; Portia, Miss Norton; Jessica, Miss Bolton. I easily prevailed upon my tutor to accompany me there; and having taken our seats in the front row of the pit—stalls were not then in prospective existence—we anxiously awaited the performance. 'He'll not appear tonight,' said an elderly gentleman who sat next to me. 'So I fear,' replied another. 'What a degradation!' exclaimed a third.

After remaining in an awful state of suspense for more than half an hour, an apology was given for Mr Cooke, who had not made his appearance at the theatre. Amidst marks of disapprobation and tumult, Mr Charles Kemble was permitted to go through the character.

For a length of time I could not drive the actor from my thoughts, and it was with sincere grief and dismay that, a few years afterwards, I read the following announcement: 'On the 26th September, 1812, at New York, George Frederick Cooke breathed his last; aged fifty-seven years and five months.'*

Thus ended the life of one gifted with the highest endowments: a warm heart, a generous nature, and a mind far above that usually allotted to mortals. Had he combined with these advantages prudence and good conduct, he would have been handed down to posterity as one of the brightest ornaments the stage ever witnessed.

WILLIAM PITT LENNOX

Editor's note: This should be fifty-six years and five months; but Lord William was probably copying Dunlap.

II

Mr Cooke

GEORGE FREDERICK COOKE kept, by fits and starts, a journal that might continue for several weeks, or, as on 23 September, 1802, close after a single morning and five words, 'Arose a quarter before seven'. The fragments show little of the 'old complaint', though there are suggestions: 'October 22, 1805.—Sciolto in *The Fair Penitent*. From the last mentioned night until the 28th of November, *from various causes*, I did not appear.' He cannot restrain his sardonic humour; but his journals have intervals of demureness almost comically staid. I have not quoted the rather dull entries from his confinement—at the plea of his creditors—in Appleby gaol, Westmorland, during the winter of 1807. On 19 December that year he wrote: 'For these ten weeks past, I have neither tasted pork, ham, bacon, poultry, fish, eggs, puddings, or game, one partridge excepted. Except my provisions being fresh, I have lived as if at sea. The bread, coals, and candles, are not good, and the wine I have drank—I wish it had been better.'

The fragments of journal are interspersed among the two volumes of the biography by William Dunlap, one of Cooke's last intimates, the American author, manager, and artist. Published in 1813, it had the comprehensive title, *The Life of George Fred. Cooke (late of the Theatre Royal, Covent Garden). Composed principally from Journals and other Authentic Documents left by Mr Cooke, and the personal knowledge of the Author. Comprising Original Anecdotes of his Theatrical Contemporaries, his Opinions of various Dramatic Writings, &c.*

The theatre at Bristol was the Theatre Royal, King Street. Orsino is in 'Monk' Lewis's melodrama, *Alfonso, King of Castile*; Bajazet is the Sultan of Turkey in Rowe's *Tamerlane*. Master

Betty, the 'Young Roscius', was fourteen when Cooke played Glenalvon to his Douglas in January 1806; they had acted the same parts in December 1804.

Bristol, September 2 1802.—AROSE BETWEEN six and seven. Employed some time in writing; altered and marked the first edition of the tragedy of *Alfonso* from the prompt-book of the Theatre. Read the letters I received the evening before; one from Mr Hutchinson, a painter at Bath; the other from a lady whom I received one from while at Plymouth, and by a strange mistake, addressed the answer to her husband. I shall neither answer the husband nor Mr H. Breakfasted and dressed; at half-past eleven went to the theatre, and rehearsed Orsino, or, rather, read it, as I have almost forgotten every line of it.

September 3.—In the evening played Orsino and Sir Archy [*Love à la Mode*]. I do not think I ever played Orsino better. This is my first and, as yet, only original part in London. The play is the production of M. G. Lewis, Esq., M.P., author of *The Castle Spectre* and the notorious romance of the Monk. This gentleman's imagination seems entirely taken up with murders, ghosts, old castles, and ancient Spanish ballads. There is certainly some good writing in *Alfonso*, but both fable and construction are miserably bad. It abounds with so many improbabilities, and even impossibilities, that to point them out would be an endless task. It is a sanguinary tale, for the four principal characters die violent deaths. One lady poisons another, and is stabbed by her lover, who, after mortally wounding his father in battle *by mistake*, stabs himself, and leaves a half-dead king behind to mourn the catastrophe. The author, resolving to be singular in every respect, published his play with a conceited, impertinent preface, *before* it was acted; and the last act, materially different from the licensed manuscript.

In the farce, the part of Mordecai was most shamefully mangled by a whiffling monkey-looking thing of the name of Treby.

Sunday, September 5.—In the 'Bristol Guide' is a copy of the playbill on the opening of the present theatre, one the 30th of May, 1766; among the respective names, not one is at present living. *The Conscious Lovers*, and the farce of *The Citizen*, are advertised, under the sanction of a concert of music, as the house was not until some years afterwards honoured with a patent. Supped between nine and ten, and ran through a novel, three volumes. I cannot much commend either the author or matter of it; in some passages I found it exceptionable. I often reprove myself for looking into a first volume of these too generally idle productions, as curiosity, however bad they are, generally impels me to pursue them to the end. In my humble opinion, a licenser is as necessary for a circulating library, as for dramatic productions intended for representation, especially when it is considered how young people, especially girls, often procure and sometimes in a secret manner, books of so evil a tendency, that not only is their time most shamefully wasted, but their morals and manners tainted and warped for the remainder of their lives. I am firmly of opinion that many females owe the loss of reputation to the insinuating, seductive, and pernicious publications too often found in those dangerous seminaries.

September 8.—Arose late, and sometime after eleven went to the theatre, and read Bajazet; looked over some pages; dined; walked out; went into a bookseller's shop and purchased 'Broad Grins', by George Colman the younger; price 5s. very dear indeed; went to the coffee-room at the Bush, drank some brandy and water, read several newspapers, went home, afterwards, to the theatre where I played Bajazet so very imperfect that I was obliged to cut out a part of the first scene in the fifth act—returned home, supped, and went to bed.

September 11.—The Scotch are certainly very national, but whether more than the English, Welsh, or Irish, I will not presume to say. They frequently carry their point, whether of good or evil tendency by a steady perseverance in adapting their behaviour to the exigence of the moment.

London, September 21.—About five, walked to the south side of Grosvenor Square, where I took my stand to see Mons. Garnerin re-ascend from St George's parade with a balloon, and a parachute attached to it, by which he was to descend; a little before six he rose in a grand and pleasing manner, and when at a great height, cut the fastening by which the parachute was attached to the balloon, and in a few minutes alighted in safety in a field near the Small-pox Hospital, St Pancras. The basket in which he descended was very much agitated as it came near the earth, and gave serious apprehensions for its safety. This is the first successful enterprise of the kind in this kingdom—returned home to tea, read, supped, then read over Falstaff—went to bed about eleven.

September 22.—The evening was warm, and the house [Covent Garden] crowded, particularly the pit and galleries. I never suffered more uneasiness on the stage. My last two acts, I am certain, must have been very bad; I was scarcely able to stand —took a coach home; supped, and went speedily to bed.—I shall defer saying any thing of the play until some future occasion.

London, December 14 1805.—Read a part of Mr G.'s comedy. Destitute of every point of dramatic merit, and totally unfit for the stage. How blinded, either by ignorance or partiality, are some who pretend to dramatic judgment!

December 16.—A clergyman, a total stranger, and a horse-dealer, etc., who was almost in the same predicament, paid me a visit at the unseasonable time of between eleven and twelve, and staid with me, drinking rum-punch, until near two in the morning. The *modesty* of some people!

January 8 1806.—A little after one o'clock went to the house inhabited by Mrs St. Leger, at the bottom of Craven Street, and viewed the funeral procession on the Thames, from Greenwich to Whitehall stairs, of the late Vice Admiral Lord Viscount Nelson. Dined with Mrs St. L. and several performers of Covent Garden Theatre. In the evening went to the theatre, accompanied by a lady, and acted Glenalvon. Douglas, by Master Betty. Douglas is the only play of Home's that keeps possession of the stage. After the play, returned with the same lady in a coach to where we dined; drank coffee, played at cards, supped, and did not get to bed till after four in the morning. Before I retired to rest, I read 'a poem on the death of Admiral Lord Nelson, with hints for erecting a national monument, etc., dedicated (by permission) to Thomas Harris Esq., by Thomas Marshall.'

January 9.—Arose in the afternoon. Dined at New Slaughter's

Coffee-house, St Martin's lane, and afterwards adjourned to the old one. The funeral procession of the late Admiral Lord Nelson to St Paul's took place this afternoon, but I did not see it.

January 11.—Arose in the afternoon. Dined at the Swan Tavern, went to the theatre between nine and ten, and heard that Mr Allingham's new comedy was damned. There are a damned set of writers at the present day.

May 14.—Answered a letter yesterday, relative to playing at Buxton. The man who writes in the name of a Mr —— who, I presume, is the manager (and possibly cannot write), asserts that the house holds £60. This is a *lie*, but is quite consistent with managerial conduct. From the first theatre to the barn (with the exception of only two within my knowledge), their intentions are the same, although, happily, there are many blockheads among them who cannot execute those intentions. After tea remained in a thoughtful confused mood till ten, when I went to bed; before dinner glanced over *my own* character, in the 7th number of a paltry biographical publication, called 'The Modern Plutarch'— some assertions true,—others the reverse. The compiler places the characters rather whimsically. I am placed between Dr Samuel Parr and the late Duchess of Devonshire.

November 25.—After coffee went to see an elegant new theatre in the Strand. A tier of boxes go round the interior, and underneath is a very commodious pit. There is not any gallery—the decorations and embellishments are handsome and well fancied. I know not if it was built for any particular purpose; but at present it is open under the title of *Sans-Pareil*, and the entertainments divided into three parts—the first, 'The Rout', consisting of recitation and singing written, composed, spoken, sung, and accompanied by a young lady who never appeared on any other stage. The second, an optical illusion in the manner of the Phantasmagoria; and the third, much the same as the second, concluding with an artificial fire-work—the second and third parts of the entertainment are very pleasing.

November 29.—A young *private* actor, who made his first *public* appearance in Pierre [*Venice Preserv'd*] at Drury Lane on Thursday last, was taught the difference between the partial approbation of friends and the impartial decision of the public.

December 1.—Went to the *Olympic Pavilion*, a new wooden building erected in Newcastle Street, in the Strand, by the celebrated Philip Astley; it is circular; the roof, with a small dome, is composed of sheets of tin, and is supported by pillars. From the centre of the top, a circular lustre of cut glass, consisting of twelve separate parts, each containing four lamps, has a very pleasing appearance. The stage is on a level with the area for horsemanship, and the orchestra rather strangely disposed up stairs, on the left of the stage. A tier of boxes go entirely round the house, with the exception of the orchestra: the pit is underneath, and behind it, a small space between is the gallery. The scenery is well painted, and the dresses are appropriate. The performances, feats on the slack-rope and dancing, were well executed, but the concluding piece, which should be the best, was the most absurd, tedious, disagreeable piece of mummery I ever witnessed. It was only displeasure that kept me from falling asleep.

December 4.—About dusk was waited on by a gentleman, whose name I have forgot, who introduced himself to me as a tragic author. His play, I find, has been twice rejected at Covent Garden, but he hoped that through my influence it might be brought forward. I endeavoured to undeceive him in that point; however, I fixed on Monday next at eleven to hear him read his play, but from what occurred at the theatre during the evening, I am afraid I shall be under the necessity of disappointing him.

December 5.—Having never seen the Royalty Theatre, determined this day should be devoted to that purpose. Passed along Cheapside, Lombard Street, Fenchurch Street, and down the Minories, until I arrived at Tower Hill, and afterwards by a circuitous route, found myself in Wellclose Square. I more than encompassed it. I saw a poor woman with grey locks, but whose face did not quite correspond with them, stoop down, pick up two or three small crumbs of bread, and put them into her mouth. I called her back and gave her a trifle, and was angry with myself afterwards that it was not more; I feel assured she was not an impostor. I looked about in vain, in the neighbourhood, for a decent house where I might dine. I then found my way to Wapping, and past for the first time the new West India docks and warehouses. The latter are an immense building, and the whole premises occupy a large space. Weary and tired, I at length found the Blacksmith's Arms tavern and Coffee house near Miller's wharf, the place of inquiry for the members of the Leith and Berwick smacks, and luckily arrived in time to partake of a warm edgebone of beef. After dining, and looking at some newspapers, inquired my way to Wellclose Square, but it being yet early, went into a pastrycook's shop, and being almost at a loss what to ask for, I bought something more than a pound of plum cake, and ate two jellies. Quitting the shop, I sauntered about, went into a public house, called for a pint of porter which I just tasted, and found the tap room in which I was sitting was frequented by thieves, as the landlady said she was obliged to remove the fireside furniture, and that the lead of the clock had recently been stolen. The doors of the theatre still remaining closed, I went to another tap opposite to it. There were two foreign sailors smoking, and two or three other foreigners. I believe Germans—it seemed a foreign house. I called for a glass of brandy and water, which I never tasted. At length I crossed the street, and as I reached the box door, Mr John Astley had just got out of a hackney coach. I entered the house with him. He gave orders at the office to admit me and my friends whenever I presented myself—I went with him to the upper house, the first tier I mean, for there is a row on each side above, I believe shut up. The theatre is very plain, but neat; the house seemed to me something larger than the Haymarket; the pit is small, but I was told the middle gallery would contain a thousand people. I went downstairs, drank two dishes of coffee in the coffee-room, and seated myself in the second row of one of the front boxes. Among other company was a very civil Jew family (there seemed many of them in the house); I presented an orange to each of the two children, and received a piece of an apple from the mistress of the family. Mr Astley came into the box, as did Mr Upton (who is, I believe, the poet of the theatre) and a young man, a relative of Mr A.'s. The performance consisted of singing, dancing, and pantomimic exhibitions, in one of which Mrs Astley performed. At the conclusion, I returned by Rosemary-lane, and re-trod the streets I had passed in the morning, and arrived at King Street, Covent Garden about half past eleven. Supped and afterwards finished the life of a Lady of Pleasure. I have not had so long a pavement walk for some time; I wish I could add that it had been a pleasant one.

December 9.—At eleven Mr —— called by appointment. From that time until it was nearly dark, he detained me with conversation; and reading his tragedy. The subject, the death of

Octavia (who gave name to the play) and the marriage of Nero to Pompaeia, by whose arts Octavia was murdered. On his former visit he said something about my acceptance of thirty pounds to hear the play read, and when he had concluded, he took from his pocket-book two banknotes, one of which seemed to be a £20, and tendered them to me—they were immediately refused. Who, or what he is, I know not; but what I have set down will appear more remarkable when I add that he lives in a trading part of the metropolis, and is descended from foreign parents. I imagine he did me the honour to suppose that it was in my power to get his play presented to the public; whatever it might be, like most writers, he seems to entertain a high opinion of it himself. On my declining his payment, he asked me if I gave instructions in the English language. I told him I did not, but if he chose would endeavour to be of service to him in that way. He asked my terms; I had none; he thanked me, and we parted.

December 10.—Went into a box at the theatre, and sat about half the first, and the second act of the *Tempest*; first altered from Shakespeare by Dryden, with the advice and approbation of Sir William Davenant, and now *revived* by Kemble. Dryden was certainly highly censurable for altering, and daring to meddle with a piece replete with the flashes of Shakespeare's genius; lowering the beautiful simplicity of Miranda, and adding his own unnatural and indecent characters of Hyppolito and Dorinda. Since the period when Garrick appeared to the present, such a despicable piece of patchwork would have met with the reprobation and contempt it so justly merits. There were several marks o disapprobation by a part of the audience, and more, I am told, on Monday last, the first night of its revival.

December 11.—Reading last night in Captain Hunter, I found eight pages missing. When I buy from a bookstall, I must be more careful in future.

December 12.—I found in the evening a polite note from ——, requesting my acceptance of a dozen claret, which accompanied the note.

January 8, 1809.—A poor old woman begging in the street, attracted my notice. I rung the bell, resolved to send her a shilling, but ere the servant appeared, changed my mind to sixpence.

January 10.—The taste for good writing is vitiated; and very small part of theatrical audiences can relish or appreciate the writings of those to whom the stage owes its present establishment. The general veneration for Shakespeare is a nominal one. His faults are by the million esteemed, and his beauties little understood.

January 14.—At night, acted Iago. The Othello of Mr Young, tho' not what is called imperfect, was yet incorrect as to the text. Very hoarse during the play, and returned home much fatigued.

January 19.—Mr De Wilde, according to appointment, came, and took a full length drawing of me in Richard III. A part of the dress, etc., I put on. This is a complacency I must give up, as it irks me much.

January 26.—Received a strange, rhyming, anonymous letter by the twopenny post; gave it what it wanted—*fire*.

January 27.—Read the first act of the *Midsummer Night's Dream*. Quince, the carpenter, in the first act, while he is distributing the parts of the interlude intended to be performed before the Duke and Duchess, is interrupted by Bottom the weaver, who wishes to act more characters than one. This reminds me of some actors (as they are called), whom I have heard of, perhaps seen some, who would willingly act more than one. I have some years ago seen a man who, I have been assured, on the same night, and at the same time, *went on* for, or as it is phrased, *doubled* Hotspur and Falstaff. Those who have only seen plays in London, cannot have an idea of the wretched and preposterous shifts to which itinerant parties are often compelled. The Athenian actors, as in this play they are drawn, were *mechanics*. So are some of our actors, even of note! Some of them very dull mechanics.

January 30.—Being caught in the rain, I stood in a passage in Pall Mall, with two men in Turkish, or rather Moorish habits, and a black. I then adjourned to Hatchet's Coffee-house, so that I breakfasted twice. How many in this great metropolis have gone without any!

G. F. COOKE, quoted by WILLIAM DUNLAP

III

The Seaport Stages

IN THE first decade of the nineteenth century, Plymouth Dock (briefly Dock, and known later as Devonport), an area separated from Plymouth by the little buffer state of Stonehouse, had its own not very reputable theatre. Plymouth itself had a similar gaff near the centre of the town, at Frankfort Place. Foulston's Theatre Royal, with its massive Ionic portico—a building that would be torn down by civic stupidity as late as the nineteen-thirties—had not yet risen, though Q, in *The Mayor of Troy*, manipulated his dates in order to let Major Solomon Hymen be press-ganged during a performance of *Love Between Decks*. Henry Francis Whitfeld, in what must be one of the fullest local histories yet written, his *Plymouth and Devonport: In Times of War and Peace* (1900), described certain perils of playgoing and acting in the seaports during the Napoleonic wars.

THE DOCK establishment speedily developed licentious features, with sailors drinking from their bottles of rum, and passing the liquor to the dissolute women who were penned apart in the hope that they would thus be amenable to some decency. The seamen threw themselves into the spirit of the plays with deadly earnestness, and during one performance of *Othello*, a remarkable scene was witnessed. Rage and sympathy filled every gallant tar. 'Is the black brute allowed to cut her life-lines?' one asked his friend, and when Desdemona was seized by the throat as she lay in bed, his companion shouted 'I'm —— if I can stand it any longer.' Throwing himself over the side of the gallery, he called upon his companions to rush to the rescue, and in a minute Desdemona was torn from the grasp of the Moor. Othello bolted into the street, and rushed in terror through the back lanes to his home—dagger in hand, and with war-paint untouched.

In the pit respectable tradesmen were the victims of insulting exclamations and showers of nuts and orange peel; and, although the magistrates asserted the right of attending to preserve the peace, 'not only for themselves and their friends', they were as impotent as the manager to stop the debauchery in which sailors, soldiers and civilians indulged . . . Disgraceful interruptions and riots occurred in the narrow and badly-constructed galleries of both theatres, and rowdyism manifested itself in the dress circles as well. At one performance at Dock in 1808 a lady was insulted when the lights were lowered; and the officers indulged in a free fight. Captain Skinner was upbraided by a lieutenant, and the middies subjected him to such offensive epithets that he left the house. Similar scenes of shame and scandal occurred in 1810, when a midshipman of the *Tartarus* created a disturbance in the upper boxes; and, on being ordered by his captain to leave the theatre, retaliated with the mutinous observation: 'No martial law here!' His fellow officers used their whips and bludgeons upon the police; but the ringleader was carried bodily to his ship, publicly stripped of the uniform 'he had so shamefully disgraced,' dismissed the service, and sentenced to solitary confinement for two years. The effect of the example was very salutary. Although Jack continued to be as demonstrative in the pit, officers showed more restraint, and 'ladies of the first quality' again patronised the performances. . . .

During the abandon of war time, Jack was always in evidence as a source of mischief; and on one occasion, when a shipwrecked hero was buffeting with the waves, a sailor rushed to the rescue with a wild cry of 'man overboard!' Scrambling over heads, shoulders, seats, and slips, he dropped upon the stage, seized Don Juan by the leg, and triumphantly hauled him to the footlights despite all his struggles. When the acting-manager remonstrated, the interrupter directed a stream of tobacco juice in his face: 'Why, there was a man overboard, and no one shall be in distress so long as I can lend a hand!' Mr Hayne, a tragedian, was often the source of unconscious fun; and he would interpolate Othello's address to the Senate with a running commentary on the conduct of the disturbers in the upper boxes; 'Most potent, grave and reverend signiors, my very noble and approved good masters. (I'll tell you what, young fellows; I'll have everyone of you in custody before you are aware of it.) That I have ta'en away this old man's daughter, it is most true. (That young woman with blue ribbons is as bad as any of you.) True, I have married her. (What, are you at it again?)' She loved me for the dangers I had passed, and I loved her that she did pity them. (Now, if there's a constable in the house, let him do his duty.)' So irritable was this artist that the temptation was irresistible to play pranks upon him; and two ladies who were smarting under one of his caustic rebukes, sewed beneath the trailing part of the robe in which he went on as Richard the Third, a long and curly tail intended for a demon scene. Advancing to the footlights, Hayne exclaimed, 'Now are our brows bound with victorious wreaths,' and twitched the robe when the tail stood out much more prominently than his crooked back. Among paroxysms of merriment, he ran from the stage with the appendage in his hand, 'projecting like a bowsprit.'

A child of the veteran Jefferson's was trained to take the part of the baby King in *Macbeth*; and little Joe, having successfully emerged from rehearsals, was held in readiness on the occasion of a visit by Kemble. The possibility that the tragedian would alarm a nervous child on approaching him, stern of aspect and weird of voice, had not been taken into account; and when the boy was sent to confront the gloomy monarch, and Kemble, in his forbidding manner, demanded to know what form was this that rose like the issue of a king, and wore upon its baby brow the round and top of sovereignty, poor Joe was struck dumb with terror. Kemble glared and muttered madly, 'Why the devil don't you speak?' and still more terrified, the child shrieked, 'Let me down, let me down!' His request had to be complied with; and to Kemble's disgust, the audience was convulsed with laughter. On another occasion, as Holman was impressively reciting the

Ode, 'Alexander's Feast', a sailor leant over the gallery, and shouted in a tone 'that might have been heard above a whirlwind', 'Hold your jaw, you lubber, and give us a hornpipe instead!' So greatly did the sailors delight in making this demand at inauspicious moments that Kemble was warned that he might be requested to oblige. 'Well', he answered, soured by previous local irreverence, 'if they ask me for a hornpipe, I shall dance one.'

HENRY WHITFELD

IV

After the Fire

THE THEATRE ROYAL, Covent Garden, which had stood since 1732, was found to be in flames about four o'clock in the morning of 20 September 1808. Twenty-two persons, including firemen, perished. Seven houses in Bow Street were destroyed. Little was saved but the receipts of the previous night's performance of *Pizarro*, stored in the box-keeper's office.

As he described in *Memoirs of the Life of John Philip Kemble, Esq.*, 1825, James Boaden, the writer, made an early call on Kemble, who was then fifty-one. He found the great actor-manager ('Black Jack', Mrs Siddons's brother) in full tragic vein: not surprisingly, for the destruction of the theatre—caused probably by a smouldering piece of wadding from a gun fired during *Pizarro*—had been a terrible blow, and he would never recover from it fully.

THE most disastrous of seasons commenced at Covent Garden Theatre on 12 September, 1808. The entertainments of the evening were *Macbeth* and *Raising the Wind*. Mr Kemble had been unwell, but was now quite recovered. Mrs Siddons had not acted for many months; indeed a notion was abroad that she had absolutely retired from the stage. She had, however, returned to it in the best health, and at all events, in such characters as were now preferred, with even *augmented power*, the silent operation of experience and time. Together, these incomparable tragedians seldom failed in their efficacy upon the town; and an audience piled to the roof attested the attraction of Shakespeare and themselves. In eight days from this great feast of dramatic excellence, the splendid site of the triumph was a mass of flaming ruins ...

In the morning after the fire, as soon as I had breakfasted, I hastened to Great Russell Street, to ascertain the state of the sufferers, and give any little aid that I might be able to render. Honest John Rousham in silence let me in, and walked up stairs before me into Mr Kemble's dressing-room. He was standing before the glass, totally absorbed, and yet at intervals endeavouring to shave himself.

Mrs Kemble was sitting in tears upon a sopha, and on seeing me exclaimed, 'O, Mr Boaden, we are totally ruined, and have the world to begin again.'

Her brother Charles, wrapt up just as he came from the fire, was sitting attentive, upon the end of the sopha;—and a gentleman, much attached to Mr Harris,* who in and about the theatre was familiarly styled *old Dives*, with his back to the wall, and leaning upon his cane, sat frowning in a corner. It was not a situation that called for speech; our salutations were like those at a funeral. I took a chair, and sat observing the manner and the look of Kemble. Nothing could be more natural than for Mrs Kemble to feel and think of their *personal* loss in this deadful calamity. Her husband, I am convinced, while I saw him, never thought of *himself* at all. His mind was rather raised than dejected, and his imagination distended with the pictured detail of all the treasures that had perished in the conflagration. At length he broke out in exclamation, which I have preserved as characteristic of his turn of mind.

'Yes, it has perished, that magnificent theatre, which for all the purposes of exhibition or comfort was the first in Europe. It is gone, with all its treasures of every description, and some which can never be replaced. That *library*, which contained all those immortal productions of our countrymen, prepared for the purpose of representation! That vast collection of *music*, composed

* *Editor's note:* Thomas Harris, Chief Proprietor of Covent Garden.

by the greatest geniuses in that science,—by Handel, Arne, and others; most of it manuscript, in the original score! That *wardrobe*, stored with the costumes of all ages and nations, accumulated by unwearied research, and at incredible expense! *Scenery*, the triumph of the art, unrivalled for its accuracy, and so exquisitely finished, that it might be the ornament of your drawing-rooms, were they only large enough to contain it! Of all this vast treasure nothing now remains but the *Arms of England* over the entrance of the theatre—and the *Roman Eagle* standing solitary in the *market place*!'

Soon after this Lord Mountjoy, I think, and other friends, called upon them, and among the topics of consolation, his Lordship turned his attention to the general sympathy that would certainly be excited by such a loss. Indeed, said he, the world in general are highly sensible of what you have done for the stage. It will be but *gratitude* for the people to compensate your loss. Mr Kemble, with great ardour and quickness, turned himself round, and thus noticed the expression: '*Gratitude*, my Lord; the gratitude of the world and the people! My Lord, Christ was *crucified*; De Wit was *assassinated*; so much for the world and the people!'

There could be no doubt about the instances he gave. The agitated and impetuous feeling of the moment will perhaps excuse one of the allusions—besides, that it was *essential* the Saviour should suffer, for a world that, be it remembered he thought worthy of so great a sacrifice. And whatever may be said, and truly said, of the gratitude of the world and the people, Mr Kemble soon had the unspeakable delight to find that there were individuals who felt even the deepest interest in his merits and his misfortune.

Would I could be more particular in alluding to the munificent conduct of the *First Person* in the realm!—the *delicacy* with which the aid was given, the princely charm, which secured its reception! The terms which his Royal Highness had the condescension to use, written with his own hand, I could wish to be at liberty to make public; but I refrain, from the respect I bear to the illustrious giver, and my deference to the decision of my invaluable friend.

[On December 30 the Prince of Wales laid the foundation stone of the new theatre.]

Mrs Siddons looked extremely well, and wore a large plume of black feathers. She expressed a great deal of anxiety for her brother, Mr Kemble, who, from having been confined to his chamber for above a month, came forward upon the occasion, accommodating his dress to the ceremony, and stood bareheaded under the rain. Mr Kemble was indefatigable in his exertions; he was full dressed in blue and white, with white stockings. Mr Smirke, the architect, and Mr Copeland, the builder, were also present.

JAMES BOADEN

V

Acting with the Siddons

EARLY IN 1812, the young actor, William Charles Macready (1793–1873), was playing in his father's company at Newcastle-upon-Tyne. Sarah Siddons, most majestic of British actresses, on her progress from Edinburgh to her farewell in London, consented to spare two nights at Newcastle, as Lady Randolph in Home's *Douglas* and Mrs Beverley in Edward Moore's *The Gamester*. William, cast as Norval ('My name is Norval; on the Grampian hills My father feeds his flocks') and as the gamester, Beverley, was terrified, and with some reason. Sarah Siddons was Melpomene herself: how could he face her sombre splendours?

Writing his recollections after his retirement—they were published posthumously (1875), in the fragment, *Macready's Reminiscences*, with extracts from his journal—he remembered clearly what had happened on those nights in the North.

AFTER several rehearsals the dreaded day of her arrival came, and I was ordered by my father to go to the Queen's Head hotel to rehearse my scenes with her. The impression the first sight of her made on me recalled the Page's description of the effect on him of Jane de Montfort's appearance in Joanna Baillie's tragedy of *De Montfort*. It was

> *So queenly, so commanding, and so noble,*
> *I shrunk at first in awe; but when she smiled,*
> *For so she did to see me thus abashed,*
> *Methought I could have compassed sea and land*
> *To do her bidding.*

The words might have been written for this interview, for my nervousness must have been apparent to her on my introduction, and in her grand but good-natured manner she received me, saying: 'I hope, Mr Macready, you have brought some hartshorn and water with you, as I am told you are terribly frightened at me,' and she made some remarks about my being a very young husband. Her daughter, Miss Cecilia Siddons, went smiling out of the room, and left us to the business of the morning.

Her instructions were vividly impressed on my memory, and I took my leave with fear and trembling, to steady my nerves for the coming night. The audience were as usual encouraging, and my first scene passed with applause; but in the next—my first with Mrs Beverley—my fear overcame me to that degree that for a minute my presence of mind forsook me, my memory seemed to have gone, and I stood bewildered. She kindly whispered the word to me (which I never could take from the prompter), and the scene proceeded.

What eulogy can do justice to her! . . . I will not presume to catalogue the merits of this unrivalled artist, but may point out, as a guide to others, one great excellence that distinguished all her personations. This was the unity of design, the just relation of all parts to the whole, that made us forget the actress in the character she assumed. Throughout the tragedy of *The Gamester*, devotion to her husband stood out as the mainspring of her actions, the ruling passion of her being; apparent when reduced to poverty in her graceful and cheerful submission to the lot to which his vice had subjected her, in her fond excuses of his ruinous weakness, in her conciliating expostulations with his angry impatience, in her indignant repulse of Stukely's advances, when in the awful dignity of outraged virtue she imprecates the vengeance of Heaven upon his guilty head. The climax to her sorrows and sufferings was in the dungeon, when on her knees, holding her dying husband, he dropped lifeless from her arms. Her glaring eyes were fixed in stony blankness on his face; the powers of life seemed suspended in her; her sister and Lewson gently raised her, and slowly led her unresisting from the body, her gaze never for an instant averted from it; when they reached the prison door she stopped, as if awakened from a trance, uttered a shriek of agony that would have pierced the hardest heart, and rushing from them, flung herself, as if for union in death, on the prostrate form before her.

She stood alone on her height of excellence, her acting was perfection, and as I recall it I do not wonder, novice as I was, at my perturbation when on the stage with her. But in the progress of the play I gradually regained more and more my self-possession, and in the last scene as she stood by the side wing, waiting for the cue of her entrance, on my utterance of the words, 'My wife and sister! well!—well! there is but one pang more, and then farewell world!' she raised her hands, clapping loudly, and calling out 'Bravo! sir, bravo!' in sight of part of the audience, who joined in her applause.

It would not be easy to describe the relief I felt when this trying night was over. The next morning I paid my required visit at her hotel, and going through the scenes of *Douglas*, carefully recorded her directions, and, in a more composed state than I had been on the previous day, took my leave. I was, in ordinary terms, 'at home' in the part of Norval, and, of course, acted with more than ordinary care and spirit; But who that had ever seen it could forget her performance of Lady Randolph? In the part of Mrs Beverley the image of conjugal devotion was set off with every charm of grace and winning softness. In Lady Randolph the sorrows of widowhood and the maternal fondness of the chieftain's daughter assumed a loftier demeanour, but still the mother's heart showed itself above all power of repression by conventional control. In her first interview with Norval, presented as Lord Randolph's defender from the assassins, the mournful admiration of her look, as she fixed her gaze upon him, plainly told that the tear which Randolph observed to start in her eye was nature's parental instinct in the presence of her son. The violence of her agitation while listening to old Norval's narration of the perils of her infant seemed beyond her power longer to endure, and the words, faintly articulated, as if the last effort of a mortal agony, 'Was he alive?' sent an electric thrill through the audience. In disclosing the secret of his birth to Norval, and acknowledging herself his mother, how exquisite was the tenderness with which she gave loose to the indulgence of her affection! As he knelt before her she wreathed her fingers in his hair, parted it from his brow, in silence looking into his features to trace there the resemblance of the husband of her love, then dropping on her knees, and throwing her arms around him, she showered kisses on him, and again fastened her eyes on him, repeating the lines,

> *Image of Douglas! Fruit of fatal love!*
> *All that I owe my sire I pay to thee!*

Her parting instructions, under the influence of her fears for her son's safety, were most affectingly delivered. When he had fallen under the treacherous stab of Glenalvon, she had sunk in a state of insensibility on his body. On the approach of Randolph and Anna she began to recover recollection. To Randolph's excuses her short and rapid reply, 'Of thee I think not!' spoke her indifference, and disregard of every worldly thing beyond the beloved object stretched in death before her. Leaning over him, and gazing with despairing fondness on his face, she spoke out in her heartrending tones—

> *My son!—my son!*
> *My beautiful, my brave! How proud was I*
> *Of thee, and of thy valour; my fond heart*
> *O'erflowed this day with transport when I thought*
> *Of growing old amidst a race of thine!*

The anguish of her soul seemed at length to have struck her brain. The silence of her fixed and vacant stare was terrible, broken at last by a loud and frantic laugh that made the hearers shudder. She then sprang up, and, with a few self-questioning words indicating her purpose of self-destruction, hurried in the wild desperation of madness from the stage.

On that evening I was engaged to a ball 'where all the beauties' —not of Verona, but of Newcastle—were to meet. Mrs Siddons after the play sent to me to say, when I was dressed, she would be glad to see me in her room. On going in, she wished, she said, 'to give me a few words of advice before taking leave of me. You are in the right way,' she said, 'but remember what I say, study, study, study, and do not marry until you are thirty. I remember what it was to be obliged to study at nearly your age with a young family about me. Beware of that; keep your mind on your art, do not remit your study, and you are certain to succeed. I know you are expected at a ball tonight, so I will not detain you, but do not forget my words: study well, and God bless you.' Her words lived with me.

W. C. MACREADY

VI

Harlequin Kean

EDMUND KEAN, then the wildest of strolling players, aged twenty-two, was engaged early in 1812 to 'act every thing' in the company at the Exeter Theatre. The passage that follows is from the first attempted biography of a difficult subject, *The Life of Edmund Kean*, written by 'Barry Cornwall' (the poet, Bryan Waller Procter), and published—at first anonymously—in 1835, two years after Kean's death at Richmond, Surrey, in May 1833.

AT EXETER he opened in Octavian [*The Mountaineers*] and played successively Shylock, Richard, Othello, and other first-rate parts. In these he delighted the critics, but he did not attract the multitude. That honour was reserved for Harlequin. Nothing else would fill the house. The chequered character, with his wand, his brown cap, his black head, and his singular costume (a glorification of the tartan!) appears to operate as a magnet in country places. When Othello is deserted, and even Romeo's love-making fails, the hero of pantomime is sure to bring a crowd. Old mothers, who frown carefully upon the soft scenes of Juliet—daughters who are cold to their rustic lovers—are drawn irresistibly towards him. He is the conqueror of all hearts, the beau ideal of all imaginations, except for the few who choose to waste their leisure in the troublesome employment of thinking.

Accordingly, our tragedian frequently played Harlequin in the provinces. When he was first put up for this important part at Exeter, he proved to be really too ill to act. He was a Harlequin of such reputation that although another person of some pretensions undertook the part, the house manifested their disappointment loudly. At last he got better, and was able to act. The announcement was made with pride. The manager, who paid him five shillings per night extra, distributed handsome placards on which were written in vast letters, 'Mr Kean will RESUME the character of HARLEQUIN THIS EVENING.' Crowds ran to witness the performance. Kean did credit to his fame, and delighted everybody. And when all was over, and the good people of Devon were trudging home to their quiet hearths, full of the pantomimic wonders that they had witnessed, our hero, with a great coat flung over his patchwork dress, and bathed in perspiration, took his customary seat at 'The Red Lion' with his brother topers, and drank strong liquors until morning.

At Exeter, Kean rented some convenient rooms over a china-shop. Miss Hake, a little feather-dresser, was his landlady. Her tenants were the china-man, Kean and Mr Cawsey, a solicitor, These persons ruled over three parts of the house; the fourth being under the jurisdiction of Miss Hake and her sister. The two ladies, besides being very little, were very precise. Had they supposed Kean capable of the sin of tippling, even in a modest degree, he would never have been a lodger over the china-shop. But they let their rooms to him in one of his sober intervals, and the wild animal was in their quiet country before they were aware. At first, all went on smoothly. He continued to drink, indeed, but his draughts were swallowed at the Red Lion; and he never returned home until long after the Misses Hake were in bed. It seemed as though the halcyon had taken their second floor and had brought tranquillity in its train.

A single night was destined to dispel this charming fancy. Kean had been acting with spirit, as it turned out, and drinking with equal vigour, when a fellow, unaware of the foibles of actors, disputed the propriety of his performance. Our hero, who was not a man to receive a reproof silently, whether merited or not, retorted in unequivocal language. The critic replied in terms bitterer than before. Thus they went on, from bad to worse, waging a fierce battle with their tongues, until Kean, who thought that words were poor things in a case of this sort, started up, intimated that he was going for his swords, and aware that his foe (now beginning to be terrified) should fight him. He left the room accordingly, and ran to his lodgings for the weapons, having on his Harlequin costume.

Whether it was that a portion of his excitement evaporated by the way, or that it took a pantomimic turn, we do not know, but on his arrival at home he became more inclined to commit a few minor extravagances than the great one of killing his adversary for a foolish speech. He mounted the steps, entered the house (the door was not fastened), ran up the stairs, and, without ceremony, jumped, Harlequin-fashion, right through a glass door at the top. It was now three o'clock in the morning, and the smashing of the glass made a tremendous noise. Mrs Kean (who had been sitting up for him) was alarmed; Mr Cawsey, the solicitor, was alarmed; both the little Misses Hake were very much alarmed. Our hero recovered himself just as Mr Cawsey, in his nightcap, was putting his head out of his bedroom door. In another instant, Mrs Kean appeared; and shortly afterwards, scarcely visible in the imperfect light, peeped forth the two little Misses Hake in their night-dresses, trembling. Fronting them all, and gazing steadfastly at Mr Cawsey, who cautiously advanced, stood the tipsy Harlequin. That personage now threw himself into a position, set his arms akimbo, began rolling his black head round and round—quick—quick—quicker still—they thought it would never stop. At last, making a sudden spring towards Cawsey, he 'cleared' the solicitor (nightcap and all) at a bound, and disappeared like a ghost.

All was cleared up by Mrs Kean's confessions in the morning when the victims of this sad frolic regained their composure, and moralised (somewhat too much) on the heinousness of the offence. As to Kean himself, notwithstanding the entreaties of his wife (who followed him to his rooms, after his exploit), he insisted upon having his swords, seized them, after a struggle, with the air of a conqueror, and went off once more to the Red Lion, with a renewed desire for vengeance.

During the three following days he was neither seen nor heard of, by his wife or family. Then he returned, saying that he had 'been doing a noble action.' One is naturally inquisitive about noble actions. Even his wife, although she was ill in bed, betrayed some curiosity on the point; whereupon he informed her gravely that he had been drinking for three days with a poor actor who was about to leave Exeter, in order 'to keep up his spirits.' In regard to his adversary at the Red Lion, he said that 'the fellow was a coward,' and had fled. His swords, therefore, were happily unstained, and in good condition, and as fit for contesting the English or Scotch crown, with the Earl of Richmond or the Thane of Fife, as formerly. His quarrel excited in him no disgust towards his old friend, the Red Lion.

The professional course of our hero, during this sojourn at Exeter, was as full of variety as his heart could have wished. He played the leading characters in tragedy; he played the Harlequin; he played the musical part of Count Belino in *The Devil's Bridge*; he played the Prince in *Cinderella*; he taught Cinderella herself to dance; he instructed the whole corps-de-ballet. His reputation in the Terpsichorean art was so great that the proprietor of an Exeter paper (who was also a bookseller) suggested that he should take a room for the purpose of teaching dancing, and promised to send his own sons there. Kean declined, but offered to give the boys the required instructions. 'All I shall ask in return', said he, 'is an old Latin dictionary which I saw in your shop.' The bargain was struck, and the young booksellers (there were five of them) came to Kean's lodgings and stamped away before him every evening; he singing during the performance, but otherwise paying little attention to the improvement of his pupils. He was rewarded in the end with the Latin dictionary, with which he busied himself for a long time afterwards, culling words and phrases from it, and using and misusing them upon every occasion. He was as proud of his little incursions into the classical country, as an Oxford or Cambridge professor.

Previously to his leaving Exeter, he took a benefit (this was on the 20th April, 1812), and played Luke in *Riches*, William in *The Sailor's Return*, and Frederick, Baron Willinghurst, in *Of Age Tomorrow*. It appears that, in the course of the second piece, there was 'a treble hornpipe by Mr Kean, Miss Quantrell, and Mr Johnson'; and that 'tickets were to be had of Mr Kean, at Miss Hake's, feathermaker, No. 211, High Street.'

'BARRY CORNWALL'

[On the night of January 26, 1814, Kean would startle London as Shylock at Drury Lane.]

VII

Strolling

EDWARD LAMBERT, known as Edward Stirling (1807–1894), was an actor who had an early gruelling in various provincial companies; a prolific dramatist, who wrote 200 plays, with many Dickens versions; and a London manager, notably at Drury Lane. His wife (Fanny Clifton, born Mary Ann Hehl), was the actress famous on the Victorian stage as Mrs Stirling. In 1894, at the age of 81, she married Sir Charles Gregory as her second husband, and died twelve months later.

Stirling himself appeared first when he was fourteen, at a small amateur theatre off Goswell Road, London. 'The late Samuel Phelps,' he said, 'was one of the amateur actors in our motley troupe. We paid to act. Prices ran high for Shakespearean heroes. Thirty shillings enabled the fortunate possessor to strut and fret his hour as Othello or Macbeth. Fifteen shillings was the price paid for the Thane of Fife. Malcolm went at seven.' In 1829, as a professional, he found himself at Ware in Hertfordshire, acting on a stage of planks fitted up in a room at the French Horn inn, with settings of calico painted by the manager, and Joseph Surface's screen (*The School for Scandal*) a clothes-horse with a tablecloth pinned over it. Later, with another company, he was on tour in the small towns of Kent and Sussex. He described his experiences in the first of two volumes of a discursive, anecdotal work (1881) called deceptively *Old Drury Lane*, but with a secondary title, *Fifty Years' Recollections of Author, Actor and Manager*.

In the ensuing extracts, *Pizarro* is the drama adapted (1799) by Richard Brinsley Sheridan from the German of Kotzebue's *The Spaniards in Peru*; John Vandenhoff (1790–1861) was a tragedian who, in spite of a long period in London, had more provincial celebrity; and Tom (T. W.) Robertson, eldest of twenty-two children, was later the dramatist of *Caste*.

My wandering career led me to Master Brooke's pretty circuit—the small towns of Kent and Sussex—commencing at Tenterden in the Weald of Kent. Brooke in his 'salad' days had played kings, nobles, peasants, etc., at Drury Lane, minus words. He married a lady vocalist, and set up business on his own account, playing your Macbeths and Romeos himself.

The Theatre Royal, Tenterden, was situated in a stable-yard; the entrance to the boxes was through a cottage kitchen, with scenes painted on both sides; these did for everything, thus wisely economising labour. Our wardrobe was well worn, scanty and of antique cut; our lights oil-lamps. Our band numbered four; the leader, first violin, played second old man, sang Irish songs, and attended to the lamps: these important offices brought Harvey one pound per week, not a large salary for this village Costa. Our prompter acted tyrants, and painted, when required, at the moderate rate of eighteen shillings. The highest salary in this very primitive concern only reached one pound five, finding your own dresses. We opened with *The Foundling of the Forest* to an audience of one boy in the gallery; his sense of solitude caused him to fall asleep. Business improved, however, and *Hamlet* brought us six pounds odd. During our few weeks' season the theatre was well attended by the resident gentry, farmers, hop-growers, etc. Nelson's neglected daughter (the vicar's wife) came frequently to witness our performances.

HARE AND HOUNDS, HASTINGS.—Brooke's Theatre Royal (Rural). A converted barn—*converted* not in a religious point of view, but by whitewash, canvas, and wreaths of paper flowers into some sort of shape; our stage, rough deals lent by a friendly theatrical enthusiast, a neighbouring builder; boxes, chairs; pit, benches; gallery, standing-places; prices high, two shillings, one shilling, and sixpence. Strange to say, the place was nightly crowded with the first families in Hastings and four miles round, and vastly they enjoyed the fun.

On one important occasion we were playing *Pizarro* with extraordinary splendour and expense (so said our bills). Six Virgins of the Sun, procured with difficulty from the Hastings fishing population; eight Peruvian armed soldiers, farm-labourers, enticed by sixpence each and an order for their sweethearts to see our acting. 'Temple of the Sun', resplendent with gold and silver foil; 'altar sacred to the god of Peru,' a tea-chest, covered with calico. The Virgins in pure white, with golden suns (paper) hung round their fair necks, symbols of virginity; high-priest Brooke, robed and bejewelled up to his eyes; army, Virgins, court, Rolla, perjured Alonzo, King Ataliba, Orozembo, Cora, Elvira, concealed in white. A few in cloaks swelled our chorus, invoking the heathen gods. All this parade was by moonlight, a large hole cut in the temple, covered with gauze; behind this luminary a country boy, perched on a ladder, held two large candles. The solemn procession entered, a death-like silence prevailed in the front of the house, and the rustic visitors in the gallery were struck with wonder and delight. A wire extending from the roof of the barn, to guide a bit of sponge dipped in spirits of wine, at a given moment descended to light the altar, that is if the god assented and the man above held the wire tight. The invocation to the sun-god commenced; High-priest Brooke, with an awful and powerful voice, sang all the parts—out of tune. After much kneeling, crossing of hands, throwing up of arms, and sundry other movements, the priest and chorus burst out: 'Give praise, give praise, our god has heard.' (he must have been very hard of hearing if he had not). Lo and behold! the moon instead of the tea-chest was on fire, displaying the boy's face grinning through it. Alarm seized the audience—screams of 'Fire! fire!' A stampede took place, everyone rushing to the barn-doors—Virgins, army, and spectators—in one wild terror. Brooke rushed up the ladder, and was seen cuffing the boy's head; he quickly descended, and heroically taking his place at the tea-chest, sang 'Give praise, give praise, our god has heard!' This calmed the affrighted people, and our play proceeded amidst thunders of applause.

Encouraged by the 'Hare and Hounds' success, Brooke built a theatre in Hastings, and failed. He played there, a good company, with Charles Kemble as star, to £20. Rayner drew £5 etc. Wisely the theatre was changed into a chapel, paying its owners.

RICHMOND, SURREY.—Joined Klanert's company, playing tragedy, comedy, etc., to our veteran manager's Macbeths, Romeos, at the ripe age of sixty-four. An actor of small parts at Covent Garden, Klanert, on his own ground at Richmond, became an actor of great proportions—so at least he thought. Always letter-perfect himself, he imagined everyone else ought to be so. Unfortunately, on one occasion, I was very remiss when playing Malcolm to Klanert's Macbeth. I failed to speak the tag perfectly, not getting any further than

> My Thanes and kinsmen,
> Henceforth be—*(a pause).*

I had forgotten what they were to be. Dead tyrant lying at my feet: 'Go on, sir.' I tried in vain to raise my kinsmen and Thanes to peerages.

> *Irate Deceased:* 'Will you go on?'
> I whispered, 'I cannot.'

Up jumped the dead king. 'I'll speak for you, sir:

> 'Henceforth be earls,
> So thanks to all at once, and to each one
> Whom we invite to see us crown'd at Scone.'

And calmly lying down, he died again, loudly applauded and laughed at. I received my *congé* on the following Saturday.

Exit from England for Scotland. Hamilton, Inverary, Stirling; William Ryder, manager. Hard work and small pay, with the advantage, however, that living was cheap. My board and lodging seldom exceeded twelve shillings per week, and this with no stint. New-laid eggs were abundant in the Burgh of Hamilton. Mistress Macfarlane, the hen-wife, supplied me with them, bringing them to my lodging for twelve for a shilling. I tried one day to get fourteen. This highly incensed and offended the puir body and she cut off the supplies. I went to the market, endeavouring to re-establish myself in the gude wife's opinion. Alas! I failed. 'Dinna ye fash, Master Stirling; ye'll ha'e nae mair o' my hen's eggs. They shall nae tak' the trouble to lay 'em for fourteen a shillin', laddie. If ye maun ha'e cheap eggs, lay 'em yoursel'.'

I next entered into an engagement with Bass and wife, or rather with wife and Bass, for she ruled the roost—in Edinburgh, Dundee, Selkirk, and Perth. My reward for playing second tragedy, first comedy, and melodrama, amounted to thirty shillings weekly (when paid, which too often it was not). Nearly five hundred miles to travel, all comedy dresses to furnish, and to live on such a stipend! Rather different an actor's position nowadays, in this year of grace, 1880, with pieces running hundreds of nights, and salaries fabulously high for very little real work. A weary journey by the 'High-flyer' coach, starting from the Saracen's Head, Snow Hill (Mr Squeers's London quarters), on a cold November morning. It rained, snowed, and hailed the whole way, three days and two nights—outside! I opened in Dundee as Mercutio, playing every night, tragedy or comedy. Books being few, we had to write out our parts, conveying the books to each other—always ladies first. Bass never played regularly; a few shillings grudgingly doled out from time to time scarce kept life and soul in us. In sober literal fact we were well-nigh starved. And let the reader recollect that escape was not easy—there were no railways or cheap steamers running them. Our labours were divided between Perth and Dundee for three winter months, a wretchedly horsed coach conveying us to and fro, a distance of twenty-five miles. Acting Macduff to Vandenhoff's Macbeth in Perth, during our desperate combat my plaided kilt fell down, exhibiting my flesh-tights, to the disgust of many and to the delight of the gallery, McDonalds, Duncans, and Sandys. Confused beyond belief, I snatched up my garment, fighting Macbeth rapidly, encouraged by the gods' applause.

'Gi' it him, laddie; strike hame. Gi' him his parritch!'

Vandenhoff declined my Thane of Fife ever after.

Returning per Leith smack southwards, I found a temporary engagement at Windsor, with Sam Penley of Drury Lane, as manager. It was Race week. Eton boys were admitted for two shillings and sixpence each from six until eight; the signal for their departure was the ringing of the college bell. A pretty game they had, laughing and talking to the actors and actresses during their performances, shooting peas at the heads of the unfortunate fiddlers, sliding down pillars from gallery to boxes, etc. Penley, however, made money by this, and his regular audience came at eight from the races.

CHELSEA, SLOANE STREET.—A person named Dalby opened a small theatre in a garden, and engaged a company on the share system. My share for acting three parts in one evening—the Stranger, Philip in *Luke the Labourer*, etc.—resulted in twopence, and a walk home to Mile End. In his younger days, Staunton the famous chess-player and editor of Shakespeare, essayed acting here, but wisely abandoned it. Othello was not his forte.

OLYMPIC THEATRE. Dr 'Blue Pill' Scott, lessee. On my applying to the doctor for employment, he referred me to his manager, Monsieur Leclerc, father of Carlotta and Rose Leclerc. After waiting a long time on the stage, the great (small) man approached me, decked in a Turkish robe, with slippers and fez to match. My business stated, Leclerc asked me to recite Shakespeare's 'Seven Ages.' This done, I was dismissed with an abrupt and authoritative 'It won't do, sir, stick to your business,' and he disappeared, robe and slippers. A little disconcerted, I groped my way out at the dingy stage-door, reflecting that I had no business to stick to. In after-life Leclerc and I reversed positions. He became the applicant, and I the employer.

CHELMSFORD RACES, ESSEX, 1829.—Quakers' metropolis for grain and salt. The Aminadabs and Obadiahs had chosen a pretty place for their 'thys' and 'thous'. Billy Hall, nicknamed 'the Surrey Beauty' for his extreme ugliness, filled the managerial throne. We had sorry houses up to eight, when the racing folks came in at half-price. A severely contested County Election helped us considerably. Hall paraded the town with a band, utilising both the candidates' colours—orange and pink—on a large flag, inscribed 'Vote for Billy Hall at the Theatre. Billy is for Whig and Tory and his pockets full of money. God save the King. Come early. Good luck to you.'

GRAVESEND, 1829.—A good theatrical town. Ships going out and coming in filled the small theatre with sailors and their sweethearts. These, together with a few townsfolk and a sprinkling of fishermen, formed a lively audience, easily pleased with my first essay in authorship—a piece founded on Scott's *Kenilworth*, artfully rechristened *Tilbury Fort; or, The Days of Good Queen Bess!* It drew a house.

My next destination was Croydon, then a small place with few inhabitants ... Edmund Kean acted two nights with raised prices and to overflowing houses, in *The Merchant of Venice* and *The Iron Chest*: Gratiano in *The Merchant* and Wilford in *The Iron Chest* were allotted to me. Having arrived at the troublous but coveted honour of stage-manager, Kean wrote to me thus:

> St John's Wood, Nov. 8, 1829
>
> Sir.—I shall not require rehearsals for my plays; but be particular in your selection of Wilford. He is all-important to me. I will run through the library scene with him when I come down. He must be young, mind.
>
> Yours obediently,
> E. KEAN.

To Mr Stirling, Theatre, Croydon.

When Kean arrived, he sent for me to his dressing-room.
'You are rather tall, sir.'
Rejoinder: 'Yes, sir, what do you wish me to do?'
Kean: 'Why, in the Library scene, sink gradually on your right knee, with your back to the audience. When I place my hand on your head to curse, mind you keep your eyes fixed on mine.'
(No very easy task to look steadily into such eyes.)
'Is that all, sir?'
Kean: 'Yes—do whatever you like after that; it will be all the same to me.'
This was not quite so elaborate an affair as some of our modern tragedians' rehearsals. I pleased Kean and the audience by my acting of Wilford, and the great little man was pleased to say that 'I did it well—very well!'
Farrell made me an offer to act at the Pavilion. Tempted by the salary—two pounds a week—I agreed, playing first-rate comedy and seconds in tragedy. Charles Freer, our leading man, brought from Nottingham, was thus modestly announced: 'Garrick came from the East, why not another star from the same hemisphere? See Freer and judge for yourselves. At six our new Roscius appears in a great character: Come early to secure good places, but don't come with children in arms!' ...
Douglas Jerrold produced his *Martha Willis,* illustrative of

London life in the seventeenth century. Our manager dressed the piece in the costumes of 1830. The author of *Mrs Caudle's Lectures* resented this anachronism by bitter sarcasm, telling Farrell (who wore Hessian boots), 'D——n it, sir, I expected brains, not boots!'

[Stirling married the actress Fanny Clifton, and they left for the North, first Liverpool, then Manchester.]

QUEENS THEATRE, MANCHESTER.—Harry Beverly's direction. Myself and wife were engaged to lead the business; this proved very bad—salaries stopped, no resources. What was to be done? It occurred to me to try my hand at writing a piece for a benefit. The subject I chose was 'Sadak and Kalasrade.' It was beautifully placed on the stage, and the scenery painted by William Beverly, the eminent artist. Beverly cleared one thousand pounds by this piece; I received sixty. Fortune smiled; my pen now went at tip-top speed—pieces written and produced plentiful as blackberries—quantity rather than quality was the order of the day. Paganini came to Manchester during our season; his wonderful performances on the one-stringed violin created a furore—a single night produced £1100. His appearance and manner were unearthly. Having no expenses, except a pianist (Miss Watson) he speedily amassed a large fortune, retired to Italy,* and died before he could enjoy it.

STALYBRIDGE, a factory village near Manchester.—During our vacation, our Company engaged to play with John Neville, a popular actor and manager, at second-class towns in Cheshire and Lancashire. The Stalybridge Temple of the Muses was a large room in the Town Hall. Two or three scenes served every purpose, much being left to the fancy and imagination of the 'factory hands,' who were our chief supporters. An egg-chest extemporised did duty for defunct Ophelia's coffin. Juliet's balcony was a large kitchen table covered with carpet.

At the small post-office, a cottage, the custom was to place all undelivered letters in the window to be claimed. The direction of one ran thus: 'To Biddy O'Shaughnessy my wife works at some Factory in some Bridge close upon Manchester in Great Britan—England—ples tell Biddy to call for it.' Postmark New Orleans, America.

* Stirling's note: Or rather, to what was then Italy. He died at *Nice*, May 1840.

Our shares grew 'beautifully less' nightly, Manager Neville sedulously looking after himself. We tried Oldham, 1834. Here I played William in *Black-Eyed Susan*. Court-martial: a table, big drum, cocked hat, and manager's son—a boy. All the witnesses and captains were spoken of, not seen; the boy admiral, or I should rather have said cocked hat, tried and condemned me offhand, telling me 'I need not trouble about witnesses.' He, the hat, knew all about me; further, having consulted with the captains, they all agreed I ought to be hung, and hung I should be at the yard-arm. 'This court now dissolves' (*loud noise on drum*). I was removed by a marine in a hussar-jacket. The ridiculous could go no further; I quitted Oldham forthwith in great disgust, and with small gain.

BOLTON.—Another of Neville's Theatres, in this case a real one. *Macbeth* acted without Macduff; Neville played Macbeth and Hecate (in a cloak), singing well. His family doctor kindly fought the tyrant in the absence of the Thane of Fife, at Manchester. Neville spoke his own part and Macduff's, addressing the astonished medical gentleman:

'You would say, then' (Shakespeare's words), 'you're not of woman born?'

He seized the trembling actor (a very old one).

'Damn'd be you if you call out enough.'

An awful fight, on Neville's side. Macduff cautiously held up his sword, to protect his grey head.

In the house where I lived there once dwelt a poor strolling actress, named Mellon: her little child, a pretty girl, daily left to the kindly protection of the landlady, who fed Harriet Mellon with her own children, principally upon porridge. Mrs Mellon, ill-paid, ill-fed, could scarcely keep herself. 'Many and many a meal I've given the poor child, when its mother was a play-acting up at playhouse,' said the good woman in her garrulous fashion. This little starveling lived to be Duchess of St Albans. When fickle Fortune smiled, be it recorded to her honour that Harriet Mellon did not forget the humble landlady at Bolton-le-Moors.

WARRINGTON, LANCASHIRE.—Our Protean Neville appeared again on the scene; he seemed to possess the genius of ubiquity. The sagacious Neville very reasonably thought that *Sadak and Kalasrade*, having brought money in Manchester, would draw in Warrington. Borrowing the dresses, banners and finery, to

Cheshire I proceeded, forwarding the luggage a day or two before. To my horror, when I arrived, our British Barnum had hung out the banners, dresses, etc., from the theatre windows in a public street, a poster explaining to the admiring crowd outside that he wished to satisfy them that the great Manchester drama with its author, Edward Stirling, was coming. No increase of prices; advising factory lads and lasses to come early and in their Sunday clothes. A gentle reminder accompanied this polite invite, viz., that bad language and short pipes must be suspended. One sensible factory-hand, vacantly looking at this Oriental tawdry, was heard to say to his mate, 'We'll spend our shilling in some'at that'll do us good, lad; Master Neville's outside is better than his inside by a long chalk.'

ASHTON-UNDER-LYNE.—Neville's towns were legion, great and small—this enterprising man took all, haphazard. If they paid, well and good; on the contrary, failing, he shut up; his actors going penniless. His system, too, often practised on the ignorant natives, was to put out a bill of astounding novelties, never before seen or dreamt of, generally issued on a Saturday (the pay-day at the cotton-mills), thus entrapping the lads and lasses. At night came an apology—sudden death, shipwreck, non-arrival of actors from London—anything; the wily manager blandly telling his disappointed hearers that he would act and sing to them in the highly entertaining piece of *The Two Gregorys; or The Orphan of Geneva*. This happened so frequently in Stockport, that whenever Neville attempted to apologise, the lads in the gallery stopped him: 'Noa, noa, Master Neville, we won't ha' "Two Gregorys" th'night.' Drinkwater Meadows (Drinkwater! what a name for a Temperance Society!) came for six nights, and played one, to eight shillings, sharing after five pounds. With tears in his eyes he offered Neville the five pounds to let him go back home to London. The delighted manager joyfully consented. Three Mondays we dismissed—no receipts. Resolved if the living would not come, I would try the dead, on the walls of a churchyard I had pictures and posters pasted for my Benefit. This had some effect. Seventeen pounds five shillings was received at the doors—goodness knows how much more! Neville being money-taker without checks or account-books.

At Preston I resided with a Mrs Wolf. Samuel Phelps, then a poor actor, not afterwards unknown to fame, had formerly occupied my rooms in the Wolf's Den. She was a perfect Sycorax, with one eye that invariably scored double her lodgers' chops, potatoes, and sundries. She had many traditional anecdotes to tell of players' privations, and of her own Christian feelings—of Phelps among the rest; his salary small, little to spare; his wife and children lived on a meat-pie for a week. Mrs Wolf had a remarkable aptitude for forgetting small change and for sharing the contents of the tea-caddy with her lodgers. Determined not to be a loser by these little peculations, I repaid this attention by forgetting her last week's rent.

LEOMINSTER, Herefordshire.—Arriving late in the evening at dark, I had to play in the after-piece. Our coach from London stopped at the Crown Inn. Inquiring of the landlady my way to the theatre, she asked if I had been in the town before? My reply, 'No.'

'Then, sir, you would never find our tumble-down old theatre; it is in a bye-lane up a stable-yard.' Ringing a bell, the ostler appears. 'Light your lantern, Jim, and show this gentleman the way to the playhouse.'

'I wool, missus. Muster Cowper's players begins tonight.'

Aided by the friendly lantern, I reached 'Muster' Cowper's theatre in time to play in a farce, *Murder and Mystery*. Ostler Jim insisted on waiting to see me back to the Crown. In this hole of a building, Lord Foley, Sir Edward Standish, and Earl Somers gave bespeaks and patronage.

(1846) With Robertson at Leicester and Sheffield. I played in my own pieces, *The Ragpicker of Paris*, and *The Wandering Jew*. At Sheffield my Benefit was to be half the receipts of the night. Mrs Robertson kindly invited me one evening to tea in a family way. Very pleasant it was—a multitude of little ones, a baby in arms, Master Tom, then about twelve years old [he was seventeen] and so on, up and down—a large family. The repast over, Mr Robertson quitted the room with all his children, leaving the baby, Mrs R., and myself *tête-à-tête*. She could talk, as will be seen. She painted a mournful picture of bad business, expenses of a home (this I believed), difficulty in paying the actors, and winding up with many anticipatory compliments on my kindness of heart (heavens, what for?) she asked me to leave my half—due to me for the Benefit—in their hands until the following week, when

Robertson would send it to me after his own Benefit had taken place. This concession would save them from ruin. Who could withstand such an appeal from a handsome woman and a smiling baby. I consented, and after receiving a shower of thanks, returned to town, minus £18 10s. Next week came, followed by another, but no tidings from Sheffield. I wrote to Robertson. His son Tom, afterwards the famous author of *Caste*, answered for his father:

Sheffield, October 2nd, 1846.

Dear Sir.—My father regrets that he could not keep his promise, but his Benefit did not turn out as well as he anticipated. His friend the sergeant-major brought the soldiers, but he was obliged to trust them for admission. He now finds great difficulty in getting the money. In a few days father will send it.

Yours, etc., TOM ROBERTSON.

E. Stirling, Esq., Theatre Royal, Covent Garden.

This was pleasant. Weeks quietly passed over. At last I wrote to Sheffield another reminder for my cash. The reply was from Tom junior again:

Sheffield, Nove. 10th, 1846.

Dear Sir.—Father desires me to say that he is in so much distress that he cannot at present send you a shilling—in fact he is giving up management to take a situation. The sergeant-major never paid the soldiers' money. Mother is greatly grieved about it, and wishes to know if you will take the money out in knives and spoons. A friend of hers would send them to you.

Yours obediently, Sir, TOM ROBERTSON.

Edward Stirling, Esq., T. R., C. Garden.

In a mercantile point of view, knives and spoons were better than nothing. But I thought it best to abandon the matter, leaving the manager and 'sergeant-major' (who had sailed with his regiment for foreign parts) to settle the matter between them. Moral—Never listen to a pretty woman's pleadings, with a very pretty baby in her arms.

EDWARD STIRLING

VIII

Comedian Off-stage

CHARLES MATHEWS senior (1776–1835) made two reputations in the English theatre: first as an eccentric comedian, later as a protean actor and mimic in his one-man *At Homes*. These developed into short plays, written by himself as a rule, though during 1817 George Colman the younger furnished him with *The Actor of All Work*. It was the right label for a stage chameleon.

Nervous, tetchy, and capricious, Mathews remained a comedian to the last. Taken ill at Plymouth in the early summer of 1835 on his return from New York, he died in lodgings near the Hoe after a month's lingering illness, and was buried in the great church of St Andrew. R. A. J. Walling says in *The Story of Plymouth* that, on his death-bed, when Mathews was parched with thirst, someone recalled a French prisoner who needed drink so badly that he drained an ink-bottle.

'What would have happened to him?' asked somebody else, and Mathews, opening his hollow eyes, murmured: 'All you'd have to do would be to swallow a piece of blotting-paper.' His son by his second wife was Charles James Mathews (1803–1878), an elegant light comedian, first married to the actress who preferred to use her former name of Madame Vestris.

The following recollections are from *A Memoir of Charles Mayne Young, Tragedian, with Extracts from his Son's Journal*. The author was the tragedian's son, Julian Charles Young, a Warwickshire parson; his zestfully discursive journal is much ampler than the preliminary memoir. My copy (1871), which the author gave to Dean Ramsay, belonged in 1917 to E. V. Lucas, who scribbled on a fly-leaf: 'This is one of the best "bed books" ever written.'

GENIUS and gentleman as Mathews was, his nervous whimsicality, his irritability about trifles, his antipathies to particular people, places, and objects, rendered him justly vulnerable to ridicule and censure. I have seen him scratch his head and grind his teeth and assume a look of anguish when a haunch of venison has been carved unskilfully in his presence. I have seen him, when in high feather and high talk, in a sunny chamber, if transferred to a badly-lighted room, withdraw into a corner and sit by himself in moody silence. He was strangely impressionable by externals. I have known him refuse permission to a royal Duke to see over his picture-gallery on Highgate Hill because the day of his call was cloudy. He was such a passionate lover of sunshine, that I have seen him 'put out' for a whole day by the lady of the house at which he was calling pulling down the Venetian blinds . . . Whenever he went out to dinner, in the good old days when moderator and sinumbra lamps were unknown, and wax-candles were in fashion, he was wont to carry in his breast-pocket a pair of small silver snuffers, so that when the wicks were long and dull, he might be able to trim them and brighten up the gloom that was gathering round the table. I have known him, without the slightest cause, appropriate remarks to himself that were intended for others, and fret his heart-strings over imaginary wrongs for hours. I have known him frenzied with rage, on discovering that a tidy housemaid had picked up from the floor of his bedroom a dirty pair of stockings which he had left there 'as a memorandum', on the same principle on which people tie knots in their handkerchiefs. And yet, with all these unhappy infirmities, I never knew a man more formed to inspire, and who succeeded more in inspiring, personal affection. . . .

The following anecdote will further illustrate his morbid sensibility to things which most people would deem insignificant. He had an appointment with a solicitor. They were to meet at a particular hour at a small inn in the city where they might hope to be quiet and undisturbed. Mathews arrived at the trysting-place a few minutes too soon. On entering the coffee-room, he found its sole tenant a commercial gentleman earnestly engaged on a round of boiled beef. Mathews sat himself down by the fire, and took up a newspaper, meaning to wile away the time until his friend arrived. Occasionally he glanced from the paper to the beef, and from the beef to the man, till he began to fidget and look about from the top of the right-hand page to the bottom of the left in a querulous manner. Then he turned the paper inside out, and, pretending to stop from reading, addressed the gentleman in a tone of ill-disguised indignation, and with a ghastly smile upon his face—'I beg your pardon, Sir, but I don't think you are aware that you have no mustard.' The person addressed looked up at him with evident surprise, mentally resenting his gratuitous interference, and coldly bowed. Mathews resumed his reading, and, curious to see if his well-meant hint would be acted on, furtively looked round the edge of his paper, and finding the plate to be still void of mustard, concluded that the man was deaf. So, raising his voice to a higher key, and accosting him with sarcastic acerbity, he bawled out with syllabic precision: 'Are — you — aw-are — Sir — that — you — have — been — eat — ing — boiled — beef — with — out — mustard?' Again a stiff bow and no reply. Once more Mathews affected to read, while he was really nursing his wrath to keep it warm. At last, seeing the man's obstinate violation of conventionality and good taste, he jumped up, and in the most arbitrary and defiant manner snatched the mustard-pot out of the cruet-stand, banged it on the table, under the defaulter's nose, and shouted out—'Confound it, Sir, you SHALL take mustard.' He then slapped his hat on his head, and ordered the waiter to show him into a private room, vowing that he never before had been under the roof with such a savage; that he had been made quite sick by the revolting sight, and that he would never sit in the room with a man who *could* eat beef without mustard....

Mathews once left me at a country inn where we had been staying together. When I was about to take my departure, I took care to ransack every possible or impossible nook or cranny behind which any article of mine might have fallen; and, in doing so, observed, secreted behind a huge old mahogany dining-table, with deep flaps, which was placed against the wall of our sitting-room, a dress-shoe, so dapper in shape and so diminutive in size, that I had no difficulty in recognising it as one of my friend's. Rejoiced at the opportunity of having a bit of fun, I enclosed it in a brown-paper parcel, and despatched it after him. Instead of thanking me for my trouble, he wrote to me and told me that I was his 'evil genius'; that, having worn out the companion pump, which was that of the foot of his lame leg, the one I had forwarded to him was of no earthly use to him; and that, in the faint hope of getting rid of it, he had placed it where I had found it; and that, in consequence of my inquisitive and officious disposition, he had been compelled to pay for the recovery of this useless article as much as would have purchased an entirely new pair.

About a month after he had left us, at Amport, I happened to go to my wardrobe in search of an old pair of trowsers which I reserved for gardening purposes. As I was putting them on, I felt that there was something in them. My first impression was that, when I had last worn them, I had left my purse in them. But on inserting my hand into the pocket, I drew out an oddly-shaped object, neatly wrapped in Bath notepaper, with these words inscribed on the outside, in the quaint but vigorous handwriting I knew so well. 'To be lost, if possible.' On opening the little packet, I found inside it a circular nailbrush, worn to the bone. It would seem that, on looking over the articles of my wardrobe, he thought the trowsers he had selected were too shabby for me ever to put on again, and therefore chose them for a hiding-place. But he was deceived. I made up another neat parcel for him, and directed it to his house in London. Unfortunately, he was on a professional tour in the provinces, where it followed him; till, by the time it reached him, the carriage had amounted to some shillings. I was not long in receiving a letter of ironical thanks 'for my kind and *dear* attention'. . . .

On the first night of one of his 'At Homes', when the theatre was packed to the very ceiling, and all his best friends and adherents were there to support him, I witnessed a singular instance of his sensibility to the opinion of others. At the end of the first part of the entertainment, Manners Sutton, the Speaker (afterwards Lord Canterbury), Theodore Hook, Gen. Phipps and others, went behind the scenes to congratulate him. . . . He accepted their compliments rather ungraciously. All they said to buoy him up, only seemed the more to depress him. At first they could not make him out, till he explained himself by blurting forth the truth. 'It is all very well, and very kind of you, who wish me success, to tell me the piece is going well; *I* know better. It ain't going well, and it can't be going well—it must be hanging fire, or that man with the bald head, in the pit in the front row, could not have been asleep the whole time I have been trying to amuse him.' 'Oh,' said the Speaker, 'perhaps he is drunk.' 'No, no, he ain't . . . I've watched the fellow, and when he opens his eyes, which he does now and then, he looks as sober as a judge, as if he disliked the very sight of me. I tell you, all the laughter and applause of the whole house—boxes, pit, and gallery put together —weigh not a feather with me while that "pump" remains dead to my efforts to arouse him.' The call bell rang; all his friends returned to their seats in front, and he to the stage. The second part opened with one of the rapid songs, in the composition of which James Smith, the author, excelled so much, and in the delivery of which no one ever equalled Mathews, except his son, who in that respect surpassed him. All the time he was singing it, as he paced from the right wing to the left, one saw his head jerking from side to side as he moved either way, his eyes always directed to one spot, till, at the end of one of the stanzas, forgetful of the audience and transported out of himself by the obstinate insensibility of the bald-pate, he fixed his eyes on him as if he were mesmerising him, and leaning over the lamps, in the very loudest key shouted at him 'Bo!' The man, startled, woke up, and observing that the singer looked *at* him, sang *to* him, and never took his eyes off him, became flattered by the personal notice, began to listen, and then to laugh—and laugh, at last, most heartily. From that instant the actor's spirits rose, for he felt he had converted a stolid country bumpkin into an appreciative listener. After such a triumph, he went home satisfied that his entertainment had been a complete success . . .

At one time he had a footman whose boundless credulity principally recommended him to his notice. A title inspired him with awe, and having seen a nobleman, now and then, at his master's table, he took it for granted that he was familiar with half the peerage. The Duke of Sussex called one day to see the picture-gallery. On announcing his Royal Highness, Mathews fully expected that he would have gone off by spontaneous combustion; for he retreated backwards, puffed out his cheeks to their fullest powers of expansion, and then poised himself on one leg, like a bird, awaiting to see the effect produced on his master by the appearance of such a visitor. Knowing his weakness, Mathews used to tell all his intimates, whenever they called, to be sure to present themselves under some assumed title. Thus Charles Kemble always announced himself as the Persian Ambassador; Fawcett called himself Sir Francis Burdett; my father was the Duke of Wellington.

This habit of jocular imposition once involved Mathews in an awkward scrape. He had no idea that there existed such a title as that of 'Ranelagh'. So that when the veritable nobleman of that name called one day on horseback at the door, and sent up a message by the manservant to say that 'Lord Ranelagh would be much obliged if Mr Mathews could step down to him, as he could not dismount,' Mathews, convinced it was one of his chums under a feigned name, sent down word to say that Lord Ranelagh must be kind enough to put up his horse in the stables, and walk up, as he could not go out of doors, having a cold, and being particularly engaged at the time with Lord Vauxhall.

Lord Ranelagh could hardly believe his ears when he received this familiar, flippant, and impertinent message. He rode off in a state of boiling indignation, and forthwith despatched a note to the offender, commenting severely on his impudence in daring to play upon his name. Of course, as soon as Mathews discovered his mistake, he wrote and explained it, and apologised for it amply.

Mathews had often told Charles Kemble of the great amusement his manservant's peculiarities afforded him, but Kemble said he had never been able to discover anything in him but crass stupidity. 'Ah,' said Mathews, 'you can't conceive what a luxury it is to have a man under the same roof with you who will believe anything you tell him, however impossible it may be.'

One warm summer's day, when Mathews had a dinner party at Highgate, and there were present, among others, Broderip, Theodore Hook, General Phipps, Manners Sutton (then

Speaker of the House of Commons), and Charles Kemble, and dessert was laid out on the lawn, Mathews, without hinting his intention, rang the bell in the dining-room, and on its being answered, told the man to follow him to the stables while he gave the coachman certain directions in his presence. The instant Mathews reached the stable door, he called out for the coachman (whom he knew was not there), looked in, and, before the man-servant could overtake him, started back, and in a voice of horror cried out, 'Good heavens! go back, go back—and tell Mr Kemble that his horse has cut its throat!'

The simple goose, infected by his master's well-feigned panic, and never pausing to reflect on the absurdity of the thing, burst on to the lawn, and, with cheeks blanched with terror, roared out, 'Mr Kemble, Sir, you're wanted directly.' Seeing Kemble in no hurry to move, he repeated his appeal with increased emphasis, 'For heaven's sake, Sir, come; your poor horse has cut his throat!'

From that time Kemble, the Persian Ambassador, admitted fully that if his friend's servant was not funny himself, he could be the fruitful cause of fun to others.

JULIAN CHARLES YOUNG

IX

A Guinea a Week

IN OLD AGE, Walter Donaldson (1793–1877) wrote his *Fifty Years of Green-Room Gossip; or, Recollections of an Actor*. A piano-maker's son, he appeared in 1807 at Crow Street Theatre, Dublin, as a sprite in 'Monk' Lewis's romantic drama of *Rugantino; or, The Bravo of Venice*. He admitted with regret that the character was 'of the most trivial quality; it was of a pantomimic nature.' But he went on from there, and in time knew most things about the arduous life of the provincial pomping folk.

In the ensuing extract, 'Robertson' is the great-uncle of T. W. Robertson and Madge Robertson (Kendal). Thomas James Serle, who died in 1889 at the age of ninety, became a dramatist and a close friend of Macready.

This passage is from the London edition of 1881.

THE OLD managers were celebrated for their wit and humour. Thornton, of the Reading circuit, was not the least among them; he was an especial favourite with George III as an actor. Thornton was particularly happy in getting through a character without knowing much of the words of the author; but, because he could be 'absent' at times, he committed strange blunders in some of his tragic attempts. One night at Gosport, while representing Biron in the tragedy of *Isabella*, he died without giving the letter which unravels the plot; and as he lay prostrate in the last scene, one of the performers on the stage whispered to him, 'Mr Thornton, the letter—the letter!' Thornton then rose up, took the letter out of his bosom, and said, 'One thing I had forgot through a multiplicity of business. Give this letter to my father; it will explain all'; and laid down again in the arms of death.

On Easter Monday 1819 I made my début at the Stockport Theatre, then under the management of John Stanton, the acknowledged best scenic artist in the provinces. Although capable of taking the first position at either of the metropolitan theatres, he preferred to lord it over the actors in his own establishment. The low comedian was one Goddard who in his day was an especial favourite with George III at Weymouth. In those days the King every summer visited the beautiful watering-place. Nor did His Majesty remain in his unpretending house on the esplanade in the cool of the evening. No; he attended, with his retinue, the little theatre, and made himself as much at ease as if seated in the national house of Covent Garden.

On one occasion, having to open Parliament, His Majesty was preparing for his departure. The very day he was to start was Goddard's benefit, and as the King was a tower of strength on such an occasion, his absence would entail a heavy loss on the unfortunate actor. Goddard screwed up his courage, and at once waited upon His Majesty. An audience was granted, and, when the comedian had stated the purport of his errand, the King, in the kindest manner, told him not to make himself unhappy—that he would remain and attend the theatre. This is a well-known fact. His Majesty performed the journey at night, sooner than be the means of inflicting an injury on a poor country actor. Goddard was a native of Birmingham, and began as an amateur actor in the same little theatre with Richard Jones. Each member of this club brought his contribution in kind, for the getting up of the theatre—one nails, another paper for the scenery. Jones, being the son of a timber-merchant, generally dropped in with a scantling under his arm. So in this humble beginning these young men started in life with equal requisites for the histrionic art. Goddard kept floundering about from one petty theatre to another; and at last, in 1819, I met him aged, broken down, surrounded by a family, and hopeless; while Jones was the leading comedian of

Covent Garden, with a fortune in the funds and a reputation of the first rank in his line of characters. But then Jones got attached, in his early struggles, to the best theatre out of London; and he was wise enough to remain there till the proper time arrived to change, and a fair field lay open for him in the metropolis.

It is not talent always that shapes a man's destiny; it is manœuvring and working—not on the stage, but off it. Trickery and bounce have a good deal to do in it. Without question Jones deserved his good fortune; and poor Goddard's ill fortune may be ascribed to circumstances over which he had no control. His Geoffrey Muffincap, in Peake's excellent farce of *Amateurs and Actors*, I have not seen equalled—not even by the original at the Lyceum. Such simple characters, it is true, are easy; but in Old Rapid, Sir Abel Handy, and many others in which Munden excelled, I have not met with any actor to be compared to him.

The Peace did not bring those blessings so fondly anticipated, and instead of bettering the condition of the working-classes in Lancashire, thousands were thrown out of employment, which brought on absolute insurrection. The drama, of course, suffered, and Stanton became a ruined man. When a manager is about to fail, the actors generally abandon him; as rats take to the water when a ship is foundering, and swim for their lives, so Stanton was left alone in his ruin, and sank to rise no more. Being an honest and straightforward man, he was free from those tricks and artifices to which others too often resort to prop their reeling fortunes.

The fate of actors, like statesmen, depends on those in power; and when the tide turns, and a reverse comes, then a new scene of action is necessary; and this scene I found in the neat and compact town of Stamford, under the direction of Manly and Robertson. *Hamlet* was performed on the opening night, in which His Majesty of Denmark, Claudius, was sustained by the writer of these Recollections; while the Prince was represented by a young gentleman, Thomas Serle, since well-known in the literary world; and the queen by Mrs Sheppard, aunt of Helen Faucit. Robertson, the manager, could write a comic song, paint a scene, dance a hornpipe, and do the low comedy. In the latter department he was a prodigious favourite in the Nottingham circuit. This I ascribe to long standing. I have known many comic actors great favourites, having no claim to distinction beyond that of being several years before the public. Robertson's conception of such characters as Acres and Tony Lumpkin was decidedly wrong. However, on the whole, I consider he was an actor of utility, and might be called a rough diamond. When he retired from the theatre, he opened a shop in Nottingham where he sold all sorts of articles, and placed over the door the following legend in large letters, 'Everything made here except a fortune.'

Manly continued the management on his own account, and made a rule never to engage married or old people. This was politic, as the walking in this circuit (I kept an account of it) in one year amounted to 500 miles. Coaching in those days was no trifling matter, and salaries being on the lowest scale, actors were obliged to walk. There was one aged man in the company, Earle, and he had been a member forty-four years. He was originally a barber, but *cut* the hair for the 'stage,' thinking it more aristocratic. By great parsimony, he saved a sum of money which he deposited in a banker's hands in Stamford. The peace came, and the banker broke, and Earle's savings were lost; yet still he kept up his spirits and walked his journeys. This task he executed alone as company was likely to drift into expense; all actors, he well knew, in their journeys through life, lived well on the road.

Certainly the means afforded by the manager did not allow of much indulgence either in eating or drinking. The salaries were £1 1s. weekly, and for this miserable stipend the actor had to find boots, shoes, buckles, silk stockings, hats, feathers, swords, canes, wigs, modern dress, long hose, gloves, military costume; and those that unfortunately possessed vocal ability were obliged to furnish the part of their songs for the orchestra; and all these articles out of a guinea a week. The actor that could sing was ever in request for glees and choruses, and was even compelled to sing the songs of other characters when certain performers were incompetent. At Nottingham, for instance, O'Keefe's opera of *The Castle of Andalusia* was performed. I represented Spado; and as the captain of the banditti, Don Caesar, was not blessed with vocal power, had to sing his songs of 'Flow, thou regal purple stream', and 'The Wolf'. Have such services ever been beneficial? Quite the contrary.—The actor that is useful is always considered a hack, and treated accordingly. . . .

No man on the stage understood the mysteries of the art better than Thomas Wilson Manly. That he was a dramatic despot, there is no denying, and a terror to those novices whom agents sent to fill the positions of experienced actors—his *hard bargains*, as he called them. Although a splendid actor himself, he studiously kept his children from the stage. One he articled to a lawyer, and another to a doctor; his daughters he trained for first-class governesses... But who can control fate, and divert man from his destiny? No one. Manly's son threw physic to the dogs and rushed on the stage; the other repudiated Coke and Blackstone for Shakespeare and Sheridan; and one of his daughters, that he had designed for an earl or a viscount, united her fate with an actor. These galling disappointments worked on a high and ambitious spirit, and in time undermined a well-knit frame and physical power of no common order, and brought him to the grave.

W. DONALDSON

X

Amateur Nights

CHARLES DICKENS (1812–1870) became the most persuaded of amateur actors: as Bobadil, for example, in Jonson's *Every Man in his Humour*. In those days he exercised his hobby as expensively as possible. When a youth he wrote on the shifts of London's 'private theatres' for the stage-struck, and his description was reprinted, on his twenty-fourth birthday, in the collected *Sketches by Boz. Illustrative of Every Day Life and Every Day People*, 1836.

'RICHARD the Third—Duke of Glo'ster, £2; Earl of Richmond, £1; Duke of Buckingham, 15s.; Catesby, 12s.; Tressel, 10s. 6d.; Lord Stanley, 5s.; Lord Mayor of London, 2s. 6d.'

Such are the written placards wafered up in the gentlemen's dressing-room, or the green-room (when there is any) at a private theatre; and such are the sums extracted from the shop-till, or overcharged in the office expenditure, by the donkeys who are prevailed upon to pay for admission to exhibit their lamentable ignorance and boobyism on the stage of a private theatre. This they do, in proportion to the scope afforded by the character for the display of their imbecility. . . .

The theatre itself may be in Catherine Street, Strand, the purlieus of the City, the neighbourhood of Gray's Inn Lane, or the vicinity of Sadler's Wells; or it may, perhaps, form the chief nuisance of some shabby street, on the Surrey side of Waterloo Bridge. The lady performers pay nothing for their characters, and it is needless to add, are usually selected from one class of society; the audiences are necessarily of much the same character as the performers, who receive, in return for their contributions to the management, tickets to the amount of the money they pay . . .

See them in the neighbouring public-house, or the theatrical coffee-shop! They are the kings of the place, supposing no real performers to be present, and roll about, hats one side, and arms a-kimbo, as if they had actually come into possession of eighteen shillings a week, and a share of a ticket night. If one of them does but know an Astley's supernumerary he is a happy fellow. The mingled air of envy and admiration with which his companions will regard him, as he converses familiarly with some mouldy-looking man in a fancy neckerchief, whose partially corked eye-brows, and half-rouged face, testify to the fact of his having just left the stage or the circle, sufficiently shows in what high admiration these public characters are held.

With the double view of guarding against the discovery of friends or employers, and enhancing the interest of an assumed character, by attaching a high-sounding name to its representative, these gentlemen assume fictitious names, which are not the least amusing part of the play bill of a private theatre. Belville, Melville, Treville, Berkeley, Randolph, Byron, St. Clair, and so forth, are among the humblest; and the less imposing titles of Jenkins, Walker, Thomson, Barker, Solomons, etc., are completely laid aside. . . .

[*On the night*]

A quarter before eight—there will be a full house tonight—six parties in the boxes, already; four little boys and a woman in the pit; and two fiddles and a flute in the orchestra, who have got through five overtures since seven o'clock (the hour fixed for the commencement of the performances), and have just begun the sixth. There will be plenty of it, though, when it does begin, for there is enough in the bill to last six hours at least.

That gentleman in the white hat and checked shirt, brown coat and brass buttons, lounging behind the stage-box on the O.P. side, is Mr Horatio St Julien, alias Jem Larkins. His line is genteel comedy—his father's coal and potato. He *does* Alfred

Highflier in the last piece, and very well he'll do it—at the price. The party of gentlemen in the opposite box, to whom he has just nodded, are friends and supporters of Mr Beverley (otherwise Loggins), the *Macbeth* of the night. You observe their attempts to appear easy and gentlemanly, each member of the party, with his feet cocked upon the cushion in front of the box! They let them do these things here, upon the same humane principle which permits poor people's children to knock double knocks at the door of an empty house—because they can't do it anywhere else. The two stout men in the centre box, with an opera-glass ostentatiously placed before them, are friends of the proprietor— opulent country managers, as he confidentially informs every individual among the crew behind the curtain—opulent country managers looking out for recruits; a representation which Mr. Nathan the dresser, who is in the manager's interest, and has just arrived with the costumes, offers to confirm upon oath if required —corroborative evidence, however, is quite unnecessary, for the gulls believe it at once.

The stout Jewess who has just entered is the mother of the pale bony little girl, with the necklace of blue glass beads, sitting by her; she is being brought up to 'the profession.' Pantomime is to be her line, and she is coming out to-night, in a hornpipe after the tragedy. The short thin man beside Mr. St. Julien, whose white face is so deeply seared with the small-pox, and whose dirty shirt-front is inlaid with open-work, and embossed with coral studs like ladybirds, is the low comedian and comic singer of the establishment. The remainder of the audience—a tolerably numerous one by this time—are a motley group of dupes and blackguards....

The little narrow passages beneath the stage are neither especially clean nor too brilliantly lighted; and the absence of any flooring, together with the damp mildewy smell which pervades the place, does not conduce in any great degree to their comfortable appearance. Don't fall over this plate basket—it's one of the 'properties' —the cauldron for the witches' cave; and the three uncouth-looking figures, with broken clothes-pegs in their hands, who are drinking gin-and-water out of a pint pot, are the weird sisters. This miserable room, lighted by candles in sconces placed at lengthened intervals round the wall, is the dressing-room, common to the gentlemen performers, and the square hole in the ceiling is *the* trap-door of the stage above. You will observe that the ceiling is ornamented with the beams that support the boards, and tastefully hung with cobwebs.

The characters in the tragedy are all dressed, and their own clothes are scattered in hurried confusion over the wooden dresser which surrounds the room. That snuff-shop-looking figure, in front of the glass, is *Banquo*, and the young lady with the liberal display of legs, who is kindly painting his face with a hare's foot, is dressed for *Fleance*. The large woman, who is consulting the stage directions in Cumberland's edition of *Macbeth*, is the *Lady Macbeth* of the night; she is always selected to play the part, because she is tall and stout, and *looks* a little like Mrs Siddons—at a considerable distance. That stupid-looking milksop, with light hair and bow legs—a kind of man whom you can warrant town-made—is fresh caught; he plays *Malcolm* tonight, just to accustom himself to an audience. He will get on better by degrees; he will play *Othello* in a month, and in a month more, will very probably be apprehended on a charge of embezzlement. The black-eyed female with whom he is talking so earnestly, is dressed for the 'gentlewoman'. It is *her* first appearance, too—in that character. The boy of fourteen who is having his eyebrows smeared with soap and whitening, is *Duncan*, King of Scotland; and the two dirty men with the corked countenances, in very old green tunics, and dirty drab boots, are the 'army'.

'Look sharp below there, gents,' exclaims the dresser, a red-headed and red-whiskered Jew, calling through the trap, 'they're a-going to ring up. The flute says he'll be blowed if he plays any more, and they're getting precious noisy in front.' A general rush immediately takes place to the half-dozen little steep steps leading to the stage, and the heterogeneous group are soon assembled at the side scenes, in breathless anxiety and motley confusion.

'Now,' cries the manager, consulting the written list which hangs behind the first P. S. wing. 'Scene 1, open country—lamps down—thunder and lightning—all ready, White?' [This is addressed to one of the army.] 'All ready.'—'Very well. Scene 2, front chamber. Is the front chamber down?'—'Yes.'—'Very well'.—'Jones' [to the other army who is up in the flies.] 'Hallo!' —'Wind up the open country when we ring up.'—'I'll take care'. —Scene 3, back perspective with practical bridge. Bridge ready, White? Got the tressels there?'—'All right.'

'Very well. Clear the stage', cries the manager, hastily packing every member of the company into the little space there is between the wings and the wall, and one wing and another. 'Places, places. Now then, Witches—Duncan—Malcolm—bleeding officer—where's the bleeding officer?'—'Here!' replies the officer, who has been rose-pinking for the character. 'Get ready, then; now, White, ring the second music-bell.' The actors who are to be discovered are hastily arranged, and the actors who are not to be discovered, place themselves, in their anxiety to peep at the house, just where the audience can see them. The bell rings, and the orchestra, in acknowledgment of the call, play three distinct chords. The bell rings—the tragedy(!) opens—and our description closes.

CHARLES DICKENS

XI

Respectable Actors

JAMES ROBINSON PLANCHÉ, dramatist and antiquarian (1796–1880) was born in London, about the time—so he said—that 'the farce begins at the Haymarket, that is, shortly after one o'clock in the morning'. A charming, garrulous personage of many gifts—he became Somerset Herald—he was a copious writer who did much for Bunn (including an English libretto of *The Magic Flute*) and for Vestris and Mathews. He was a forerunner of Gilbert: certainly we can trace the Nightmare Song in *Iolanthe* to Planché's 'A Dream', originally an imitation of James Smith's style and later altered for the extravaganza of *Theseus and Ariadne*:

> I dreamed I was walking
> With Homer, and talking
> The very best Greek I was able—
>   was able,
> When Lord Liverpool, he
> Came in very coolly,
> And danced a Scotch jig on the table—

The Royal Kent Theatre, mentioned in this extract from *Recollections and Reflections* (1872) existed off Kensington High Street between 1831 and 1850; unassumingly neat, it had a 'royal entrance' in a mews. Denvil's career was a failure; he dwindled to a check-taker at a minor theatre and died in obscurity. (One of his daughters, Alice Denvil, was celebrated in later life with the Benson company.) Bertram was the principal character, created by Edmund Kean, in R. C. Maturin's tragedy (1816), *Bertram; or, The Castle of St Aldobrand*. Of John Cooper (1790–1870), George Augustus Sala wrote: 'He had a curious intonation, and I can still hear a line of his as Henry VIII: "What poiles of wealth hath he not accumulated."'

During the autumn of 1834, accident led me to visit a little theatre which had been opened in the 'Court Suburb', as Leigh Hunt has called it, of Kensington. In this curious little nook, wherein the drama had furtively taken root, I witnessed the performance of a piece, entitled *The Queen's Lover*, by a company of actors all previously unknown to me, even by name, but who generally exhibited talent, and one, in my humble-opinion, genius.

I was sufficiently impressed by what I had seen, to induce Madame Vestris to accompany me on a second visit, and Mr. Bunn on a third; and I had the pleasure to find my opinion confirmed by both these important theatrical potentates.

Mr. Bunn, who at that time had just succeeded to the throne of the united stage-kingdoms of Drury Lane and Covent Garden, had arranged with me for the adaptation of Fenimore Cooper's novel, *The Bravo*, introducing the music, by Maliarni, of an Italian opera on the same subject, performed in Paris, and in which Madame Grisi had been greatly successful. The old obstacle, the want of a singer who could act, immediately presented itself. There was no longer at Drury Lane a popular melo-dramatic performer like James Wallack; but in *The Queen's Lover*, I fancied I had discovered the man we wanted. Bunn thought so too, and engaged him immediately. This was Henry Gaskell Denvil; and had Mr. Bunn been guided by common prudence, there was stuff enough of the right sort in this poor fellow—starving as he was when I lighted upon him—to have recruited the fortunes of Drury Lane Theatre, and to have made his own. Instead, however, of reserving him for the melodramatic character, which I designed him for, Bunn, fancying he had secured a second Edmund Kean, insisted on his making his first appearance as Shylock. Denvil came to me in the greatest distress. 'He is putting me,' were his words, 'on a pinnacle to break my neck; but what can I do? I have, for weeks past, walked Kensington Gardens without a dinner in order that my wife and little ones should not lose a crumb to me. Mr. Bunn offers me five pounds per week, which is affluence to us—salvation! How can I refuse it?' How could he, indeed? I could only encourage him to make the attempt.

He did make it, and puzzled the press. The diversity of opinion, not only as to the extent of his abilities, but respecting almost every scene of his performance, is, perhaps, scarcely to be equalled in the annals of criticism. After three performances of Shylock, he appeared as *Richard III* and *Bertram*, with the same result; the conflicting evidence of the *Times, Herald, Chronicle*, and *Morning Post*, being most amusingly summed up by the *True Sun*, in the evening. In these, and other characters, he had to endure comparison with Edmund Kean; but, in Lord Byron's *Manfred*, which was subsequently produced, he had the advantage of an original part, and united the suffrages of the critics. The remainder of his brief career—his ill-treatment by Bunn, and melancholy exit from the stage of life, I must leave untold in these pages. I have only here to express my regret that I was deprived of the services of an excellent actor, whom I had singled out for my hero, without the consolation of seeing him permanently established in the higher position which, notwithstanding many disadvantages, he had attained, and might have secured under a more judicious management.

I was, consequently, condemned to accept Mr. Cooper as the only available exponent of my unfortunate 'Bravo'; one of those highly respectable actors who are always 'clean and perfect', and who may be thoroughly depended upon for everything except acting. John Cooper was a model of his class—a class I believe indigenous to England; natives to the *manner* born. I have seen on foreign stages, good, bad, and indifferent actors; but in the worst there was always discernible a glimpse of the *artist*—a creditable conception of the character, however faulty might be the execution. The author was, at least understood, and more or less ably interpreted. Otherwise, indeed, the actor would not have been permitted to appear on the stage. Now, the misfortune of the 'respectable actor' in this country is, that, possessing fairly enough the commonplace qualifications for his profession, he plods through his part to the satisfaction of the general public, but to the agony of the author, who, though every syllable of it is distinctly spoken, scarcely recognises his own language from the style of its delivery, in many cases, as I know to my cost, conveying to the audience an entirely different notion of the character it was intended to illustrate.

I remember asking Charles Young one day, when I met him in Paris, how he accounted for the superiority of the general run of French actors to those of our own country. His answer was, 'My dear fellow, *they understand the value of words.*' No definition could be more perfect. That is 'the heart of the mystery.' That is the precise knowledge of which the class of actors I am alluding to are woefully and hopelessly ignorant. They get the words by heart, and utter them distinctly, and to the general ear with sufficient propriety; but of the effect to be imparted to the most commonplace sentence, by some particular emphasis or intonation, they have not the slightest conception. Let me hasten to do justice to the great body of actors of the present day—very few of the class I have been describing are now to be found. The 'walking gentleman' of forty years ago has walked off, and his successor *is* a gentleman who can walk and talk like one; and there is scarcely a theatre in London where what used to be considered a 'respectable actor', could now command an engagement.

J. R. PLANCHÉ

XII
Dolphin and Fotheringay

IN THE FOURTH chapter of William Makepeace Thackeray's novel *Pendennis* (1849), young Arthur Pendennis and his friend Foker visit the Theatre Royal at Chatteris, for which we can read Exeter. There—the period is the eighteen-thirties—an actress known as Miss Fothcringay is appearing as Mrs Haller in Benjamin Thompson's version of Kotzebue's *The Stranger*, hack piece of many stock companies. Pen falls violently in love; but later his uncle Major Pendennis manages not only to break the alliance but also to provide for Miss Fotheringay a new professional engagement. Hence the arrival at Chatteris of the 'famous London Impresario' called Dolphin.

Thackeray's description of him, in the fourteenth chapter of the novel, is based upon Alfred ('Poet') Bunn, the genial vulgarian who in his time—the eighteen-thirties and forties were his heyday—managed both Drury Lane and Covent Garden Theatres. Macready, angered by Bunn's insolence, knocked him down in his Drury Lane office on a famous April night in 1836. A facile versifier, he wrote the libretto of *The Bohemian Girl* ('I dreamt that I dwelt in marble halls') to Balfe's music; he put on anything that might get a public, from *Hamlet* to lion-taming. In 1860, his luck gone, he died of apoplexy at Boulogne, and the *Daily Telegraph* obituary notice described him (not everyone would have agreed) as a 'person of singularly courteous and gentlemanlike demeanour'.

Here is the first visit of Arthur Pendennis to the Chatteris theatre. It is followed after a few weeks by Dolphin's.

THEY had almost their choice of places in the boxes of the theatre, which was no better filled than country theatres usually are, in spite of the 'universal burst of attraction and galvanic thrills of delight' advertised by Bingley in the playbills. A score or so of people dotted the pit-benches, a few more kept up a kicking and a whistling in the galleries, and a dozen others, who came in with free admissions, were in the boxes where our young gentlemen sate. Lieutenants Rodgers and Podgers, and young Cornet Tidmus, of the Dragoons, occupied a private box. The performers acted to them, and these gentlemen seemed to hold conversation with the players when not engaged in the dialogue, and applauded them by name loudly.

Bingley, the manager, who assumed all the chief tragic and comic parts except when he modestly retreated to make way for the London stars who came down occasionally to Chatteris, was great in the character of the 'Stranger'. He was attired in the tight pantaloons and Hessian boots which the stage legend has given to that injured man, with a large cloak and beaver and a hearse-feather in it drooping over his raddled old face, and only partially concealing his great buckled brown wig. He had the stage-jewellery on too, of which he selected the largest and most shiny rings for himself, and allowed his little finger to quiver out of his cloak with a sham diamond ring covering the first joint of the finger, and twiddling in the faces of the pit. Bingley made it a favour to the young men of his company to go on in light comedy parts with that ring. They flattered him by asking its history. The stage has its traditional jewels, as the Crown and all great families have. This had belonged to George Frederick Cooke, who had it from Mr Quin, who may have bought it for a shilling. Bingley fancied the world was fascinated with its glitter.

He was reading out of the stage-book—that wonderful stage-book which is not bound like any other book in the world, but is rouged and tawdry like the hero and heroine who holds it; and who holds it as people never do hold books; and points with his finger to a passage, and wags his head ominously at the audience, and then lifts up eyes and finger to the ceiling, professing to derive some intense consolation from the work between which and heaven there is a strong affinity.

As soon as the Stranger saw the young men he acted at them; eyeing them solemnly over his gilt volume as he lay on the stage bank showing his hand, his ring, and his Hessians. He calculated the effect that every one of these ornaments would produce upon his victims; he was determined to fascinate them, for he knew they had paid their money; and he saw their families coming in from the country and filling the cane chairs in his boxes.

As he lay on the bank reading, his servant, Francis, made remarks upon his master.

'Again reading,' said Francis; 'thus it is from morn till night. To him nature has no beauty—life no charm. For three years I have never seen him smile' (the gloom of Bingley's face was fearful to witness during these comments of the faithful domestic). 'Nothing diverts him. O, if he would but attach himself to any living thing, were it an animal—for something man must love.'

[*Enter Tobias from the hut.*] He cries, 'O, how refreshing, after seven long weeks, to feel these warm sunbeams once again. Thanks, bounteous heaven, for the joy I taste!' He presses his cap between his hands, looks up, and prays. The Stranger eyes him attentively.

Francis to the Stranger: 'This old man's share of earthly happiness can be but little. Yet mark how grateful he is for his portion of it.'

Bingley: 'Because though old, he is but a child in the leading-string of hope.' (He looks steadily at Foker, who, however, continues to suck the top of his stick in an unconcerned manner.)

Francis: 'Hope is the nurse of life.'

Bingley: 'And her cradle—is the grave.'

The Stranger uttered this with the moan of a bassoon in agony, and fixed his glance on Pendennis so steadily, that the poor lad was quite put out of countenance. He thought the whole house must be looking at him; and cast his eyes down. As soon as ever he raised them Bingley's were at him again. All through the scene the manager played at him. How relieved the lad was when the scene ended, and Foker, tapping with his cane, cried out, 'Bravo, Bingley!'

'Give him a hand, Pendennis; you know every chap likes a hand,' Mr Foker said; and the good-natured young gentleman, and Pendennis laughing, and the Dragoons in the opposite box, began clapping hands to the best of their power.

A chamber in Wintersen Castle closed over Tobias's hut and the Stranger and his boots; and servants appeared, bustling about with chairs and tables—'That's Hicks and Miss Thackthwaite,' whispered Foker. 'Pretty girl, ain't she, Pendennis? But stop—hurray—bravo! here's the Fotheringay!'

The pit thrilled and thumped its umbrellas; a volley of applause was fired from the gallery; the Dragoon officers and Foker clapped their hands furiously; you would have thought the house was full, so loud were their plaudits ... Pen's eyes opened wide and bright, as Mrs Haller entered with a downcast look, then rallying at the sound of the applause, swept the house with a grateful glance, and, folding her hands across her breast, sank down in a magnificent curtsey. More applause, more umbrellas; Pen this time, flaming with wine and enthusiasm, clapped hands and sang 'Bravo', louder than all. Mrs Haller saw him and everybody else, and old Mr Bows, the little first fiddler of the orchestra (which was this night increased by a detachment of the band of the Dragoons, by the kind permission of Colonel Swallowtail), looked up from the desk where he was perched, with his crutch beside him, and smiled at the enthusiasm of the lad.

Those who have only seen Miss Fotheringay in later days, since her marriage and introduction into London life, have little idea how beautiful a creature she was at the time when our friend Pen first set eyes on her. She was of the tallest of women, and at her then age of six-and-twenty—for six-and-twenty she was, though she vowed she was only nineteen—in the prime and fullness of her beauty. ...

She was dressed in long flowing robes of black, which she managed and swept to and fro with wonderful grace, and out o the folds of which you only saw her sandals occasionally; they were of rather a large size; but Pen thought them as ravishing as the slippers of Cinderella. ...

She stood for a moment—complete and beautiful—as Pen stared at her. 'I say, Pen, isn't she a stunner?' asked Mr Foker.

'Hush!' Pen said, 'She's speaking.'

She began her business in a deep sweet voice. Those who knew the play of the 'Stranger' are aware that the remarks made by the various characters are not valuable in themselves, either for their sound sense, their novelty of observation, or their poetic fancy.

Nobody ever talked so. If we meet idiots in life, as will happen, it is a great mercy that they do not use such absurdly fine words. The Stranger's talk is sham, like the book he reads, and the hair he wears, and the bank he sits on, and the diamond ring he makes play with—but, in the midst of the balderdash, there runs that reality of love, children, and forgiveness of wrong, which will be listened to wherever it is preached, and sets all the world sympathising.

With what smothered sorrow, with what gushing pathos, Mrs Haller delivered her part! At first, when as Count Wintersen's housekeeper and preparing for his Excellency's arrival, she had to give orders about the beds and furniture, and the dinner, etc., to be got ready, she did so with the calm agony of despair. But when she could get rid of the stupid servants, and give vent to her feelings to the pit and the house, she overflowed to each individual as if he were her particular confidant, and she was crying out her griefs on his shoulder: the little fiddler in the orchestra (whom she did not seem to watch, though he followed her ceaselessly), twitched, twisted, nodded, pointed about, and when she came to the favourite passage, 'I have a William, too, if he be still alive— Ah, yes, if he be still alive. His little sisters, too. Why, Fancy, dost thou rack me so? Why dost thou image my poor children fainting in sickness, and crying to—to their mum-um-other,'—when she came to this passage little Bows buried his face in his blue cotton handkerchief, after crying out 'Bravo.'

All the house was affected. Foker, for his part, taking out a large yellow bandanna, wept piteously. As for Pen, he was gone too far for that. He followed the woman about and about—when she was off the stage, it and the house were blank; the lights and the red officers reeled wildly before his sight. He watched her at the side-scene where she stood waiting to come on the stage, and where her father took off her shawl: when the reconciliation arrived, and she flung herself down on Mr Bingley's shoulders, whilst the children clung to their knees, and the Countess (Mrs Bingley) and Baron Steinforth (performed with great liveliness and spirit by Garbetts)—while the rest of the characters formed a group round them, Pen's hot eyes only saw Fotheringay, Fotheringay. The curtain fell upon him like a pall. He did not hear a word of what Bingley said, who came forward to announce the play for the next evening, and who took the tumultuous applause, as usual, for himself. Pen was not even distinctly aware that the house was calling for Miss Fotheringay, nor did the manager seem to comprehend that anybody but himself had caused the success of the play. At last he understood it—stepped back with a grin, and presently appeared with Mrs Haller on his arm. How beautiful she looked! Her hair had fallen down, the officers threw her flowers. She clutched them to her heart. She put back her hair, and smiled all round. Her eyes met Pen's. Down went the curtain again, and she was gone. Not one note could be heard of the overture which the brass band of the Dragoons blew by kind permission of Colonel Swallowtail.

'She *is* a crusher, ain't she now?' Mr Foker asked of his companion.

Pen did not know exactly what Foker said, and answered vaguely. He could not tell the other what he felt; he could not have spoken, just then, to any mortal. Besides, Pendennis did not quite know what he felt yet; it was something overwhelming, maddening, delicious; a fever of wild joy and undefined longing.

And now Rowkins and Miss Thackthwaite came on to dance the favourite double hornpipe, and Foker abandoned himself to the delights of this ballet, just as he had to the tears of the tragedy, a few minutes before. Pen did not care for it, or indeed think about the dance, except to remember that that woman was acting with her in the scene where she first came in. It was a mist before his eyes. At the end of the dance he looked at his watch and said it was time for him to go.

'Hang it, stay to see "The Bravo of the Battle-Axe",' Foker said, 'Bingley's splendid in it; he wears red tights, and has to carry Mrs B. over the Pine-bridge of the Cataract, only she's too heavy. It's great fun, do stop.'

Pen looked at the bill with one lingering fond hope that Miss Fotheringay's name might be hidden, somewhere, in the list of the actors of the after-piece, but there was no such name. Go he must. He had a long ride home. He squeezed Foker's hand. He was choking to speak, but he couldn't. He quitted the theatre and walked frantically about the town, he knew not how long; then he mounted at the George and rode homewards, and Clavering [Ottery St Mary] clock sang out one as he came into the yard at Fairoaks.

[Pendennis meets the Fotheringay, who is the daughter of a shabby 'Captain'; he sees her as Ophelia. ('She made the most charming corpse; and while Hamlet and Laertes were battling in her grave, she was looking out from the back scene with some curiosity towards Pen's box, and the family party assembled in it'.) He proposes; things seem bad; but his uncle, Major Pendennis, handles the affair smartly and it is soon over. Pen goes again to the Chatteris theatre on the night that the manager from London is there.]

Mr Manager Bingley was performing his famous character of Rolla, in 'Pizarro', to a house so exceedingly thin that it would appear as if the part of Rolla was by no means such a favourite with the people of Chatteris as it was with the accomplished actor himself. Scarce anybody was in the theatre. Poor Pen had the boxes almost to himself, and sate there lonely, with bloodshot eyes, leaning over the ledge and gazing haggardly towards the scene, when Cora came in. When she was not on the stage, he saw nothing. Spaniards and Peruvians, processions and battles, priests and virgins of the sun, went in and out, and had their talk, but Arthur took no note of any one of them; and only saw Cora whom his soul longed after. . . . There he sate then, miserable, and gazing at her. And she took no more notice of him than he did the rest of the house.

The Fotheringay was uncommonly handsome, in a white raiment and leopard skin, with a sun upon her breast, and fine tawdry bracelets on her beautiful glancing arms. She spouted the few words of her part, and looked it still better. The eyes, which had overthrown Pen's soul, rolled and gleamed as lustrous as ever; but it was not to him that they were directed that night. He did not know to whom, or remark a couple of gentlemen, in the box next to him, upon whom Miss Fotheringay's glances were perpetually shining.

Nor had Pen noticed the extraordinary change which had taken place on the stage a short time after the entry of these two gentlemen into the theatre. There were so few people in the house that the first act of the play languished entirely, and there had been some question of returning the money. The actors were perfectly careless about their parts, and yawned through the dialogue, and talked loud to each other in the intervals. Even Bingley was listless, and Mrs B. in Elvira spoke under her breath.

How came it that all of a sudden Mrs Bingley began to raise her voice and bellow like a bull of Bashan? Whence was it that

Bingley, flinging off his apathy, darted about the stage and yelled like Kean? Why did Garbetts and Rowkins and Miss Rouncy try, each of them, the force of their charms or graces, and act and swagger and scowl and speak their very loudest at the two gentlemen in box No. 3?

One was a quiet little man in black, with a grey head and a jolly, shrewd face—the other was in all respects a splendid and remarkable individual. He was a tall and portly gentleman with a hooked nose and a profusion of curling brown hair and whiskers; his coat was covered with the richest frogs, braidings, and velvet. He had under-waistcoats, many splendid rings, jewelled pins, and neck-chains. When he took out his yellow pocket-handkerchief with his hand that was cased in white kids, a delightful odour of musk and bergamot was shaken through the house. He was evidently a personage of rank, and it was at him that the little Chatteris company was acting.

He was, in a word, no other than Mr Dolphin, the great manager from London, accompanied by his faithful friend and secretary Mr William Minns; without whom he never travelled. He had not been ten minutes in the theatre before his august presence there was perceived by Bingley and the rest; and they all began to act their best and try to engage his attention. Even Miss Fotheringay's dull heart, which was disturbed at nothing, felt, perhaps, a flutter, when she came in the presence of the famous London Impresario. She had not much to do in her part, but to look handsome, and stand in picturesque attitudes encircling her child; and she did this work to admiration. In vain the various actors tried to win the favour of the great stage Sultan. Pizarro never got a hand from him. Bingley yelled, and Mrs Bingley bellowed, and the Manager only took snuff out of his great gold box. It was only in the last scene when Rolla comes in staggering with the infant (Bingley is not so strong as he was, and his fourth son Master Talma Bingley is a monstrous large child for his age)—when Rolla comes staggering with the child to Cora, who rushes forward with a shriek and says—'O God, there's blood upon him!'—that the London manager clapped his hands, and broke out with an enthusiastic bravo.

Then having concluded his applause, Mr Dolphin gave his secretary a clap on the shoulder, and said, 'By Jove, Billy, she'll do.'

'Who taught her that dodge?' said old Billy, who was a sardonic old gentleman—'I remember her at the Olympic, and hang me if she could say Bo to a goose.'

It was little Mr Bows in the orchestra who had taught her the 'dodge' in question. All the company heard the applause, and, as the curtain went down, came round her, and congratulated and hated Miss Fotheringay.

Now Mr Dolphin's appearance in the remote little Chatteris theatre may be accounted for in this manner. In spite of all his exertions, and the perpetual blazes of triumph, coruscations of talent, victories of old English comedy, which his play-bills advertised, his theatre (which, if you please, and to injure no present susceptibilities and vested interests, we shall call the Museum Theatre) by no means prospered, and the famous Impresario found himself on the verge of ruin. The great Hubbard had acted legitimate drama for twenty nights, and failed to remunerate anybody but himself; the celebrated Mr and Mrs Cawdor had come out in Mr Rawhead's tragedy, and in their favourite round of pieces, and had not attracted the public. Herr Garbage's lions and tigers had drawn for a little time, until one of the animals had bitten a piece out of the Herr's shoulder; when the Lord Chamberlain interfered and put a stop to this species of performance; and the grand Lyrical Drama, though brought out with unexampled splendour and success, with Monsieur Poumons as first tenor, and an enormous orchestra, had almost crushed poor Dolphin in its triumphant progress; so that great as his genius and resources were, they seemed to be at an end. He was dragging on his season wretchedly with half salaries, small operas, feeble old comedies; and his ballet company; and everybody was looking out for the day when he should appear in the Gazette.

One of the illustrious patrons of the Museum Theatre, and occupant of the great proscenium-box, was a gentleman whose name has been mentioned in a previous history; that refined patron of the arts, and enlightened lover of music and drama, the Most Noble the Marquis of Steyne. His lordship's avocations as a statesman prevented him from attending the playhouse very often, or coming very early. But he occasionally appeared at the theatre in time for the ballet, and was always received with the greatest respect by the Manager, from whom he sometimes condescended to receive a visit in his box. It communicated with the stage, and when anything occurred there which particularly pleased him, when a new face made its appearance among the *coryphées*, or a fair dancer executed a *pas* with especial grace or agility, Mr Wenham, Mr Wagg, or some other aide-de-camp of the noble Marquis, would be commissioned to go behind the scenes and express the great man's approbation, or make the inquiries which were prompted by his Lordship's curiosity, or his interest in the dramatic art. He could not be seen by the audience, for Lord Steyne sate modestly behind a curtain and looked only towards the stage—but you could know he was in the house by the glances which all the corps-de-ballet, and all the principal dancers, cast towards his box....

One night this great Prince surrounded by a few choice friends was in his box at the Museum, and they were making such a noise and laughter that the pit was scandalised, and many indignant voices were bawling out silence so loudly, that Wagg wondered why the police did not interfere to take the rascals out. Wenham was amusing the party in the box with extracts from a private letter which he had received from Major Pendennis, whose absence in the country at the full London season had been remarked, and, of course, deplored by his friends.

'The secret is out', said Mr Wenham, 'there's a woman in the case. "Dear Wenham," he begins, "as you have had my character in your hands for the last three weeks, and no doubt have torn me to shreds, according to your custom, I think you can afford to be good-humoured by way of variety, and to do me a service. It is a delicate matter, *entre nous, une affaire de cœur*. There is a young friend of mine who is gone wild about a certain Miss Fotheringay, an actress at the theatre here, and I must own to you, as handsome a woman, and, as it appears to me, as good an actress as ever put on rouge. She does Ophelia, Lady Teazle, Mrs Haller—that sort of thing. Upon my word, she is as splendid as Georges in her best days, and, as far as I know, utterly superior to anything we have on our scene. *I want a London engagement for her.* Won't you get your friend Dolphin to come and see her, to engage her, to take her out of this place? A word from a noble friend of ours (you understand) would be invaluable, and if you would get the Gaunt House interest for me—I will promise *anything* I can in return for your service—which I shall consider one of the greatest *that can be done to me*. Do, do this now as a good fellow, which I *always said you were*; and, in return, command yours truly, A. PENDENNIS.'"

'It's a clear case,' said Mr Wenham, having read this letter; 'old Pendennis is in love.'

'And wants to get the woman up to London—evidently,' continued Mr Wagg....

'Stuff,' said the great man. 'He has relations in the country, hasn't he? He said something about a nephew, whose interest could return a member. It is the nephew's affair, depend upon it. The young one is in a scrape. I was myself—when I was in the fifth form at Eton—a market-gardener's daughter—and swore I'd marry her. I was mad about her—poor Polly!' Here he made a pause, and perhaps the past rose up to Lord Steyne, and George Gaunt was a boy again not altogether lost. 'But I say, she must be a fine woman from Pendennis's account. Have in Dolphin, and let us hear if he knows anything of her.'

At this Wenham sprang out of the box, passed the servitor who waited at the door communicating with the stage, and who saluted Mr Wenham with profound respect; and the latter emissary, pushing on and familiar with the place, had no difficulty in finding out the manager, who was employed, as he not infrequently was, in swearing and cursing the ladies of the corps-de-ballet for not doing their duty.

The oaths died away on Mr Dolphin's lips, as soon as he saw Mr Wenham and he drew off the hand which was clenched in the face of one of the offending *coryphées*, to grasp that of the new-comer. 'How do, Mr Wenham! How's his lordship tonight? Looks uncommonly well,' said the manager, smiling, as if he had never been out of temper in his life; and he was only too delighted to follow Lord Steyne's ambassador and pay his personal respects to that great man.

The visit to Chatteris was the result of their conversation; and Mr Dolphin wrote to his Lordship from that place, and did himself the honour to inform the Marquis of Steyne, that he had seen the lady about whom his Lordship had spoken, that he was as much struck by her talents as he was by her personal appearance, and that he had made an engagement with Miss Fotheringay, who would soon have the honour of appearing before a London audience, and his noble and enlightened patron, the Marquis of Steyne.

Pen read the announcement of Miss Fotheringay's engagement in the Chatteris paper where he had so often praised her charms. The editor made very handsome mention of her talent and beauty, and prophesied her success in the metropolis. Bingley, the manager, began to advertise 'The last night of Miss Fotheringay's engagement'. Poor Pen and Sir Derby Oaks were very constant at the play: Sir Derby in the stage-box, throwing bouquets and getting glances—Pen in the almost deserted boxes, haggard, wretched, and lonely. Nobody cared whether Miss Fotheringay was going or staying except those two—and perhaps one more, which was Mr Bows of the orchestra.

He came out of his place one night, and went into the house to the box where Pen was; and he held out his hand to him, and asked him to come and walk. They walked down the street together; and went and sate upon Chatteris bridge in the moonlight, and talked about Her. 'We may sit on the same bridge,' said he: 'We have been in the same boat for a long time. You are not the only man who has made a fool of himself about that woman. And I have less excuse than you because I'm older and know her better. She has no more heart than the stone you are leaning on; and it or you or I might fall into the water, and never come up again, and she wouldn't care. Yes—she would care for me, and will be forced to send for me from London. But she wouldn't if she didn't want me. She has no heart and no head, and no sense, and no feelings, and no griefs or cares, whatever. I was going to say no pleasures—but the fact is she does like her dinner, and she is pleased when people admire her.'

'And you do?' said Pen, interested out of himself, and wondering at the crabbed homely little old man.

'It's a habit, like taking snuff, or drinking drams,' said the other. 'It was I made her. If she doesn't send for me, I shall follow her: but I know she'll send for me. She wants me. Some day she'll marry, and fling me over, as I do the end of this cigar.'

The little flaming spark dropped into the water below, and disappeared, and Pen, as he rode home that night, actually thought about somebody but himself.

W. M. THACKERAY

XIII
A Pint of Porter

ONLY a few weeks after the outraged Macready had knocked down Alfred Bunn, the buoyant manager was back in Drury Lane, upon crutches, for the final rehearsals of *The Maid of Artois*. Maria Malibran appeared as Isoline, the Maid, in this opera for which Michael William Balfe had written the music, and Bunn himself the libretto. Two lines from one of its songs, a second act ballad for the Marquis,

> The light of other days is faded,
> And all their glory past

are now among the entries under Bunn's name in *The Oxford Dictionary of Quotations*. The others are 'Alice, where art thou?' (a song title) and two snatches from the libretto of *The Bohemian Girl*, 'I dreamt that I dwelt in marble halls, With vassals and serfs at my side,' and 'When other lips, and other hearts, Their tales of love shall tell.'

During the third act, in the desert of Guiana, the Maid of Artois uses the last drop of water to bathe her insensible lover's wound before breaking into what the *Morning Post* called 'a paroxysm of exultation that "the light is in his eye again, the beating at his heart."' She is in danger of yielding to thirst; but fortunately help arrives, and everybody is reconciled to everyone else. The *Morning Post* said Malibran 'gave the finale, "the rapture swelling," with inexhaustible fire and energy. Three octaves did she call into requisition in this masterpiece of execution, reaching E in alt, and making a prolonged shake, if we mistake not, on B flat in alt. It was, in sooth, a wondrous burst, and it was cruel to demand it a second time.' But the audience did, and Malibran responded.

Bunn, in *The Stage: Both Before and Behind the Curtain* (1840) recalls this encore on the night of 26 May, 1836.

HOWEVER troublesome and tedious the progress of recovery from so sudden an attack on a frame by no means so thin and genteel as it was wont to be, the delay it occasioned in the production of the new opera for Madame Malibran was a much more important affair. I could not entrust that production to any other because, as author and manager, the entire preparation had devolved upon me, and it would have taken me more time, even had my condition admitted of it, to have instilled my crude notions into the noddle of another, than it did in the first instance to devise them. It should be borne in mind that Madame Malibran could not remain in England beyond a given time, and that even if she could the London season was waning fast apace. There were but two characters, La Sonnambula and Fidelio, in which she was prepared, and although their attraction was but slightly abated, every repetition of either tended to abate it the more. I went to the Drury Lane stage upon crutches to attend the last six rehearsals of *The Maid of Artois*, which was eventually represented on the 26th May. The effect produced by Malibran upon the town in the character of Isoline made amends for every indignity, and for every pang that had been endured.

I had occasion during the last rehearsal but one to express myself in strong terms when Malibran left the stage for more than an hour and a half, to go and gain £25 at a morning concert. Neither the concerted pieces of music, nor the situations of the drama in which she was involved, could possibly be proceeded with, and the great stake we were then contending for was likely to be placed in jeopardy by an unworthy grasp at a few pounds, to the prejudice of a theatre paying her nightly five times as much. She knew she had done wrong, and she atoned for it by her genius, while her pride would not have permitted her to have done so. She had borne along the two first acts on the first night of performance in such a flood of triumph, that she was bent, by some almost superhuman effort, to continue its glory to the final fall of the curtain. I went into her dressing-room previous to the third act to ask how she felt, and she replied, 'Very tired, but' (and here her eye of fire suddenly lighted up) 'you angry devil, if you will contrive to get me a pint of porter in the desert scene, you shall have an encore to your music.' Had I been dealing with any other performer, I should perhaps have hesitated in complying with a request that might have been dangerous in its application at the moment; but to check *her* powers was to annihilate them.

I therefore arranged that behind the pile of drifted sand on which she falls in a state of exhaustion, towards the close of the desert scene, a small aperture should be made in the stage; and it is a fact that, from underneath the stage through that aperture, a pewter pint of porter was conveyed to the parched lips of this rare child of song, which so revived her, after the terrible exertion that the scene led to, that she electrified the audience, and had strength to repeat the charm, with the finale to *The Maid of Artois*.

The novelty of the circumstance so tickled her fancy, and the draught itself was so extremely refreshing, that it was arranged, during the run of the opera, for the Negro slave, at the head of the governor's procession, to have in the gourd suspended to his neck the same quantity of the same beverage, to be applied to her lips, on his first beholding the apparently dying Isoline.

[Four months later, Malibran, who had returned to England from Brussels, for the Manchester Music Festival, died at the Moseley Arms Hotel, Manchester, 23 September 1836. She was twenty-eight.]

ALFRED BUNN

XIV

Green-Room

GEORGE VANDENHOFF (1813–1885) was the son of a tragedian, John Vandenhoff, who, in spite of a long London career, was famed particularly in the provinces. George made his début in 1839 as Mercutio at Covent Garden (he described the Green-Room of the theatre in his sometimes astringent *Dramatic Reminiscences*, 1860). He acted for more than a decade in America, returned to England, and in 1856 practically retired from the stage. At Covent Garden he acted under the management of Madame Vestris (1797–1856) and her second husband, Charles Mathews the younger (1803–1878). James Sheridan Knowles (1784–1862) was the actor and dramatist—author of *The Hunchback*—who in later life became a Baptist preacher. James Henry Leigh Hunt (1784–1859), essayist and poet, had been one of the first major drama critics; the play *A Legend of Florence* appeared at Covent Garden in 1840.

IT MUST be understood that in Covent Garden and Drury Lane Theatres, there were a *first* and *second* Green-Room; the first, exclusively set apart for the *corps dramatique* proper—the actors and actresses of a certain position; the second, belonging to the *corps de ballet*, the pantomimists, and all engaged in that line of business—what are called the *little people*—except the principal male and female dancer (at that time, at Covent Garden, Mr and Mrs Gilbert), who had the privilege of the first Green-Room.

The term Green-Room arose originally from the fact of that room being carpeted in green (baize, probably), and the covering of the divans being green-*stuff*. But the first Green-Room in Covent Garden Theatre was a withdrawing-room, carpeted and papered elegantly; with a handsome chandelier in the centre, several globe lights at the sides, a comfortable divan, covered in figured damask, running round the whole room, large pier and mantel-glasses on the walls, and a full-length moveable swing-glass; so that, on entering from his dressing-room, an actor could see himself from head to foot at one view, and get back, front, and side views by reflection, all round. This is the first point to attend to on entering the Green-Room, to see if one's dress is in perfect order, well put on by the dresser, hanging well, and perfectly *comme il faut*. Having satisfied him or herself on these interesting points, even to the graceful drooping of a feather, the actor or actress sits down, and enters into conversation with those around, which is interrupted every now and then by the shrill voice of the *call-boy* 'making his calls.' The call-boy is a most important 'remembrancer'—he may be named the prompter's Devil, as the boy in a printing office who calls for copy is yclept the printer's devil. His business is to give the actors and actresses notice, by calling at the door of the Green-Room (he is not allowed to enter those sacred precincts in a London theatre) the names of the persons whose presence is required on the stage. This he does by direction of the prompter, who about five minutes, or three lengths (120 lines) before a character has to enter on the stage, finds marked in his prompt-book of the play a number thus (3). He then says to his attendant imp, who has a list in his hand (a call-list—very different from a New Year's call-list), 'Call *three*'; the boy looks at his list, walks to the Green-Room door, and calls the character marked (3) in that act; or the prompter orders him to call 4, 5, 6, 7; he consults his list for the act, finds these numbers, and at the Green-Room door calls the characters they represent, thus: Hamlet, Horatio, Marcellus, Ghost. The gentlemen who represent these characters, on being thus called, rise, leave the Green-Room, and go and stand at the wing—the side-scene—at which they are presently to enter. All the calls are made at the Green-Room door, and it is at an actor's peril to take notice of them; it is only on a change of dress that he is entitled to be called at his dressing-room, except *stars*, and they insist on being always called there, as well as in the Green-Room; and the point is conceded to them.

In many theatres the calls are made by the name of the actor or actress representing the character called. It was so, if I recollect, at Covent Garden; at the Haymarket it is otherwise; and generally throughout the theatres of the United States, the calls are made by the names of the characters; and it is the safer plan, and less liable to mistakes on the part of the call-boy.

The Green-Room was exceedingly comfortable during the Mathews and Vestris management. Indeed I must pay them the compliment of saying that their arrangements generally for the convenience of their company, the courtesy of their behaviour to the actors, and consideration for their comforts, formed an example well worthy to be followed by managers in general; who are not, I am sorry to say, usually remarkable for these qualities. In fact, the reign of Vestris and her husband might be distinguished as the *drawing-room management*. On special occasions—the opening night of the season, for example, or a 'Queen's visit'—tea and coffee were served in the Green-Room; and frequently, between the acts, some of the officers of the guard, or gentlemen in attendance on the royal party, would be introduced, which led, of course, to agreeable and sometimes advantageous acquaintances.

The Green-Room, too, is the place where new plays that have been accepted by the management, are read by the author to the ladies and gentlemen who are to be engaged in their performance. Here I heard Leigh Hunt read his elegant and poetical play of *A Legend of Florence*, which was admirably played, as he himself delighted to acknowledge—Miss Tree, a gentleman named Moore (a new man), Anderson, and myself were in the cast; and here also I heard Sheridan Knowles read his play of *Old Maids* the season after, in which Mrs Nisbett, Madame Vestris, Charles Mathews, and myself played.

Leigh Hunt was a charming, genial, kind-hearted, simple-mannered gentleman, 'soft as summer', with rather long hair tinged with grey (later white as snow, I am told) with something of a Lorenzo de Medici look, softened; and he read clearly and pleasingly, with just emphasis, but without any aim at effect. Sheridan Knowles, on the contrary, was a hearty, rather boisterous old fellow; of strong, rather coarse features; reminding one of the traditional portraits of Ben Jonson; and he read his play in a loud, rollicking style, with marked emphasis, a theatrical effect, and strong dashes of the brogue.

Leigh Hunt looked like a poet of the gentle elegiac school; you could well conceive him as the teller of the tale of Rimini in such sweet words; and you would not doubt that he wept over them himself. Knowles, on the contrary, looking anything but poetical; brusque in manner, slovenly in dress, absent in mind, quick and rapid in utterance, he gave you rather the idea of an Irish school-master. But he had great power as a dramatist; deep poetic feeling; and a nervous, energetic diction, when he was not misled by the affectation of imitating the old dramatists, into an involved and inverted style, most painful to the actor to learn, unpleasing in the delivery, and difficult for an audience to follow. In reading a play, he could produce strong effects by his earnest intensity; and though you might sometimes laugh at his abruptness and his brogue that would peep out, you would not unfrequently catch yourself weeping at his touches of natural pathos and the deep feeling he knew how to throw into his tenderest passages. The stage owes him much for what he has done for it, in spite of what he is doing against it by his pulpit denunciations.

Some authors, new to the *coulisses*, are terribly embarrassed on being presented to the Green-Room, to read their play under the battery of so many sparkling eyes and the criticism of so many captious ears. The actors are usually courteous in attention, if not always encouraging in applause; and they sit, silently watchful, and picking out by degrees, the part that each thinks will be allotted to him. The reading being closed, the parts are then and there distributed in manuscript; and then is made manifest the disappointment of some who find they have not got the parts they expected, and the disgust of others, who have got just the very parts that they dreaded and detested in the reading. It is then the acting manager's business—no easy one, sometimes—to smoothe these difficulties, and to smoothe their discontented spirits. His is the task to persuade Miss Jenkins that her part will *act* much better than it *reads*; and that it is ('really now') a much more effective part than Mrs Timkins's; and

'Consider, my dear, the change of dress; besides breeches in the first act.'

Then the leading actor is to be reconciled to his part, which he thinks very much below his abilities.

'My dear sir,' says the manager, 'it's just the thing for you, you will produce a great effect in the third act.'

'But', objects the actor, 'it falls off so confoundedly in the fifth act; the lady has it all to herself.'

'Well, well,' says the ready manager, 'we'll get the author to write you up in the fifth act; and we'll give you the tag to speak' (the *tag* is the closing lines of the play), and so the great man is smoothed down.

Then comes up an actor, third or fourth-rate, but thinking a great deal more of himself than audience or manager can be brought to do, with a very scanty manuscript in his hand, which he opens to show how little writing there is in it, exclaiming in a voice of suffering innocence, 'Why! Mr Bartley, my part is all *cues*; there are only ten lines to speak, and I am on in every scene in every act.'

'It's not a long part, my boy, I know,' replies the plausible manager, 'but it's a very responsible one, and you'll be splendidly dressed.'

That last consideration reconciles the youth to his bad part, with the consolation that he will, at all events, have an opportunity of exhibiting his own appearance to advantage; and he is smoothed over.

Then Mrs Shady thinks that 'she really ought not to be called on to play *old women*.'

'Old women, my dear,' says he, 'what do you mean? Your part's not an old woman; she's a young, dashing widow, my dear; that's the reason I cast you for it.'

'Young!' exclaims Mrs Shady, 'she must be fifty, at least; she has a daughter married.'

'Nonsense, my dear,' says the manager. 'Fifty! She's not more than thirty. She was married young, of course, and so was her daughter. In the period of this play, and in Spain, girls married at thirteen; so did you and your daughter. *Play* it young, my dear; as young as you like; I've no objection.'

And Mrs Shady collapses, out-answered, and feeling herself the victim of oppression and managerial injustice (to say nothing of that odious Mrs Middleton, who will triumph over her); has a good cry, and goes home and studies her part.

GEORGE VANDENHOFF

XV
Mannerism

JOHN COLEMAN, who died in 1904 at the age of seventy-two, was like every old-actor joke, collected, indexed, and bound in leather. He was known to address a super with the words, 'My dear sir, when you ascend the raking piece and leave the stage, be good enough to emit a greasy laugh of truculent defiance.' But he was on terms with most people in the Victorian theatre; and though he spoke and wrote with the rumble of a cannon-ball rolling down the thunder-track, he could often be shrewd. Nobody could ignore a man of his generous good-nature, his romantic view of the profession, and his blotting-paper memory for the nonsense of stock melodrama. He could have been a model (though he was not) for Pinero's Telfer in *Trelawny of the 'Wells'*. Samuel Phelps (1804–1878) was his hero; and towards the end of Coleman's life he realized his ambition to be the first man since Phelps to present *Pericles, Prince of Tyre*. His production of his own adapted and bowdlerized version at Stratford-upon-Avon in April 1900 remains one of the principal jokes of Stratford history. Honest John wrote copious reminiscences, and the ensuing extract is from *Players and Playwrights I Have Known*, 1888.

George Vandenhoff, whom I also quote on mannerism, disliked Macready; Macready disliked him. The play *Gisippus* (Drury Lane, 1842) was by an Irish dramatist, Gerald Griffin.

MANNERISM

THOUGH straight and lithe of motion, Phelps had but a meagre figure. Its slenderness, however, became an advantage as he grew older, and his singularly abstemious habits, combined with his regular mode of living, enabled him to present to the last an elasticity of gait and a singular youthfulness.

Certain criticasters, legitimate descendants of the 'common cry of curs' who, ages ago, yelped at great Caesar's heels because his brow was bald, and who later carped at the wart upon the brow of the mighty Oliver, and whose representatives today measure Gladstone's genius by the dimensions of his shirt-collar, maintained with 'damnable iteration' that Phelps's demeanour was bourgeois, that his eyes were colourless and lacked lustre, that his features were commonplace and inexpressive; yet even these small fry were compelled to admit that his brow was lofty and arched like the dome of a temple, that the nasal column was straight and strong, and that his mouth and chin were firm, powerful, and determined.

Though his hands were large-boned, gnarled, and even ugly, he made them eloquently expressive, and he had taught every muscle of his body to respond instinctively to the motion of his mind. His voice, which he assured me was originally a piping, weak, reed-like thing, had by constant application been trained into a potent, resonant organ, capable of expressing every varying mood of tragic or comic art. That he was a mannerist his greatest admirers will never seek to deny. It is remarkable that his mannerisms should have assimilated so closely to those of Macready, when it is remembered the two men never met until Phelps was thirty-four years of age when one would have thought his style was fixed.

At Sadler's Wells all the young actors glided irresistibly into the Phelps mannerism, and at the Princess's, during the representation of that delightful and magnificent spectacle, *A Midsummer Night's Dream*, although the Keans did not act in the play, yet when Helena and Hermia, Lysander and Demetrius were lost in the wood, and out of sight of the audience during the changing scene, their various voices emitted from different sides of the stage such unconscious burlesque imitations of Mr and Mrs [Charles] Kean's most marked peculiarities as to evoke roars of laughter through the entire house. It is unfortunate that on these occasions the scholar's zeal invariably induces him to reproduce the exaggerations and not the excellences of his master.

The most remarkable thing about the Phelps mannerism was the fact that it persistently asserted itself in his tragic assumptions, while in comedy he obliterated it so effectively as to efface his own personal identity. For my own poor part, the only drawback I ever experienced to my perfect enjoyment of his acting was his mannerism.

When I discussed this peculiarity one day with the veteran dramatist, Palgrave Simpson, speaking of a mutual friend who had not succeeded according to his deserts, Pal broke out:

'K. is too good an actor to be a great one. I admit he looks like a man, and speaks like a gentleman; so much the worse. He ought to growl, or grunt, or stutter, or have a French, or at least a provincial, accent; in fact, he ought to be a mannerist. No man has ever been a popular favourite in my time unless he was a pronounced mannerist. Charles [Mayne] Young was a mellifluous, mouthing mannerist; Charles Kemble was a silver-tongued, sententious mannerist; Edmund Kean was a stuttering, spasmodic mannerist; then he got drunk, my boy, and people had the delicious excitement and uncertainty of doubt as to whether he was "half seas over or wholly gone." Macready and Phelps were always grim and growling over their bones; Charles Kean had a chronic cold in his head; Lemaitre was always drunk or delirious (what could be more exciting than that?), Keeley was sleek and sleepy, Bucky [Buckstone] was a chuckler, and always loose in the text; Compton was as funny as a funeral; Ben Webster was always imperfect, and had a Somerset dialect; Mathews was Mephisto in kid gloves and patent-leather boots—and nothing but Mephisto (but you know "the Prince of Darkness is a gentleman," so was Charley); Ryder was a roarer; in fact, all these great actors owed their popularity to the fact of their being more or less pronounced mannerists. Ergo, your friend Phelps owed a great deal of his hold upon the public to the fact that he was a confirmed mannerist.'

JOHN COLEMAN

George Vandenhoff wrote in his *Dramatic Reminiscences*:

The slavish copying of Macready was pushed to such an extent at his own theatre, that the very supers who carried a banner adopted 'the eminent tragedian's' rolling walk; and the man who delivered a message gave it out with 'the eminent's' extrasyllabification of utterance. It was really a singularly strange thing to see, in the tragedy of *Gisippus*, for example (which Mr Macready brought out at Drury Lane with great care and taste), at one view, a whole company surrendering their own identities with plastic subservience, and melting themselves down into the Macready mould.

There was [James] Anderson in Fulvius, who had caught the master's tones, slides and angularities, sway and action, till they seemed almost his own; the assumption was so complete, that some people would have it that he was Mac's son. Then came Hudson as Chraemes, who had been indoctrinated into the same routine, only on a higher pitch, with a dash of flippancy thrown in, like an acid, to give effervescence to the mixture; then came Helen Faucit, as Sophronia, who, having commenced her career under 'the eminent's' management, was entirely made up of his mannerisms, 'subdued even to the very quality of her lord,' redeemed only by the charms of her own feminine sweetness;— and last, George Bennett as Lycias, a violent exaggeration of every singularity, angularity, and formality of the Macreadian method.

These were the principal characters. Then came the subordinates and supers, all formed on the same model, crying in the same tune, and rolling with the same swinging gait. It was a perfect babel of confusion to the mind, on an *inverse principle*, from a puzzling general communion of identity—one could scarcely separate the interests and positions of people who were so much alike. When they came together, it was a great organ, and you had to watch the mouths of the speakers to see which *stop* was playing; nor could you always keep your mind clear as to how all these people could be engaged in plots and counterplots for intermarrying with, or destroying each other, when it seemed evident that they were all members of the same family, and so ought to be barred, by ties of consanguinity, from schemes of love or intrigue.

XVI

Palace by the Lake

ONE OF THE most popular show-pieces in the nineteenth-century theatre was a passage for Claude and Pauline from the first scene of the second act of the then Edward Lytton Bulwer's *The Lady of Lyons; or, Love and Pride*. Macready and Helen Faucit acted the parts at Covent Garden on the night of 15 February 1838.

The scene is Lyons, the period 1795, post-Revolution. Claude Melnotte, a peasant who has vainly loved a proud beauty, Pauline ('as pretty as Venus, and as proud as Juno'), is wooing her in his disguise of the Prince of Como. The trick has been planned by two of Pauline's rejected suitors, Beauseant and Glavis, to discredit her; but, given his chance, Claude speaks to Pauline (who had never known him as the gardener's son) with a lover's passionate eloquence. They are married; there is a fatal revelation; then, two years and a half later, Claude (now a Colonel and a hero) and his wife are happily reunited.

The dramatist has a careful note to the wooing scene: 'The reader will observe that Melnotte evades the request of Pauline. He proceeds to describe a home, which he does not say he possesses, but to which he would lead her "could Love fulfil its prayers." This caution is intended as a reply to a sagacious critic who censures the description because it is not an exact and prosaic inventory of the characteristics of the Lake of Como! When Melnotte, for instance, talks of birds "that syllable the name of Pauline" (by the way, a literal translation from an Italian poet), he is not thinking of ornithology, but probably of the Arabian Nights. He is venting the extravagant, but natural, enthusiasm of the Poet and the Lover.'

Melnotte: You can be proud of your connexion with one who owes his position to merit—not birth.
Pauline: Why, yes; but still—
Melnotte: Still what, Pauline!
Pauline: There is something glorious in the Heritage of Command. A man who has ancestors is like a Representative of the Past.
Melnotte: True; but, like other representatives, nine times out of ten he is a silent member. Ah, Pauline! not to the Past, but to the Future, looks true nobility, and finds its blazon in posterity.
Pauline: You say this to please me, who have no ancestors; but you, Prince, must be proud of so illustrious a race!
Melnotte: No, no! I would not, were I fifty times a prince, be a pensioner on the Dead! I honour birth and ancestry when they are regarded as the incentives to exertion, not the title-deeds to sloth! I honour the laurels that overshadow the graves of our fathers;—it is our fathers I emulate, when I desire that beneath the evergreen I myself have planted, my own ashes may repose! Dearest! could'st thou but see with my eyes!
Pauline: I cannot forego pride when I look on thee, and think that thou lovest me. Sweet Prince, tell me again of thy palace by the Lake of Como; it is so pleasant to hear of thy splendours since thou didst swear to me that they would be desolate without Pauline; and when thou describest them, it is with a mocking lip and a noble scorn, as if custom had made thee disdain greatness.
Melnotte: Nay, dearest, nay, if thou would'st have me paint
The home to which, could Love fulfil its prayers,
This hand would lead thee, listen!—A deep vale
Shut out by Alpine hills from the rude world;
Near a clear lake, margin'd by fruits of gold
And whispering myrtles! glassing softest skies
As cloudless, save with rare and roseate shadows,
As I would have thy fate!
Pauline: My own dear love!
Melnotte: A palace lifting to eternal summer
Its marble walls, from out a glossy bower
Of coolest foliage musical with birds,
Whose songs should syllable thy name! At noon
We'd sit beneath the arching vines and wonder

Why Earth could be unhappy, while the Heavens
Still left us youth and love! We'd have no friends
That were not lovers; no ambitions, save
To excel them all in love; we'd read no books
That were not tales of love—that we might smile
To think how poorly eloquence of words
Translates the poetry of hearts like ours!
And when night came, amidst the breathless Heavens
We'd guess what star should be our home when love
Becomes immortal; while the perfumed light
Stole through the mists of alabaster lamps,
And every air was heavy with the sighs
Of orange-groves and music from sweet lutes,
And murmurs of low fountains that gush forth
I' the midst of roses!—Dost thou like the picture?
Pauline: Oh! as the bee upon the flower, I hang
Upon the honey of thy eloquent tongue!
Am I not blest? And if I love too wildly,
Who would not love thee like Pauline?
Melnotte: (*bitterly*)   Oh, false one!
It is the *prince* thou lovest, not the *man*:
If in the stead of luxury, pomp, and power,
I had painted poverty, and toil, and care,
Thou hadst found no honey on my tongue,—Pauline,
That is not love!
Pauline: Thou wrong'st me, cruel Prince!
At first, in truth, I might not have been won,
Save through the weakness of a flatter'd pride;
But *now*,—Oh! trust me,—could'st thou fall from power
And sink—
Melnotte: As low as that poor gardener's son,
Who dared to lift his eyes to thee?—
Pauline: Even then,
Methinks thou would'st be only made more dear
By the sweet thought that I could prove how deep
Is woman's love! We are like the insects, caught
By the poor glittering of a garish flame;
But, oh, the wings once scorch'd, the brightest star
Lures us no more; and by the fatal light
We cling till death!

Melnotte: Angel!
  (*Aside*) O conscience! conscience!
  It must not be:—her love hath grown to torture
  Worse than her hate. I will at once to Beauseant,
  And—ha! he comes.—Sweet love, one moment leave us.
  I have business with these gentlemen—I—I
  Will forthwith join you.
Pauline: Do not tarry long! (*Exit*)
  Enter Beauseant and Glavis.
Melnotte: Release me from my oath,—I will not marry her!
Beauseant: Then thou art perjured.
Melnotte: No, I was not in my senses when I swore to thee to marry her! I was blind to all but her scorn!—deaf to all but my passion and my rage! Give me back my poverty and my honour!
Beauseant: It is too late,—you must marry her! and this day. I have a story already coined, and sure to pass current. This Damas suspects thee,—he will set the police to work;—thou wilt be detected—Pauline will despise and execrate thee. Thou wilt be sent to the common gaol as a swindler.
Melnotte: Fiend!
Beauseant: And in the heat of the girl's resentment (you know of what resentment is capable) and the parents' shame, she will be induced to marry the first that offers—even perhaps your humble servant.
Melnotte: You! No; that were worse—for thou hast no mercy! I will marry her—I will keep my oath. Quick, then, with the damnable invention thou art hatching;—quick, if thou would'st not have me strangle thee or myself.
Glavis: What a tiger! Too fierce for a prince,—he ought to have been the Grand Turk.
Beauseant: Enough—I will despatch; be prepared.

E. L. BULWER

XVII

Imogen and Pauline

HELEN FAUCIT (1817–1898) made her début at Covent Garden in 1836 as Julia in Sheridan Knowles's *The Hunchback*. She was often Macready's leading actress and created Pauline in *The Lady of Lyons* (1838). She acted Imogen in *Cymbeline* under his management at both Covent Garden and Drury Lane. At one point she was clearly infatuated with him; but ultimately, in 1851, she married Theodore Martin, later the Prince Consort's biographer, and knighted. In later years she used the name Helena.

This extract is from her book, *On Some of Shakespeare's Female Characters* (1885). 'Mr Elton' is the actor Edward William Elton, who was drowned (on a voyage from Leith) when the *Pegasus* was wrecked on the Farne Islands in 1843. The production was the Covent Garden *Cymbeline* of September 1838. Macready wrote in his journal (26 September): 'Spoke to Miss Faucit about her boy's dress for Imogen, and suggested to her, on the supposition that her legs were rather thin, the use of a pair of fleeced stockings "such as Malibran used to wear." I managed this "delicate negotiation" as dexterously as I could, and reconciled her easily to the experiment; went out and purchased a pair for her . . .'

I CANNOT quite remember who acted with me in *Cymbeline*, but I can never forget Mr Macready's finding fault with my page's dress, which I had ordered to be made with a tunic that descended to the ankles. On going to the theatre at the last rehearsal, he told me, with many apologies and much concern, that he had seen my page's dress, and had given directions to have it altered. He had taken the liberty of doing this, he said, without consulting me, because, although he could understand the reasons which had weighed with me in ordering the dress to be made as I had done, he was sure I would forgive him when he explained to me that such a dress would not tell the story, and that one-half the audience—all, in fact, who did not know the play—would not discover that it was a disguise, but would suppose Imogen to be still in woman's attire. Remonstrance was too late, and, with many tears, I had to yield, and to add my own terror to that of Imogen, when first entering the cave. I managed, however, to devise a kind of compromise, by swathing myself in the 'franklin housewife's riding-cloak,' which I kept about me as I went into the cave; and this I caused to be wrapped round me afterwards when the brothers carry in Imogen—the poor 'dead bird, which they have made so much on.'

I remember well the Pisanio was my good friend Mr. Elton, the best Pisanio of my time. No one whom I have since acted with has so truly thrown into the part the deep devotion, the respectful manly tenderness and delicacy of feeling which it requires. He drew out all the nicer points of the character with the same fine and firm hand which we used to admire upon the French stage in M. Regnier, that most finished of actors, in characters of this kind. As I write, by some strange association of ideas—I suppose we must have been rehearsing *Cymbeline* at the time—a little circumstance illustrative of the character of this good Mr Elton comes into my mind. This helpful friend did not always cheer and praise, but very kindly told me of my mistakes. We were to appear in *The Lady of Lyons*, which was then in its first run, and had been commanded by the Queen for a State performance. I had never acted before Her Majesty and Prince Albert; and to me, young as I was, this was a great event. Immediately I thought there ought to be something special about my dress for the occasion. Now, either from a doubt as to the play's success, or for some good financial reason, no expense had been incurred in bringing it out. Mr Macready asked me if I had any dresses which could be adapted for Pauline Deschappelles. He could not, he said, afford to give me new dresses, and he would be glad if I could manage without them. Of course I said I would willingly do my best. Upon consulting with the excellent Mr Dominic Colnaghi, the print-seller in Pall Mall, who always gave me access to all his books of costume, I found as I had already heard, that the dress of the young girl of the period was simple in material and form—fine muslin, with lace *fichus*, ruffles, broad sashes, and the hair worn in long loose curls down the back, my own coming in naturally for this fashion. As it was in my case, so I suppose it was with the others—the costumes, however, being all true to the period. The scenery was of course good and sufficient, for in this department Mr Macready never failed. And thus, with trifling cost, this play, which was to prove so wonderfully successful, came forth to the world unassisted by any extraneous adjuncts, depending solely upon its own merits and the actors' interpretation of it.

It must have been written with rare knowledge of what the stage requires, for not one word was cut out, nor one scene rearranged or altered after the first representation. The author was no doubt lucky in his interpreters, Mr Macready, though in appearance far too old for Claude Melnotte, yet had a slight, elastic figure, and so much buoyancy of manner, that the impression of age quickly wore off. The secret of his success was, that he lifted the character, and gave it the dignity and strength which it required to make Claude respected under circumstances so equivocal. This was especially conspicuous in a critical point early in the play (Act ii.), where Claud passes himself off as a prince. Mr Macready's manner became his dress. The slight confusion, when addressed by Colonel Damas in Italian, was so instantly turned to his own advantage by the playful way in which he laid the blame on the Colonel's bad Italian, his whole bearing was so dignified and courteous, that it did not seem strange he should charm the girlish fancy of one who was accustomed to be courted, but whose heart was hitherto untouched. He made the hero, indeed, one of nature's exceptional gentlemen, and in this way prepossessed his audience, despite the unworthy device to which Claude lends himself in the first frenzy of wounded vanity. Truth to say, unless dealt with poetically and romantically, both Claude and Pauline drop down into very commonplace people—indeed I have been surprised to see how commonplace. . . .

But to return to the evening of the Royal Command, and what I was going to say. I had nothing especially new and fresh to wear; so in honour of the occasion I had ordered from Foster's some lovely pink roses with silver leaves, to trim the dress I wore in the second act. I had hitherto used only real roses—friends, known and unknown always supplying me with them. In my mind was always the idea that Pauline loved flowers passionately. It was in the garden among his flowers that Claude first saw and loved her. I never was without them in the play; even in the sad last act, I had violets on my plain muslin dress. You remember how Madame Deschappelles reproaches Pauline for not being *en grande tenue* on that 'joyful occasion'.

I thought my new flowers, when arranged about my dress, looked lovely—quite fairy-like. When accosted with the usual 'Good evenings' while waiting at the side scenes for the opening of the second act, I saw Mr Elton looking at me with a sort of amused wonder. I said at once, 'Do you not think my fresh flowers pretty?' 'Oh', he said, '*are* they fresh? They must have come a long way. Where do they grow? I never saw any of the kind before. They must have come out of Aladdin's garden. Silver leaves! How remarkable! They may be more rare, but I much prefer the home-grown ones you have in your hand.' Ridicule of my fine decoration! Alas! alas! I felt at once that it was deserved. It was too late to repair my error. I must act the scene with them—before the Queen too!—and all my pleasure was gone. I hid them as well as I could with my fan and handkerchief, and hoped no one would notice them. Need I say how they were torn off when I reached my dressing-room, never to see the light again? I never felt more ashamed and vexed with myself.

Like many pleasures long looked forward to, the whole of the evening was a disappointment. The side scenes were overcrowded with visitors, Mr Macready having invited many friends. They were terribly in the way of the exits and entrances. Worse than all, those who knew you insisted on saluting you; those who did not, made you run the gauntlet of a host of curious eyes—and this in a place where, most properly, no stranger had hitherto been allowed to intrude. Then, too, though of course I never looked at the Queen and the Prince, still their presence was felt by me more than I could have anticipated. It overawed me somehow—stood between me and Pauline; and instead of doing my best, I could not in my usual way, lose myself entirely in my character, so that, on the whole I never acted worse or more artificially—too like my poor flowers!

It was well I had a handkerchief on this occasion to help to screen my poor silver leaves; but as a general rule I kept it in my pocket—and for this reason. In the scene in the third act—where Pauline learns the infamous stratagem of which she is the victim—on the night the play was first acted, I tore my handkerchief right across without knowing that I had done so; and in the passion and emotion of the scene it became a streamer, and waved about as I moved and walked. Surely any one might have seen that this was an accident, the involuntary act of the maddened girl; but in a criticism on the play—I suppose the day after, but as I was never allowed to have my mind disturbed by theatrical criticisms, I cannot feel sure—I was accused of having arranged this as a trick in order to produce an effect. So innocent was I of a device which would have been utterly at variance with the spirit in which I looked at my art, that when my dear home master and friend asked me if I *had* torn the handkerchief in the scene, I laughed and said, 'Yes, at the end of the play my dresser had shown me one in ribbons.' 'I would not,' was his remark, 'have you carry one again in the scene, if you can do without it'; and I did not usually do so. It was some time afterwards before I learned his reason, and I then continued to keep my handkerchief mostly in my pocket, lest the same accident should happen again; for, as I always allowed the full feeling of the scene to take possession of me, I could not answer but that it might. There would have been nothing wrong in acting upon what strong natural emotion had suggested in the heat of actual performance; but all true artists will, I believe, avoid the use of any action, however striking, which may become by repetition a mere mechanical artifice.

It was different with another suggestion which was made to me as to the way I acted in the same scene. As I recalled to Claude, in bitter scorn, his glowing description of his palace by the Lake of Como, I broke into a paroxysm of hysterical laughter, which came upon me, I suppose, as the natural relief from the intensity of the mingled feelings of anger, scorn, wounded pride, and outraged love, by which I found myself carried away. The effect upon the audience was electrical because the impulse was genuine. But well do I remember Mr Macready's remonstrance with me for yielding to it. It was too daring, he said; to have failed in it on a first representation might have ruined the scene (which was true). No one, moreover, should ever, he said, hazard an unrehearsed effect. I could only answer that I could not help it; that this seemed the only way for my feelings to find vent; and if the impulse seized me again, again, I feared, I must act the scene in the same way. And often as I played Pauline, never did the situation fail to bring back the same burst of hysterical emotion; nor, so far as I know, did any one ever regard my yielding to it as out of place, or otherwise than true to nature. Some time afterwards I was comforted by reading a reply of the great French actor Baron, when he was blamed for raising his hands above his head in some impassioned scene, on the ground that such a gesture was contrary to the rules of art. 'Tell me not of art', he said. 'If nature makes you raise your hands, be it ever so high, be sure nature is right, and the business of art is to obey her.' When playing with Mr Macready the following year at the Haymarket, I noticed a chair placed every evening at the wing as I went on the stage for this act. On inquiry, I found it was for Mrs Glover, the great actress of comedy, who afterwards told me that she came every night to see me in this scene, she was so much struck by the originality of my treatment of it. She said it was beyond anything she had ever known; and yet it was always as fresh and new, that each time it moved her as if she had not seen it before. Nature spoke through me to her—no praise to me.

HELENA FAUCIT

XVIII

A Forgotten Hamlet

EDWARD OTWAY, like an earlier and even more resolute amateur actor, 'Romeo' Coates, was determined to be heard. Alfred Bunn, who—probably to his surprise—let him play Hamlet for one Drury Lane performance towards the end of 1837, described in the second volume of *The Stage: Both Before and Behind the Curtain* (1840) the tactics Otway used to reach the theatre.

I HAD long been subject to a species of persecution, even to a greater extent than the managers of Covent Garden and the Haymarket theatres, from a half madman by the histrionic appellation of Otway. I hope I am as fond of a bit of fun as any of my neighbours; but between the ravings, the conceit, the ignorance (as to stage matters), the ridicule, the foolery, mixed up in his actions, there is no fun whatever.

By birth, connexion and education, I believe Capt. Hicks (his real name) to be a perfect gentleman; I have never heard the breath of slander pass over him—but on the one point—of the drama—he is a decided lunatic. Yet, with the cunning for which all such unfortunate people are remarkable, he places you occasionally in a difficult position to deal with, by the adoption of an apparently sound reasoning. Mr Otway has thrust himself so repeatedly before the public with the same luckless result, that he is a fair subject for examination. His first appearance before a London audience was under the management of Elliston, in his pet character of Hamlet; and owing to his disappointing the audience both by his performance and his non-performance, a young actor in the company, yclept Hamblin, played the part for him—memorable only from the circumstance of Elliston calling that actor into the green-room, and addressing him to this effect: 'Young man, you have not only pleased the public, but you have pleased me; and as a slight token of my regard and good wishes, I beg your acceptance of a small piece of plate.' It was beyond any question a *very* small piece, for it was a silver toothpick.

I missed the worthy captain, after this occurrence, for several years, when in the year 1833 he perched himself one morning in my room, and favoured me with his view of London management, and his opinion of his own acting; and from that day I could never get rid of him. Though he failed at one house, could not complete his failure at another, and got thoroughly laughed at in both, still he stuck to me like a leech; and as mischievous persons were to be found ready to insert in some public prints any trash he thought proper to write, I at last became the subject of his scurrilous attacks. He then beset me at the stage-door, in the box-office, and even in the streets; and I have more than once resolved on sending him to some station-house. Finding his importunities thus far fruitless, he induced the editor of the *Observer* to insert this letter in his columns:

To Alfred Bunn, Esq.,
of the Theatre Royal, Drury Lane

Saturday, October 28, 1837.

Sir.—As I presume you have now completed, with the exception of Mr Charles Kean (prior to his appearance some time will elapse), the trial of those aspirants who seek for metropolitan favour as tragedians, in spite of the opposition you have manifested towards my employment hitherto, my services are still at your command; and as the line I would attempt leaves ample scope for such characters as, probably, Mr Kean hopes to excel in, it might not be ill-timed for you to make the experiment of my ability. I should have no objection to take either of the principal characters in *Julius Caesar* for my debut, to be followed by *Coriolanus*, grounding the value of my services upon the only estimate competent to determine them, viz., *public approbation*, having, at the same time, regard to your nightly receipts: not fearing that, could I once appear before you, our parting would be as unwilling as our approximation has been rendered unfortunately difficult.

In looking to the opposition *which has been forced upon me in self-defence*, and from which, on my terms, *no possible good could have arisen to me* in which you would not have been the main recipient; (you cannot fail to see the redeeming quality,—that my efforts *have been fair and above-board*); and if I have been severe in my strictures upon *measures of a bad tendency*, yet I flatter myself you have no stronger partisan in anything that admits of just approbation. I have thought this letter, for various reasons, to be the best public.

I am, Sir, your obedient servant,
EDWARD OTWAY

He followed up this nonsensical public tirade by the subjoined private note, commencing with the familiarity of 'Dear Sir,' after all the vulgar abuse of which he had been so lavish; conceiving evidently that the failure of Planché's *Caractacus* had created a chasm that he was capable altogether of filling up;

Dear Sir.—I presume you will readily comprehend the motives which have impelled my public letter to you in *The Observer*, viz., in the first place to obviate the difficulty of any acquiescence on your part by the application originating with me; and secondly not to afford a plea that any *unbecoming compromise* had taken place on either side. If you like to underline me for *Hamlet* on Friday, which is to be played at the 'Garden', I will do my best for you; but the action will be so short, that you must not be disappointed if we should fail in a house; but please God you would have another sort of one on the Monday. I merely, however, suggest this, feeling that you must be in some difficulty by the reception of last night's play; and I apprehend whatever I may do will not interfere with Mr Kean, as it is *his name* that is to do you good in the first place, and because *Hamlet* could at once be got up.

Yours, dear sir, obediently,
EDWARD OTWAY

A. Bunn, Esq., 25, Bow-street,
Tuesday, Nov. 7, 1837.

What was to be done with such an irredeemable booby on stage tactics as this unfortunate man? The public had conveyed *their* opinion to him; I had repeatedly conveyed *mine*; he would not admit the one, and thought the other prejudice. I therefore deemed it best, for the purpose of silencing him for the future, and to prevent the possibility of his few partisans laying a charge of prepossession against me, to give the opportunity he so doggedly fought for, of appearing on the boards of Drury Lane Theatre. I did this against my judgment, and was determined, in conceding the point, to record my opinion, and to publish that opinion in the paper which had permitted Mr Otway to favour me at various times with so much of his abuse. I therefore sent this reply to Mr Otway's last letter, and a copy of it to his ally, the editor of the *Observer*:

Theatre Royal, Drury Lane,
November 8, 1837

Sir.—Without entering upon the question of your gross and unfounded attacks upon me, which I am told have from time to time appeared in the public prints, and are utterly beneath even contempt, I reply to the renewed offer of service contained in your public letter to the *Observer* on Sunday last, and your private communication to me of yesterday. *You* believe yourself to be one of the best performers of the day, *I* believe you to be one of the worst; but as the manager of a theatre should never act upon prejudice, I will leave the public to judge between us, by announcing you for Hamlet, as soon as you have entered into the necessary arrangement with me for doing so.

I am, Sir, your obedient servant,
A. BUNN

E. Otway, Esq.

Instead of taking any angry notice of this effusion, Mr Otway waited upon me at the theatre; and being aware of the kind of man I had to deal with, I requested Mr Russell, the stage manager, to hear what passed, in order that no perversion of my remarks might appear in print, well knowing that he would not circulate what I *did say*.

My worthy friend, Jerry (the nomenclature by which Mr Russell's admirable performance in *The Mayor of Garrett* has long since distinguished him), laughed immoderately at the interview, from the extreme placidity with which Mr Otway received the fire he had himself been the cause of being directed against him; and it ended in his being announced, under sundry restrictions, to play *Hamlet* the following Monday. One of the main limitations imposed upon him was, that he should on no consideration address the audience; knowing that silly harangues very often lead to serious consequences.

He pledged his honour, and he violated his pledge; for on his re-entry, after killing Polonius, setting the audience on the titter, he told them the fault was none of his, for the scene had not been set for him at rehearsal. Certainly it had not that day, because no part of *Hamlet* beyond the scenes with Ophelia was rehearsed that day, a full rehearsal having taken place on the preceding Saturday. However, the curtain fell, and the audience fell too, laughing, hissing, and mocking, and heroically applauding, mixed with the genuine approbation of a few pitying varlets, who were witnesses of a man born and bred a perfect gentleman, and entitled to move in society, so lost as to come forward, and mistaking, or choosing to mistake, such a scene for an ebullition of public favour, to bow repeatedly in acknowledgement of so much kindness. Poor fellow! Divested of this fearful mania, there is a pleasing manner, a gentlemanly address, and a melancholy replete with interest, pervading every action of Mr Otway.

ALFRED BUNN

XIX
Lola Montez Obliges

THIS IS an example of sheer good luck; a capricious and beautiful young woman's generosity to an amiable routine dramatist she had met only once. He was Edward Fitzball (1792–1873), now among nineteenth-century writers one of the most readily and most resolutely forgotten. I have always found him endearing for his description of Macready ('he was so confoundedly classic') refusing to go under a ladder in Long Acre. 'I entertain an insurmountable dislike to passing under a ladder,' said Macready. 'It is a failing, if it be a failing, which I have imbibed from childhood; excuse me, therefore, if I go round.'

In the summer of 1843, when working for Covent Garden, Fitzball wanted urgently an attraction for his benefit performance (from which he would get most of the night's proceeds). But, as he explained in *Thirty-Five Years of a Dramatic Author's Life* (1859), where could he find the right name?

Just before this there had been dancing in London a tempestuous woman, self-christened Lola Montez. Born in barracks at Limerick, she was actually the daughter of an Irish ensign and a Spanish mother, and her name was Eliza Gilbert. She had eloped to an unhappy marriage with an Army captain. When she appeared in London she claimed to come from the Teatro Real in Seville; but the manager of Her Majesty's, learning the truth, refused to allow her to appear again, though her single night was triumphant.

It was just after this that she responded to Fitzball. Later she danced through the European capitals, became the mistress of the mad King Ludwig of Bavaria whose policy she dictated for a year (1847–8), and finally, after alarums in America and Australia (where she thrashed the editor of the *Ballarat Times*), died in New York, a penitent, during 1861.

IN MAKING what is called a benefit, people who are unsophisticated in theatrical affairs should know that everyone is anxious to secure everything like an attraction within his grasp, especially in a theatre where the expenses are, sometimes, from two to three hundred pounds. Benefit had followed benefit; at both houses [Covent Garden and Drury Lane] every novelty had been resorted to; nothing new was left to me. This benefit, which I fully expected would prove to me a decided loss, annoyed me sadly; I was sauntering up Regent Street when I met Stretton, the popular singer, whose benefit was just coming off. He assured me that he had secured every attraction worthy of the public, and that there was no hope left for me unless, indeed, he added satirically, turning back, you could secure the Lola Montez.

'The Lola Montez,' reiterated I, 'pray what is *that*,' in my ignorance, not knowing.

'Lola Montez is a lady who appeared the other night, at Her Majesty's Theatre, the Opera in the Haymarket, a dancer. Owing to some aristocratic disturbance, she has quitted the place in disgust; the papers were full of it; I have offered her fifty pounds to dance for me, and met with a decided refusal, so, as I observed just now, I see no hope for *you*.'

Thus ended our conversation, except my enquiring the address of the beautiful, enraged Lola Montez which, having obtained, I repaired at once to her apartments, and simply by my sending up my card, was graciously admitted. She was sitting for her portrait, a charming likeness, but far less charming than the original.

I explained my errand and was at once, as Stretton had foretold, left without hope. It was, perhaps, that a look of disappointment, if not something of distress, crossed my features, but in an instant her look changed; her voice also. 'I will, however,' she continued blandly, 'ask my mamma,' I think she said mamma, 'what she thinks of it; give me your address. I will write to you.' I thanked her very cordially; made my bow, and my exit, carrying with me to the theatre very little anticipation of a good result. I was occupied at the rehearsal of the opera; two hours, perhaps; Balfe and his sensitive and gifted wife were there and pressed me strongly to dinner; but as I never in my life absented myself from my own dinner table at home without specifying the same, being a very punctual man, I knew my remaining out would cause great anxiety; therefore, home I went. Judge of my surprise on entering the drawing-room, at finding Madame Lola Montez, seated on the sofa, chatting with my wife as familiarly as if they had known each other for years. She had already made up her mind to dance for me! When I mentioned terms, she refused to hear me, and in fact intended, and did dance for me for *nothing*. When the announcement appeared, everybody was astonished, and everybody was calculating the enormous amount of the sum I had consented to give for the attraction; and a great attraction it proved; the theatre was crammed. After all, my hopeless benefit proved the best of the season; and the usual remark was made, a remark invariably applied to any success of mine, that from downright good luck, I had as usual alighted on my feet.

Lola Montez arrived on the evening in a splendid carriage, accompanied by her maid, and without the slightest affectation entered the dressing-room prepared for her reception. When she was dressed to appear on the stage, she sent for me, to enquire whether I thought the costume she had chosen for the occasion would be approved of by my friends. I have seen sylphs appear, and female forms of the most dazzling beauty, in ballets and fairy dramas, but the most dazzling and perfect form I ever did gaze upon was Lola Montez in her splendid white and gold attire, studded with diamonds, that night.

Her bounding before the public was the signal of general applause and general admiration of her beauty—and general admiration of her dancing which was quite unlike anything the public had ever seen; so original, so flexible, so graceful, so indescribable. At the conclusion of her performance, I need scarcely add, how rapturous and universal was the call for her reappearance; after which, when I advanced with delighted thanks, again holding up her hand in graceful remonstrance, she refused to hear me, and in half-an-hour, in the same carriage, had quitted the theatre; from that time I have never again had the exceeding pleasure of seeing the *generous*, the beautiful Madame Lola Montez. Singular as are the various reports respecting her, which have reached us in different papers, to me at least, as I have here set down, she was all that was generous, ladylike, and gentle.

EDWARD FITZBALL

XX

The Eccentric Mr Knowles

JAMES SHERIDAN KNOWLES (1784–1862) has vanished into the mists; but in the mid nineteenth century he was a popular and busy dramatist, author of such plays as *Virginius* (acted by Macready) and *The Hunchback*. R. H. Horne hit off Knowles's style in a note on *Virginius*: 'We have Roman tunics, but a modern English heart—the scene is the Forum, but the sentiments those of the "Bedford Arms."' Knowles, an Irishman, was an odd personage, first a schoolmaster, then an actor, and late in life a Baptist preacher. Always a Bohemian, he was the chairman of various convivial societies named after fishes, beasts, and fowls of the air, as Edward Stirling put it. One, which used to meet at a tavern near Drury Lane, was 'The Owls.' Knowles would write to Stirling invitingly: 'Come to our Nest next Tuesday; I shall mount my perch at nine sharp. All our old Owls and several unfledged Owlets will be there. Jolly whooping and woo-wooing, depend... Nine, Tuesday—woo—woo.'

James Robinson Planché remembers him here in *Recollections and Reflections* (1872).

SHERIDAN KNOWLES had already won his spurs in the dramatic world by the production of *The Hunchback*; and during the Covent Garden management of Madame Vestris three of his plays were produced, *Love*, *John of Procida*, and *Old Maids*, all of which I had the pleasure of putting on the stage, I believe to his satisfaction. Of all the eccentric individuals I ever encountered, Sheridan Knowles was, I think, the greatest. Judge, gentle reader, if the following anecdotes may not justify my assertion. Walking one day with a brother-dramatist, Mr Bayle Bernard, in Regent's Quadrant, Knowles was accosted by a gentleman in these terms:— 'You're a pretty fellow, Knowles! After fixing your own day and hour to dine with us, you never make your appearance, and from that time to this not a word have we heard from you!' 'I couldn't help it, upon my honour,' replied Knowles; 'and I've been so busy ever since I haven't had a moment to write or call. How are you all at home?' 'Oh, quite well, thank you; but come now, will you name another day, and keep your word?' 'I will—sure I will.' 'Well, what day? Shall we say Thursday next?' 'Thursday? Yes, by all means—Thursday be it.' 'At six?' 'At six. I'll be there punctually. My love to 'em all.' 'Thank ye. Remember, now. Six next Thursday.' 'All right, my dear fellow; I'll be with you.' The friend departed, and Knowles, relinking his arm with that of Bayle Bernard, said, 'Who's that chap?' not having the least idea of the name or residence of the man he had promised to dine with on the following Thursday, or the interesting 'family at home,' to whom he had sent his love.

Upon one occasion when he was acting in the country he received an anxious letter from Mrs. Knowles, informing him that the money—£200, which he had promised to send up on a certain day, had never reached her. Knowles immediately wrote a furious letter to Sir Francis Freeling, at that time at the head of the Post-office, of which, of course, I cannot give the precise words, but beginning 'Sir', and informing him that on such a day, at such an hour, he himself put a letter into the post-office at such a place, containing the sum of £200 in bank-notes, and that it had never been delivered to Mrs Knowles; that it was a most unpardonable piece of negligence, if not worse, of the post-office authorities, and that he demanded an immediate inquiry into the matter, the delivery of the money to his wife, and an apology for the anxiety and trouble its detention had occasioned them. By return of post he received a most courteous letter from Sir Francis, beginning, 'Dear Sir,' as, although they were personal strangers to each other, he had received so much pleasure from Mr Knowles' works, that he looked upon him as a valued friend, and continuing to say that he (Knowles) was perfectly correct in stating that on such a day and at such an hour he had posted a letter at — containing banknotes to the amount of £200, but that, unfortunately, he had omitted not only his signature inside, but *the address outside*, having actually sealed up the notes in an envelope containing the words, 'I send you the money,' and posted it without a direction! The consequence was that it was opened at the chief office in London, and detained till some inquiry was made about it. Sir Francis concluded by assuring him that long before he would receive his answer the money would be placed in Mrs Knowles' hands by a special messenger. Knowles wrote back, 'My dear sir, you are right and I was wrong. God bless you! I'll call upon you when I come to town.'

One day also in the country, he said to Abbot, with whom he had been acting there, 'My dear fellow, I'm off tomorrow. Can I take any letter for you?' 'You're very kind,' answered Abbot; 'but where are you going to?' '*I haven't made up my mind.*'

Seeing O. Smith, the popular melodramatic actor on the opposite side of the Strand, Knowles rushed across the road, seized him by the hand, and inquired eagerly after his health. Smith, who only knew him by sight, said, 'I think, Mr Knowles, you are mistaken; I am O. Smith'. 'My dear fellow', cried Knowles, 'I beg you ten thousand pardons—I took you for your namesake, T. P. Cooke!'

An opera was produced at Covent Garden during my engagement, the story of which turned upon the love of a young count for a gipsy girl, whom he subsequently deserts for a lady of rank and fortune; and in the second act there was a fête in the gardens of the château in honour of the bride-elect. Mr. Binge, who played the count, was seated in an arbour near to one of the wings witnessing a ballet. Knowles, who had been in front during the previous part of the opera, came behind the scenes; and, advancing as near as he could to Binge without being in sight of the audience, called to him in a loud whisper, 'Binge!' Binge looked over his shoulder. 'Well, what is it?' 'Tell me. Do you marry the poor gipsy after all?' 'Yes,' answered Binge, impatiently, stretching his arm out behind him, and making signs with it for Knowles to keep back. Knowles caught his hand, pressed it fervently, and exclaimed, 'God bless you! You are a good fellow!' This I saw and heard myself as I was standing at the wing during the time.   J. R. PLANCHÉ

XXI
Mems. by Bunn

ALFRED BUNN'S cheerfully malicious *The Stage: Both Before and Behind the Curtain* (1840) is interspersed with what he called 'Mems. of a Manager'. Some of the personages in these extracts are: Charles Kean (1811–1868), Edmund's son; Maria Theresa Bland (1769–1838), ballad singer long popular at Drury Lane ('Sally in our Alley' as she sang it, said Edward Stirling, never failed to move her audience to tears); Clarkson Stanfield (1793–1867), the marine artist, friend of Macready and Dickens, who was originally a scene designer and painter; John Reeve (1799–1838), the comedian; J. B. Buckstone (1802–1879), comedian and dramatist, in whose plays Reeve had acted at the Adelphi; Julia Glover (1781–1850), whom Macready called a 'rare thinking actress'; and of course Macready himself—then actor-manager at Covent Garden—who was always much on Bunn's mind.

JANUARY 7, 1838.—Charles Kean called on me today, during one of my paroxysms of intense suffering—he's in an established funk about the result of to-morrow; it is momentous to him and all of us; but 'funking' will only make it more so. He has good qualities in him, with a very gentlemanly mind; Eton has done that part of the business for him—he'll get well through—doing much himself, and we helping him with the rest. I liked some of his Hamlet when I saw it at Brighton in September last. 'Is it the King?' will hit others, I guess, as it hit me. Miss Charles, whose real name is Pettingall, has thrown up her engagement, because, at Mr Kean's suggestion and request, I put Miss Romer into the part of Ophelia, instead of her sweet self—she'll be sorry before *I* shall.

January 8.—Charles Kean makes what may be termed his début in *Hamlet*, prepared with new scenes, dresses, and paraphernalia. His appearance and his performance elicited a degree of enthusiasm never heard of but in the case of his father, for he might truly say, as his sire said before him, 'the pit rose at me'— receipt of the house, despite reduced prices and without taking annual boxes into account, £453 10s. Though suffering from the effects of severe illness, I flannelled up, and went down to see the sight. A very earnest actor, with most of the peculiarities (not the intenseness, mind) and all the faults of his renowned papa. By perseverance, talent, and conduct, he has at length managed 'to climb the steep where Fame's proud temple shines afar.' His fencing perfect—plenty of *foils* provided by the rest of the company. This play will run, and like some other things that *run*, will *draw*; which two isolated words are part of the favourite slang of a histrio's vocabulary.

January 10.—The Royal Exchange burnt down—the 'whereby' not yet known . . . Kean fidgety, lest the attraction of his second night should suffer by the event.

January 15.—Mrs Bland died this day, aged 73 [she was 69]: she married the brother of Mrs Jordan; but the chances are, that those who never aided her living are not likely to mourn for her dead! Bravo—'O world, thy slippery turns'—what a ballad singer! in appearance like a fillet of veal on castors—it was 'vox et preterea nihil'—but *what* a vox!

January 20.—They tell me that Macready has sent Stanfield £300 for painting a diorama in the pantomime of *Peeping Tom*— that Stanfield has retained one-half and has returned the other, and that Macready has caused the said other half to be expended in a piece of plate, to be presented to Stanfield. The two reasons why I doubt this report* are, that I never yet heard of Macready giving away money, nor of Stanfield refusing it. This scenepainter's salary with me was £16 per week; and although his

* *Editor's note*: Stanfield took £150; Macready added a salver.

present work has certainly been the salvation of the pantomime and the season, there is some difference between this *salary* and that *sum*.

January 24.—John Reeve died in the evening of this day, at his house in Brompton. His great favouritism with the public enabled him to take great liberties with them; he was only fitted for the Adelphi Theatre, where a fine salary and a funking manager completely spoiled him; he was born in 1799, and was therefore in his fortieth year. His acting was a striking illustration of the vast difference there is between a *farceur* and a comedian. Poor John was the *Bottle Imp* of every theatre he ever played in. The last time I saw him, he was posting at a rapid rate to a City dinner, and on his drawing up to chat, I said, 'Well, Reeve, how do you find yourself today?' and he returned for answer, 'The Lord Mayor *finds* me today.'

January 26.—Her Majesty visited Drury Lane Theatre to see Charles Kean in *Hamlet*—the house was a choker—£463 3s. 6d. The Queen looked well, and, better still, was received well. Charles improveth by practice and patronage, and the loss of fear —it is literally a relief to see a Hamlet not having a stocking dangling at his heel to prove the distemper of his mind.

January 27.—Heard of the death of William Dimond, which took place at Paris more than three months ago, and has been kept a secret by his friends, who, though they rejoiced at his decease, were ashamed of his existence, and *ergo* were silent. He possessed great knowledge of the stage, as his pieces of *The Foundling of the Forest, Doubtful Son, Conquest of Taranto, Lady and Devil*, and some twenty others attest. His last piece, I believe, was *The Novice*, brought forth the beginning of this season at Covent Garden Theatre. His enormities are said to have broken his mother's heart, and to have been the cause of his father cutting his throat. He succeeded that most respected parent in the management of the Bath Theatre; but was compelled by General Palmer, the larger proprietor, to relinquish it altogether in 1823, since which period he has been in many jails (in Horsemonger Lane, under the name of James Bryant), and tried in many courts (he was tried at Croydon assizes under the name of William Dimer) under many names, for heinous crimes—out of all of which he escaped by mere miracles; his deeds at Bath, the early and great scene of his profligacy, would fill a volume.

January 30.—Buckstone has published a very silly letter in this day's *Herald*, to endeavour to prove that poor John Reeve was not a drunkard—he might much more easily have proved that he was seldom sober.

February 1.—Macready sick 'of thick coming fancies that keep him from his rest'; he was leeched this evening, I hear, after playing—he'll be bled more than that, if he remains much longer a manager.

February 3.—Mrs Glover, the best living actress by many degrees, has had a fall from one of the Coventry stage-coaches, and is much smashed—sorry for it indeed—when she falls in reality from the stage, she will not leave a successor behind her—her line will be extinct.

February 5.—Charles Kean appeared in *Richard the Third*, which tragedy was produced with great care and expense; house £409 5s.; he will do fully as well, if not better, in this part as he has thus far done in *Hamlet*.—Her Majesty was present from the rise to the fall of the curtain, and commanded me to express to Master Charley how delighted she was with his performance.

February 12.—They hiss Mr King nightly for his performance of Richmond; and yet I have Shakespeare's authority for putting him in the part:

> Henry the Sixth
> Did prophesy that Richmond should be King.

March 10.—We brought forward for the first time in an English garb, Mozart's opera *The Zauberflöte* [*The Magic Flute*]; and, as a mere matter of opinion, regardless of what others do not think, I deem it to be one of the most perfectly 'got up' affairs our stage has seen, being long and properly studied in every respect, and elaborately prepared in every department.... I bethought me at this time of the repeated and unjust attacks levelled at me for neglecting the legitimate drama, and the fulsome compliments paid the rival lessee for his support of it; and I could not but contrast the causes which led to so much illiberality, falsehood, and injustice; for while Covent Garden was exhausting its resources in the preparation of Auber's opera of the *Domino Heir*, which proved an utter failure, Drury Lane was giving some one of Shakespeare's plays every night, backed by this celebrated composition, Mozart's *Magic Flute*, which completely filled the theatre.　　　　　　　　　　　　　　　ALFRED BUNN

XXII

From the Theatre Royal

DURING the late eighteen-forties, John Coleman, as a very young actor, received an offer of a guinea a week from William Robertson, Manager of the Lincoln circuit. Coleman, with sadly battered hat, joined the company at Leicester. More than half a century later he recalled the engagement—it was his second—in *Fifty Years of an Actor's Life*, published in 1904. Here the Victorian pomping folk are in fullest cry.

IT WAS market-day, and Leicester was all alive. Though the season commenced on Monday, there was not a play-bill out, nor an announcement of any description. I had not been advised as to my opening part or parts, so I made my way at once to the theatre, then an almost new, and somewhat imposing, edifice in Horse-Fair Street. The doors were locked, and there was no one about from whom I could obtain any information whatever. Just as I had arrived at the conclusion that I had made a mistake in the date, and was turning away in despair, a bill-poster came up and began to post on the wall the announcement of the coming season: 'Mr. Robertson has the honour to announce to the nobility, gentry, and inhabitants of Leicester,' etc.

This was the good old flunkeyish style in which the advent of the players was announced by the managers of the period. The opening play was a Lyceum drama by Bayle Bernard, which I have never met since, entitled *The Farmer's Story*. There was a goodly lot of names—the one, however, which attracted me most was 'The Hon. Mr. Derby—Mr Coleman, from the Theatre Royal, Olympic [very much from the Olympic], Derby'.

The bill-poster was loquacious enough, but totally ignorant of the movements of the Robertson troupe. He guessed they were in Oundle, or Stamford, or Peterborough, or Boston, or Lincoln. But the coach had come in from all those places; consequently there was no probability of the company arriving that night; possibly the 'pub round the corner' might be better informed. Round the corner I went. The landlady, fat, fair, and forty, informed me that there were many letters *for* Mr. Robertson, but none *from* him, and there was no communication whatever for me.

This was a bad look-out. I had expected to have found a book of *The Farmer's Story*, or at least a part of the Hon. Mr. Derby, and it was my intention to have studied my part before I went to bed that night, which reminded me that I must set out and look for a lodging at once. After an hour's hunt, I found myself comfortably installed in a couple of decent rooms, at the modest honorarium of five shillings a week. I got a boy to bring my bag and luggage from the station—nearly half a mile—for a couple of pence.

It now became necessary to apprise my landlady that I had been disappointed in my remittances. She was a kind, motherly soul, and sympathised with the situation. . . .

In the early morning I went to the 'pub round the corner.' Still no news of the Robertson troupe. The last train from Lincoln, however, was due at six o'clock. At eleven we went to the Catholic church; in the evening I was destined to be an unwilling Sabbath-breaker. At six I put in a second appearance at the 'pub'—a detestable place to me at all times, more especially on Sunday. Here, with some difficulty, I found the prompter, a Mr Norman, from whom I obtained the Prompt-book, and trotted home to copy out my part, which was, as well as I can remember, that of a miserable masher of the period. Before I got to bed I was letter perfect.

I slept little, was up at daybreak, and went for a long walk, going carefully and repeatedly over my part. A dreadful anxiety oppressed me: my impending interview with the autocrat of the Lincoln circuit was overshadowed by the condition of my hat. The 'call' was for ten o'clock, and there was no time (even if I had the money) to get my battered beaver restored to its normal shape. I went home to breakfast and was on the stage sharp at ten to introduce myself to my manager. I don't think we were either of us much impressed with the other. He was a tall, broad-shouldered, broad-browed, square-chinned, neutral-complexioned man of forty or forty-five, with fiery eyes, which seemed to be on the look-out for a pretext to become angry. His costume struck me as being rather eccentric, at any rate for morning wear: he wore a broad-brimmed, almost clerical hat, a black dress-coat and vest, white choker, with pepper-and-salt continuations. While I was taking stock of him, he was taking stock of me and—my hat.

I was modest and deferential; he was curt and dictatorial. He brusquely inquired how old I was, where, and what I had acted. Candour constrains me to confess that my answers were not entirely veracious. I added considerably to my years, and my experience; but evidently he was not impressed with either the one or the other, and he dismissed me abruptly with a vicious glance at my unfortunate beaver.

The Farmer's Story was what is called a 'stock piece'; consequently my scenes were the only ones rehearsed, and it was quite evident that the company, who knew their parts backwards, and had played them over and over again, wished the newcomer at Hong-Kong or anywhere but Horse-Fair Street. The rehearsal was so slipshod and perfunctory that it was enough to have upset an old stager, let alone a novice.

'Mrs Robertson!' called the Prompter.

'Mrs Robertson is looking out the checks. Read for her,' grimly remarked Mr Robertson.

'Gabble-gabble,' commenced the Prompter—'gabble! Now, sir, that's your cue: on you come from behind the centre arch.'

'Where will the arch be?'

'Where will the arch be, Casson?' inquired the Prompter.

'Second grooves,' replied the master carpenter.

'It will be a drawing-room. Here is a chair; there a table,' continued the Prompter.

'But I don't see either the one or the other,' I replied.

'No, but you will at night.'

'Shall I?'

'Oh, yes! it will be all right at night.'

Oh that 'all right at night'! From that day to this I've been fighting against it. I've killed it a million times, but it always comes to life again.

I take off my hat as I bid the Prompter, who is standing up for the heroine, 'Good morning!'

'Mind you leave your 'at in the 'awl, sir!' says the Prompter patronisingly.

'But this is a morning call!'

'Morning or evening, it don't signify; a gentleman always leaves his 'at in the 'awl!'

'Not always,' I reply politely; 'but if you'll kindly give me the cue, I'll try to get on.'

'Gabble gabble—squeak. Cross to right, then to left and up centre. Mind you give Mrs Robertson the stage: she wants plenty of elbow-room. Now, Mr Rogers, if you please.'

Mr Rogers, a short, thick-set man of fifty, with an enormous head and a huge bull-neck, who was known for many years after at the Haymarket as a sound, sensible actor of old men and character parts, is the interesting hero, Stephen Lockwood. This gentleman sits upon me, warns me to give him the stage and to keep my eye on him, and begins to gabble and growl. I respond to the best of my ability, and am about to make my exit on the left-hand side.

'No, my good young man, not that way,' interposes the adipose tragedian with dignity.

The 'good young man' is intended to be patronising, but it is reassuring, for he calls me a man, at any rate.

'Which side is it, Norman?' inquires the great Rogers.

'Right hup-her hentrance.'

'Then I will cross in front to the left, and you, sir, go up to the right. No, no, not that way! Don't turn your back to the audience. Whatever you do, don't turn your back to the audience.'

Thus I am put through my paces by every one concerned, and then contemptuously dismissed. No one speaks a civil word or gives me a kind look, and, considerably crestfallen, I retire and watch the remainder of the rehearsal to see if I can learn anything.

This is the little comedy which takes place:

Prompter. Now, your song, Mrs Este.

Mrs Este. Thank you! All right. A chord in G., Mr Stannard, please, and keep the brass down.

(Mrs Este *warbles*!)

Prompter. Now, Miss Wright—Miss Rosina Wright. We are waiting to try your dance.

Miss Wright (*from her dressing-room*). I'm putting on my practising things, Mr Norman.

The Leader. Surely the whole band needn't be kept waiting while this London ballet-girl is putting on her skirts!

Miss Wright. The London ballet-girl has got 'em on, you old bear! (*and on bounds the fair Rosina, who was* 'always Rosy *and always* Right').

Always susceptible to grace and beauty, I remain to admire the fair Rosina's pirouettes. We strike up an acquaintance, and commence a friendship which lasts for years.

At last the rehearsal is over and I am off.

Although I was not 'on' until the second act of the play, I was at the theatre an hour or more before the doors were opened, and I was dressed long before the time. Had I followed that wretched Prompter's *ipse dixit* and left my 'at in the 'awl, I should not have come to grief as I did. Just as the overture was about to commence, there was some difficulty about the gas, which went out, and left the house in total darkness. The audience were kicking up a row; and the manager was going about 'like a roaring lion seeking whom he might devour,' when, as my ill-luck would have it, at the very instant the lights went up, he came in contact with me—and my hat.

He had a poetic imagination and a copious vocabulary, by means of which he was enabled without effort to improvise a few florid compliments. Having taken my breath away by the vigour of his vituperation, he renewed the attack by stigmatising me as an impostor and a swindler, and demanded to know how I dared introduce myself into his theatre with such a hat! Fully conscious of the iniquity of my conduct, and convinced that I ought at least to be hung, drawn and quartered for having attempted to obtain a guinea a week under false pretences, I beat an ignominious retreat into the green-room.

Unfortunately he pursued me there. Two ladies were there also; a further exchange of compliments of a still more florid character took place, with the result that my worthy manager unexpectedly found himself on his back, while I was going for him with the poker!

Those two dear ladies (both young and beautiful then, both

angels in heaven, I hope, now) intervened and separated the belligerents; whereupon the manager retired, ordering me out of the theatre. The ladies took pity on my youth and misery, soothed and even caressed me, until at last I broke down, burst out crying like a child, and rushed from the theatre. Years after, whenever I went to 'star' in Leicester, that very room was always allotted for my dressing-room, and, year after year, I never entered it, but I went through that dreadful scene again.

The night was dark and stormy; but, taking no heed of that, I walked on till I found myself on the banks of the river. The future seemed so hopeless that there were only two alternatives open to me—either to drop quietly into the water and end my troubles at once, or to enlist as a soldier. Coleridge and Cobbett had enlisted before me, so there was no lack of good precedents. My mind was made up: I would take the Queen's shilling on the morrow. Having arrived at this conclusion, I made my way home, slunk in unobserved, went hungry and supperless to bed, and cried myself to sleep....

Next morning a thundering rat-tat came at the door, and 'Mr Tom Robertson' was announced. The future author descended upon me, with his father's compliments, intimating that for both our sakes it would be better for me to carry out my engagement, and to take the usual month's notice. A month—a whole month! The proposal was a godsend, and I jumped at it.

Mr Tom responded with dignity, 'In that case you will do Paul in *The Bohemians of Paris* to-night. Here is a book; you had better get your part out and be at the theatre by twelve sharp for rehearsal. Till then, au revoir.'

The Bohemians was a new piece and all the company groped their way both in the words and the business. I didn't do either. I rehearsed letter perfect, which staggered the old stagers, who, when we started fair, didn't have so much the advantage; in fact, while they were mumbling and stumbling over the words at night, I spoke mine. As to acting—ah! that is an art which isn't learnt in a week, or a year! Anyhow, finding me obliging and attentive, Mr and Mrs Robertson magnanimously condoned the scene in the green-room. Tom and I fraternised and became sworn chums. We had the same tastes and the same aspirations; he wrote poetry, so did I, though, mind you, we were both pretty bad—I scarce know even now which was the worst. We were to have written a play together upon a famous local murder; but we couldn't agree as to the treatment, so our collaboration fell through. Notwithstanding, we both resolved to be great authors and great actors. Though he never became a great actor, he left his mark 'upon the form and body of the time' as an admirable author.

[A little later in his career Coleman was engaged as Juvenile Tragedian for the Theatre Royal, Greenock.]

Looking out for the bill of the play, I saw myself advertised in large letters after this fashion:

TO-MORROW NIGHT THE CELEBRATED JUVENILE TRAGEDIAN, MR J.C., FROM [very much from*] THE THEATRE ROYAL, DRURY LANE, WILL MAKE HIS FIRST APPEARANCE IN THIS CITY [why city?] IN THE PART OF ALONZO IN SHERIDAN'S GRAND TRAGIC PLAY OF 'PIZARRO; OR, THE DEATH OF ROLLA.'

To be sure there was one alloy—I had never seen or heard of the play, and was much exercised in my mind as to who Alonzo was, and what relevance the death of Rolla bore to Pizarro. . . .

JOHN COLEMAN

* The interpolations are Coleman's.

XXIII

Fanny Kemble on Tour

FRANCES ANNE (FANNY) KEMBLE (1809–1893) was the daughter of Charles Kemble and niece of John Philip and of Sarah Siddons. A great success at Covent Garden and in the American theatre when she was young, she left the stage on her marriage in 1834 to an American, Pierce Butler, whom she divorced in 1845 after an unhappy experience.

In these extracts from her *Records of Later Life* (1882), she describes her return to the stage after thirteen years: a tour of the English provinces in such parts as Juliet, Lady Macbeth, Julia in *The Hunchback*, and Juliana in *The Honeymoon*. Her maid accompanied her; it was hardly the kind of touring known to a Stirling or Donaldson or Coleman.

The letters were addressed to her life-long friend, Harriet (Hal) St Leger.

MANCHESTER, February 11, 1847: Everybody in the theatre is civil and good to me, and I am heartily grateful to them all.... My dressing-room is wretched in point of size and situation, being not much larger than this sheet of paper, and up a sort of steep ladder staircase: in other respects it is tidy enough, and infinitely better than the dark barrack-room you remember me dressing in when I was in Manchester years ago, when I was a girl. It is not the same theatre, but a new one built by the Mr Knowles who engaged me to act here, and one of the prettiest, brightest, and most elegant playhouses I ever saw; admirable for the voice and of a most judicious size and shape. Unfortunately, a large hotel has been built immediately adjoining it (I suspect by the same person, who is a great speculator, and apt, I should think, to have many, if not too many, irons in the fire), and the space that should have been appropriated to the accommodation of the actors, behind the scenes in the theatre, has been sacrificed to the adjoining building, which is a pity.

If I were to tell you the names of the people who act with me, you would be none the wiser. The company is a very fair one indeed, and might be an excellent one, if they were not all too great geniuses either to learn or to rehearse their parts. The French do not put the flimsiest vaudeville upon the stage without rehearsing it for *three months*: here, however, and everywhere else in England, people play such parts as Macbeth with not more than three rehearsals; and I am going to act this evening in *The Honeymoon* [by John Tobin] with a gentleman who, filling the principal part in the piece, has not thought fit to attend at the rehearsal; so that though I was there, I may say in fact that I have had no rehearsal of it,—which is businesslike and pleasant.

I write this after my first night's performance [she played Julia* in *The Hunchback*]. How I wondered at myself, as I stood at the side scene, without any quickening of the pulse or beating of the heart—thanks to the far other experiences I have gone through, which have left me small sensibility for stage apprehensions; and yet I could hardly have believed it possible that I should have been as little nervous as I was. When I went on, however, I had to encounter the only thing I dreaded; and the loud burst of public welcome (suggestive of how many associations, and what a contrast!) shocked me from head to foot, and tried my nerves to a degree that affected my performance unfavourably through several scenes.

* *Editor's note:* She created this part, in Sheridan Knowles's play, at Covent Garden in 1832.

But this was my first appearance after thirteen years of absence from the stage; and, of course, no second emotion of the kind awaits me. The exertions and exposure of the performance gave me a violent cold and sore throat, and I have been obliged to send for a doctor. I had *two* rehearsals yesterday, which did not mend matters, but I have bolstered myself up *pro tem.*, and what with inhaling hot water and swathing my throat in cold, and lozenges and gargles, etc., I hope to fight it through without breaking down.

February 25: Your inquiry about my health I cannot answer very triumphantly. I am not well, and my feet and ankles swell so before I have stood five minutes on the stage, that the prolonged standing in shoes, which, though originally loose for me, became absolute instruments of torture, like those infamous 'boots' of martyrising memory, is a terrible physical ordeal for either a tragic or comic heroine—who had need indeed to be something of a real one to endure it. Some of this trouble is due to general debility, and some to the long unaccustomed effect of so much standing, and will, I trust, gradually subside as I grow stronger and more used to my work. I acted Juliet last night, and I am very weary today, but thankful to have my most arduous part well over.

LIVERPOOL. March 7: I am swallowing ipecacuanha lozenges by the gross.

DUBLIN, March 14: The houses at Liverpool were crammed, but here last night there was a very indifferent one, partly, they say, owing to the fact that the Lord Lieutenant bespeaks the play for to-morrow night; but I should think it much more rational to account for it by the deplorable condition to which the famine has reduced the country, which ought to affect the minds of those whose bodies do not suffer, with something like a sympathetic seriousness, inimical to public diversions.

[*Later in the year*]

BIRMINGHAM, May 29: From Liverpool to Crewe I had companions in the ladies' carriage in which I was; after that, I had it to myself, and lay stretched on the ground for rest the whole of the rest of the way. I got here [Queen's Hotel] a little after three. The house is upside down with cleaning processes, by reason of which I am put (till a smaller one can be got ready for me) into an amazingly lofty large room, with some good prints hung on the walls, and a pianoforte; seeing which privileges I have declined transferring myself to any other apartment, and shall be made to pay accordingly.

BRISTOL, May 30: Only think, my dear, on arriving here, and inquiring for Hayes [her maid] I recollected that I had sent her to Bath and not to Bristol. 'Consekens is,' as Mr Sam Weller says (but alas for you! you don't know *Pickwick*), that I have had to send off a porter from this house to Bath, per railway, to reclaim my erring maid and fetch her thither; and, being a Sunday, fewer trains go between the two places than usual, and she cannot get here till near four o'clock this afternoon, until which time I dare not trust myself to think of the state of mind of the abandoned (in the perfectly honest sense of the word) Bridget or Biddy Hayes; indeed I shall not get her here until six this evening, and I only hope that I may then.

What a moon there was last night! and how it made me think of you as it shone into the dark, lofty room at Birmingham, where I sat playing and singing very sadly all by myself! The sea must have been as smooth as glass, and you cannot have been sick, even with your best endeavour.

The road from Birmingham here is quite pretty; the country in a most exquisite state of leaf and blossom; the crops look extremely well along this route; and the little cottage gardens, which delight my heart with their tidy cheerfulness, are so many nosegays of laburnum, honeysuckle, and lilac. The stokers on all the engines that I saw or met this morning had adorned their huge iron dragons with great bunches of hawthorn and laburnum, which hung their poor blossoms close to the hissing hot breath of the boilers, and looked wretched enough. But this dressing up the engines, as formerly the stage-coach horses used to be decked with bunches of flowers at their ears on Mayday, was touching. I suppose the railroad men get fond of their particular engine, though they can't pat and stroke it as sailors do their ship.

BRISTOL, May 31: After all, I had directed my poor maid perfectly *write* (look how I've spelt this in the tumult of my feelings and confusion of my thoughts), and she arrived, but not till three o'clock in the afternoon, paper in hand, with the direction I had myself written as large as life, 'The Great Western Hotel, Bristol'. The fact is, that I had made so sure that she would be here before I was, that not finding her on my arrival, I made equally sure that I had misdirected her to Bath, and despatched one of the hotel porters thither to hunt for her, which he did, sans intermission, for two hours, and on his return had the pleasure of finding her here. What a capital thing a clear head is, to be sure! at least I imagine so. . . .

BATH, June 2: You would have been amused yesterday evening if you had been at the theatre with me. The weather was so beautifully bright that I could not bear to shut the shutters and light the gas, so I dressed by the blessed light of heaven, and was sitting all rouged and arrayed for my part, working, with my back to the window, when a small mob of poor little ragged urchins, who had climbed over a railing that separated the theatre from a mean-looking street behind it, collected round, and, clambering on each other's shoulders, clustered and hung like a swarm of begrimed bees at the window, which was near the ground, to enjoy the sight of me and my finery. Bridget, who is kind-hearted and fond of children, turned the dresses that were hanging up right side out for the edification of the poor little ragamuffins, and their comments were exceedingly funny and touching. We could hear all that they said through the window—how they wondered if I put *them* beautiful dresses on one by one, or over each other; the rose in my hair, which you gave me, and the roses in my shoes, made them scream with delight; and if you could have heard the pathetic earnestness with which one of them exclaimed, 'Oh, my! don't you wish them 'ere windies was cleaner!' for the dirt-dimmed glass obstructed the full glory of the vision not a little!

PLYMOUTH, June 16: *All* the theatres where I act—indeed, as far as I can see, all the theatres throughout the country—are Theatres Royal; and with very good reason, for they are certainly all equally patronised by royalty. . . . The weather is cold, rainy, windy, in short odiously tempestuous; in spite of which I went into the sea yesterday, and shall do every day while I am here; the freshness of the salt water is delicious.

EXETER, June 21: This inn is in the middle of the town, and an old, dingy, dull house; and I have an old, dingy, dark sitting-room, and the only trees I see are two fine felled elm trunks, which I have been industriously sketching.

The cathedral here is a grand old church, and I went yesterday afternoon to service there; but the choir was full, so I sat on a sort of pauper's wooden bench, just outside the choir, and under the beautiful porch that forms the entrance to it; and heard the chanting, but nothing else. I had Hayes with me, and she earnestly entreated me to sit with my feet upon hers, to protect myself from the cold stone pavement; was not that touching and nice of her?

FANNY KEMBLE

XXIV

In Those Days

EDMUND YATES (1831–94), for some years a contemporary of Anthony Trollope in the Post Office, was writer, dramatist, and at length the founder of a weekly journal, *The World*. Because of permitting an unlucky libel early in 1883, he served (two years later) seven weeks of a four months' prison sentence in Holloway. As a 'first-class misdemeanant' his circumstances were luxurious: a room furnished by Maple's, and 'no private servants . . . more zealous or more respectful' than his two warders.

This contentious figure was the son of Frederick Yates, the actor-manager (for some time at the Adelphi Theatre) and the actress Mrs (Elizabeth Brunton) Yates. As with Macready, says their son, they 'had no great liking' for their profession; but Edmund grew into a persuaded playgoer and man about the theatre. In his autobiography, *Edmund Yates: His Recollections and Experiences* (1884) he described early memories (from the late eighteen-forties) of theatres he knew. Among those mentioned in these extracts, the Princess's was on the north side of Oxford Street, east of the Circus; the Olympic was in Wych Street (destroyed in the creation of Aldwych) and the Surrey was a famous transpontine house. Jenny Lind (1820–1887), known as 'the Swedish Nightingale', made her English début in May 1847; Louisa Nisbett (Lady Boothby) was the comedienne (1812–1858); and Gustavus Vaughan Brooke (1818–1866), a talented, reckless, and fatally intemperate tragedian.

Her Majesty's: I made up my mind to be present on the night when Jenny Lind should make her first bow to the English public. Every retainable seat had been retained for weeks; but I was young and strong and active, and at a few minutes before noon on Tuesday, the 4th May, I took my place among twenty persons, then gathered round the gallery door of the opera house in the Haymarket. The twenty soon swelled into two hundred, into five hundred, into uncountable numbers; and there we stood, swaying hither and thither, joking, chaffing, panting, groaning, until the doors were opened at 7 p.m., and away we went with a rush. I had brought some sandwiches and a pocket-flask with me, and was in good condition luckily; for anything like that crowd I have never experienced. There were women among us, and just as I neared the door I heard a feeble whisper in my ear, 'For God's sake, help me! I'm fainting!' I could not move my arms, which were pinioned to my sides, but I turned my head as best as I could, and said, 'Catch hold of me, and I'll pull you up.' The woman—I never saw her face—put her arms round my waist, and, thus burdened, I struggled on. I reached and mounted the staircase; I put my hand, with the exact admission money in it, into the hole in the pay-box, whence at first it was swept out, with a score of other hands, by the maddened money-taker; but I succeeded. I got my pass-check, and, still burdened, I fought to the top of the staircase where my check was demanded. It was then discovered that my unfortunate passenger had not paid her money, and had received no check. She released me; she was refused admittance, and was literally carried off on the human tide. I heard no more of her. When I reached my goal—the third row in the gallery—I sat down there, perspiring and exhausted, and, following the example of all round me, I took off my coat. The first notes of the overture to *Robert Le Diable* found the gallery in its shirt-sleeves; but we were clothed and in our right minds before the opera began.

Drury Lane: The great *Monte Cristo* row occurred in the summer of 1848, and I was present. The troupe of the Théâtre Historique, from Paris, were announced for a short series of performances, but on the opening night a band of opponents took possession of the pit, and prevented a syllable being heard throughout the evening. The riot was renewed the next night, and one of the leaders of the malcontents, being arrested, proved to be Sam Cowell, an actor and comic singer. There was a great deal of free fighting, and as one of the incidents I remember a huge strawberry pottle being hurled at Albert Smith who had just issued a sixpenny book called *A Pottle of Strawberries*, and who was conspicuously active on the side of the Frenchmen.

Haymarket: I saw Mrs Nisbett as Constance in *The Love Chase*, with Webster as Wildrake and Mrs Glover as Widow Green. This was on the occasion of Mrs Nisbett's return to the stage, after the death of her second husband, Sir William Boothby. She was a very lovely woman of the ripe-peach style, large eyes and pouting lips. One night I went behind the scenes and was presented to her by my mother: 'Lady Boothby, this is my boy'. 'How wonderfully like his father!' and her Ladyship inclined her lovely face and gave me a kiss. 'Lucky fellow,' said Webster, who was standing by; 'you'll remember in after-years that you've kissed Mrs Nisbett!' 'I've forgotten it already,' I said, lifting up my face for a reminder. Mrs Nisbett laughed and acceded; and Webster, turning to her so that my mother could not hear, muttered, 'Very like his father!'

Princess's: At the time when I first knew it, and for many years after, it was under the management of a Hebrew gentleman, whose name appeared at the head of the playbills as J. M. Maddox, and whose short stout figure and very marked features, with a cigar always protruding from under his very prominent nose, was a constant source of delight to the caricaturists. His real name was, I imagine, Medex—at least that was the name painted over a tobacconist's shop immediately facing the theatre, which was avowedly kept by the lessee's brother, and there, seated on a tub or lounging against the counter, Mr Maddox was constantly to be found. Stories of his wonderful fertility of resource in saving money were rife. Among other things it was said that all the lighter pieces produced at the Princess's were the work of a jobbing author, who was kept on the premises—some said chained by the leg to his desk—and who for a small salary was compelled to produce two French translations weekly.

Under the Maddox regime, and the theatrical name of Wynn, was a very strange man, Charles Kerrison Sala, brother of the author [George Augustus Sala], largely endowed with the family talent, and with more than an average supply of the family eccentricity. For some reason or other, he was most objectionable to Macready. When at rehearsals Wynn appeared on the stage, Macready's eyes were tightly closed until he disappeared, when he would ask the prompter, 'Has it gone?' Now it happened that, on the revival of Shakespeare's *Henry VIII*, with Macready as Cardinal Wolsey, the part of Cardinal Campeius was allotted to Mr Wynn. It had been represented by the manager that Mr Macready's costume would be correct and splendid, more especially as regards some magnificent point-lace, and it had been suggested that something extra should be done to make the other Cardinal respectable. But Mr Maddox thought some old scarlet robes fudged up from the wardrobe would suffice; and, as to point-lace, silver tissue-paper, deftly snipped and sewn on, would have much the same appearance when viewed from a distance. At the dress rehearsal Macready, enthroned in a chair of state, had the various characters to pass before him; he bore all calmly until, clad in the scarlet robes bordered by silver tissue-paper, and wearing an enormous red hat, Wynn approached. Then, clutching both arms of his chair and closing his eyes, the great tragedian gasped out: 'Mother Shipton, by ———!'

Adelphi: The entertainment scarcely ever varied. It began at seven o'clock with a melodrama in three acts, which was over before ten, after which there were a couple of farces. About nine, or as soon after as could be managed without too much disturbing the performance, the 'half-price' was admitted—that is to say, a considerable reduction was accepted in the entrance fee to the boxes and pit. In small theatres the half-price was a very important consideration to the management; for money was not so rife in those days, and there were numberless young men who, while they would have been bored by spending the entire evening in the theatre, and would have grudged a large disbursement for a comparatively short time, were willing to pay the reduced price; so that, though the drama was the staple portion of the entertainment, the farces were no mere affairs to fill up the bill, but had their own value and their own audience.

Olympic: My first regular recollection is of going to the pit to see a man who had taken the town by storm as Othello. Gustavus Vaughan Brooke was his name, and he remains in my memory as the best representative of the character I have ever seen: manly, soldierly, with all Salvini's gallantry and pathos, without a suggestion of Salvini's repulsive violence, with a voice now capable of the softest modulation in love or pity, now trumpet-toned in command. He soon dropped away, poor fellow—became a heavy drinker, of stout and porter mostly, and lost his gallant bearing, and his voice grew thick and muddy. Though he played for years afterwards, he was virtually a lost man in his first season. He went down in the *London*, a ship which foundered in the Bay of Biscay on her way to Australia, and when last seen, after most strenuous exertions at the pumps, was leaning over the bulwarks, calmly awaiting his doom.

Surrey: The manager, a Mr Levi, one day asked my father what piece he proposed to produce next, and my father, mentioning *The Admirable Crichton*, a version of Ainsworth's novel which had been successful at the Adelphi, Mr Levi said: 'That's a capital notion—*The Admiral Crichton*: and we've something in the wardrobe that'll just do for it. Jones, step up to the wardrobe and fetch that admiral's uniform I bought last week.' When I visited the Surrey as a young man, it was under the joint management of Mr Shepherd and Mrs Vincent, 'the acknowledged heroine of domestic drama,' as she used to be called in the bills, a lady whose great part was Susan Hopley, a virtuous servant-maid. On my being presented as the son of the late, etc., to Mr Shepherd, that gentleman affably remarked, 'Oh indeed! glad to know you, sir! *Did your father leave your mother pretty well off?*'

EDMUND YATES

XXV

Acting with Macready

WHEN, for a month, Fanny Kemble became William Charles Macready's leading lady at the Princess's Theatre in Oxford Street during the spring season of 1848, friends warned her that he was a terrifying partner who might go berserk if a part dominated him, and maul his actresses black and blue (he had always been a violent player). Fanny described her experiences in letters to her devoted friend, Harriet St Leger, published in *Records of Later Life* (1882).

From a letter of February 10, 1848:
I had a three hours' rehearsal this morning, and Macready was there. . . . He is unnecessarily violent in acting which I had always heard, and congratulated myself that in Lady Macbeth I could not possibly suffer from this; but was much astonished and dismayed when at the exclamation, 'Bring forth men-children only,' he seized me ferociously by the wrist and compelled me to make a demi-volte, or pirouette, such as I think that Lady did surely never perform before, under the influence of her husband's admiration.

February 23, 1848:
Macready is not pleasant to act with, as he keeps no specific time for his exits or entrances, comes on while one is in the middle of a soliloquy, and goes off while one is in the middle of a speech

to him. He growls and prowls, and roams and foams, about the stage, in every direction, like a tiger in his cage, so that I never know on what side of me he means to be; and keeps up a perpetual snarling and grumbling like the aforesaid tiger, so that I never feel quite sure that he *has done*, and that it is my turn to speak....

I do not know how Desdemona might have affected me in other circumstances, but my only feeling about acting it with Mr Macready is dread of his personal violence. I quail at the idea of his laying hold of me in those terrible passionate scenes; for in *Macbeth* he pinched me black and blue, and almost tore the point lace from my head. I am sure my little finger will be re-broken, and as for that smothering in bed, 'Heaven have mercy upon me!' as poor Desdemona says. If that foolish creature wouldn't persist in *talking* long after she has been smothered and stabbed to death, one might escape by the off side of the bed and leave the bolster to be questioned by Emilia, and apostrophised by Othello; but she will uplift her testimony after death to her husband's amiable treatment of her, and even the bolster wouldn't be stupid enough for that.

Did it ever occur to you what a witness to Othello's agony in murdering his wretched wife his inefficient clumsiness in the process was—his half smothering, his half stabbing her: *That* man not to be able to kill *that* woman outright, with one hand on her throat, or one stroke of his dagger, how tortured he must have been, to have bungled so at his work!

February 24, 1848:

My rehearsal of Desdemona tried me severely, for I was frightened to death of Macready, and the horror of the play itself took such hold of me that at the end I could hardly stand for shaking, or speak for crying; and Macready seemed quite mollified by my condition, and promised not to re-break my little finger, *if he could remember it.* He lets down the bed-curtain before he smothers me and as the drapery conceals the murderous struggle, and therefore he need not cover my head at all, I hope I shall escape alive.

February 26, 1848:

I got through Desdemona very well, as far as my personal safety was concerned; for though I felt on the stage in real hysterics at the end of one of those horrible scenes with Othello, Macready was more considerate than I had expected....

I really believe Macready cannot help being as odious as he is on the stage. He very nearly made me faint last night in *Macbeth* with crushing my broken finger, and, by way of apology, merely coolly observed that he really could not answer for himself in such a scene, and that I ought to wear a splint; and truly, if I act much more with him, I think I shall require several splints, for several broken limbs. I have been rehearsing *Hamlet* this morning with him for three hours. I do not mind his tiresome particularity on the stage, for, though it all goes to making himself the only object of everything and everybody, he works very hard, and is zealous, and conscientious, and laborious in his duty, which is a merit in itself. But I think it is rather *mean* (as the children say) of him to refuse to act in such plays as *King John, Much Ado About Nothing*, which are pieces of his own too, to oblige me; whilst I have studied expressly for him, Desdemona, Ophelia, and Cordelia, parts quite out of my line, merely that his plays may be strengthened by my name.

March 8, 1848:

My little finger has recovered from Macready. It is gradually getting much better, but he certainly did it an injury. With regard to his 'relenting,' he is, I am told, quite uncommonly gracious and considerate to me.

I was told by a friend of mine who was at *Hamlet* the other evening, that in the closet scene with his mother, he had literally knocked the poor woman down who was playing the Queen. I thought this an incredible exaggeration, and asked her afterwards if it was true, and she said so true that she was bruised all across her breast with the blow he had given her; that, happening to take his hand at a moment when he did not wish her to do so, he had struck her violently and knocked her literally down; so I suppose I may consider it 'relenting' that he never yet has knocked me down.

FANNY KEMBLE

[Macready, after deciding in his journal that Fanny Kemble was 'most unnatural and bad,' softened a little when he considered her admirable intentions as Desdemona, but ended by deciding that she was 'a very indifferent actress to be placed in a prominent position.']

XXVI

The Curate's Daughter

WILKIE COLLINS, the novelist, was twenty-six when, during the late summer of 1850, he toured Cornwall with his artist-friend, Henry C. Brandling. They were, in Cornish idiom, 'trodgers,' or what we now call, less happily, hikers; and Collins recorded the tour in a book (1851) that he entitled *Rambles Beyond Railways; or, Notes in Cornwall Taken A-foot*. At this period the railway went no further than Plymouth. Then, in the following year, the trains came. Cornwall was discovered, and Collins said wryly that by the time a second edition appeared his title was already out of date.

During the tour he descended the copper mine at Botallack; but he had one of his most cheerful experiences, not long afterwards, at a performance of a drama named *The Curate's Daughter* (author unknown) in what was nobly called the Sans Pareil Theatre at Redruth. Here are the pomping folk in high flourish. Students may like to compare the costume worn by 'good h'Adam Marle' with that chosen by John Coleman, at Greenock a few years earlier, as Alonzo in *Pizarro*: 'A nice Romeo dress ... a jaunty hat and feather, a sword, a pair of smart gauntlets, a Vandyke collar, a pair of White Berlin pantaloons,' and a pair of Hessian boots coated with yellow oil paint and varnished.

I DOUBT much whether we should not have passed as unceremoniously through the large town of Redruth—the capital city of the mining districts—as we passed through several towns and villages before it, had not our attention been attracted and our departure delayed by a public notice, printed on rainbow-coloured paper, and pasted up in the most conspicuous part of the market-place.

The notice set forth that 'the beautiful drama of *The Curate's Daughter*' was to be performed at night in the 'unrivalled Sans Pareil Theatre,' by 'the most talented company in England,' before 'the most discerning audience in the world.' As far as we were individually concerned, this theatrical announcement was remarkably tempting and well-timed. We were now within one day's journey of Piran Round, the famous amphitheatre where the old Cornish Miracle Plays used to be performed. Anything connected with the stage was, therefore, a subject of particular interest in our eyes. The bill before us seemed to offer a curious opportunity of studying the dramatic tastes of the modern Cornish, on the very day before we were about to speculate on the dramatic tastes of the Ancient Cornish, among the remains of their public theatre. Such an occasion was too favourable to be neglected; we ordered our beds at Redruth, and joined the 'discerning audience' assembled to sit in judgment on *The Curate's Daughter*.

The Sans Pareil Theatre was not of that order of architecture in which outward ornament is studied. There was nothing florid about it; canvas, ropes, scaffolding-poles, and old boards, threw an air of Saxon simplicity over the whole structure. Admitted within, we turned instinctively towards the stage. On each side of the proscenium boards was painted a knight in full armour, with powerful calves, weak knees, and an immense spear. Tallow candles, stuck round two hoops, threw a mysterious light on the green curtain, in front of which sat an orchestra of four musicians, playing on a trombone, an ophicleide, a clarionet, and a fiddle, as loudly as they could—the artist on the trombone, especially, performing prodigies of blowing, though he had not room enough to develop the whole length of his instrument. Every now and then great excitement was created among the expectant audience by the vehement ringing of a bell behind the scenes, and by the occasional appearance of a youth who gravely snuffed the candles all round, with a skill and composure highly creditable to him, considering the pertinacity with which he was stared at by everybody while he pursued his occupation.

At last the bell was rung furiously for the twentieth time; the curtain drew up, and the drama of *The Curate's Daughter* began.

Our sympathies were excited at the outset, We beheld a lady-like woman who answered to the name of 'Grace'; and an old gentleman, dressed in dingy black, who personated her fat father, the Curate; and who was, on this occasion (I presume through unavoidable circumstances), neither more nor less than—drunk. There was no mistaking the cause of the fixed leer in the reverend gentleman's eye; of the slow swaying in his gait; of the gruff huskiness in his elocution. It appeared, from the opening dialogue, that a pending law-suit, and the absence of his daughter, Fanny, in London, combined to make him uneasy in his mind just at present. But he was by no means so clear on this subject as could be desired—in fact, he spoke through his nose, put in and left out his *h*s in the wrong places, and involved the dialogue in a long labyrinth of parentheses whenever he expressed himself at any length. It was not until the entrance of his daughter Fanny (just arrived from London: nobody knew why or wherefore), that he grew more emphatic and intelligible. We now observed with pleasure that he gave his children his blessing and embraced them both at once; and we were additionally gratified by hearing from his own lips, that his 'daughters were the h'all on which his h'all depended—that they would watch h'over his 'ale autumn; and that whatever happened the whole party must invariably trust in heabban's obdipotent power!'

Grateful for this clerical advice, Fanny retired into the garden to gather her parent some flowers; but immediately returned shrieking. She was followed by a Highwayman with a cocked hat, mustachios, bandit's ringlets, a scarlet hunting-coat, and buff boots. This gentleman had shown his extraordinary politeness—although a perfect stranger—by giving Miss Fanny a kiss in the garden; conduct for which the Curate very properly cursed him, in the strongest language. Apparently a quiet and orderly character, the Highwayman replied by beginning a handsome apology, when he was interrupted by the abrupt entrance of another personage who ordered him (rather late in the day, as we ventured to think) to 'Let go his holt, and beware how he laid his brutal touch on the form of innocence!' This newcomer, the parson informed us, was 'good h'Adam Marle, the teacher of the village school.' We found 'h'Adam', in respect of his outward appearance, to be a very short man, dressed in a high-crowned modern hat, with a fringed vandyck collar drooping over his back and shoulders, a modern frock-coat, buttoned tight at the waist, and a pair of jackboots of the period of James the Second. Aided by his advantages of costume, this character naturally interested us; and we regretted seeing but little of him in the first scene, from which he retired, following the penitent Highwayman out, and lecturing him as he went. No sooner were their backs turned, than a waggoner, in a clean smock-frock and high-lows, entered with an offer of a situation in London for Fanny, which the unsuspicious Curate accepted immediately. As soon as he had committed himself, it was confided to the audience that the waggoner was a depraved villain, in the employ of that notorious profligate, Colonel Chartress, who had commissioned a second myrmidon (of the female sex) to lure Fanny from virtue and the country to vice and the metropolis. By the time the plot had 'thickened' thus far, the scene changed, and we got to London at once.

We now beheld the Curate, Chartress's female accomplice, Fanny, and the vicious waggoner, all standing in a row, across the stage. The Curate, in a burst of amiability, had just lifted up his hands to bless the company, when Colonel Chartress (dressed in an old *naval* uniform, with an opera hat of the year 1800), suddenly rushed in, followed by the Highwayman, who, having relapsed from penitence to guilt, had, as a necessary consequence, determined to supplant Chartress in the favour of Miss Fanny. These two promptly seized each other by the throat; vehement shouting, scuffling, and screaming ensued; and the Curate, clasping his daughter round the waist, frantically elevated his walking-stick in the air. Was he about to inflict personal chastisement on his innocent child? Who could say? Before there was time to ask the question, the curtain fell with a bang on the crisis of the first act.

In act the second, the first scene was described in the bills as Temple Bar by moonlight. Neither Bar nor moonlight appeared when the curtain rose—so we took both for granted, and fixed our minds on the story. The first person who now confronted us was 'proud h'Adam Marle.' The paint was all washed off his face; his immense spread of collar looked grievously in want of washing; and he leaned languidly on an oaken stick. He had been walking—he informed us—through the streets of London for six consecutive days and nights, without sustenance, in search of Miss Fanny, who had disappeared since the skirmish at the end of act the first, and had never been heard of since. Poor dear Marle! how eloquent he was with his white handkerchief, when he fairly opened his heart, and confided to us that he was madly attached to Fanny; that he knew he was 'nothink' to her; and that, under existing circumstances, he felt inclined to rest himself on a doorstep. Just as he had comfortably settled down, the valet of the profligate Chartress entered, in the communicative stage of intoxication; and immediately mentioned all his master's private affairs to 'h'Adam.' It appeared that the Colonel had carried off Miss Fanny, and then got tired of her, and had coolly handed her over to a Jew, in part payment of a 'little bill.' Having ascertained the Jew's address, the indefatigable Marle left us (still without sustenance) to rescue the Curate's daughter, or die in the attempt.

The next scene disclosed Fanny, sitting conscience-stricken and inconsolable, in a red polka jacket and white muslin slip. Mr Marle, having discovered her place of refuge, now stepped in to lecture and reclaim. Vain proceeding! The Curate's daughter looked at him with a scream, exclaimed 'Cuss me, h'Adam, cuss me!' and rushed out. 'H'Adam', after a despondent soliloquy, followed with his eloquent handkerchief to his eyes; but, while he had been talking to himself, our old friend the Highwayman had been on the alert, and had picked Fanny up, fainting in the street. And what did he do with her after that? He handed her over to his 'comrade in villainy.' And who were his comrades in villainy? They were the trombone and ophicleide players from the orchestra, and the 'Miss Grace' of act first, disguised as a bad character in a cloak, with a red pocket-handkerchief over her head. And what happened next? A series of events happened next. Miss Fanny, recovered of a sudden, perceived what sort of company she had about her, rushed out a second time into the street, fell fainting a second time on the pavement, and was picked up on this occasion by Colonel Chartress—in the interests, it is to be presumed, of his friend, the Jew moneylender. Before, however, he could get clear off with his prize, the indefatigably vicious Highwayman and the indefatigably virtuous Marle, precipitated themselves on the stage, assaulting Chartress, assaulting each other, assaulting everybody. Fanny fell fainting a third time in the street; and before we could find out who was the third person who picked her up, down came the curtain in the midst of the catastrophe.

Act the third was opened by the heroine, still injured, still inconsolable, and still clad in the polka jacket and white slip. We thought her a very nice little woman, with a melodious, genteel-comedy-voice, trim ankles, and a habit of catching her breath in the most pathetic manner, at least a dozen times in the course of one soliloquy. While she was still assuring us that she felt the most forlorn creature on the face of the earth, she was suddenly interrupted by no less a person than the Curate himself. We had seen nothing of the reverend gentleman throughout the second act; but 'h'Adam' had casually informed us that his time had been passed at his parsonage, 'sittun with his 'ed between his knees, sobbun!' Having now wearied of this gymnastic method of indulging in parental grief, he had set forth to seek his lost daughter, and had accidentally stopped at the very inn where she had taken refuge. Nothing could be more piteous than his present appearance; he was infinitely more tipsy, infinitely more dignified, and infinitely more parenthetical in his mode of expressing himself, than when we last beheld him. A streak of burnt cork running down each side of his venerable nose, showed us how deeply grief had increased the wrinkles of age; and our pity for him reached climax when he cast his clerical hat on the floor, sank drowsily into a chair, and began to pray in these words: 'O heabben! hear a solemn and a solid prayer—hear a solemn heart who wants to embrace his darling Fanny!'

All this time, the lost daughter was hiding behind the forlorn father's chair; an awful and convenient darkness being thrown on the stage by the introduction of a plank between the actors and the tallow candles. In this striking situation, Miss Fanny told her sad story, and pleaded her own cause as a stranger, under disguise of the darkness. Useless—quite useless! The reverend gentleman, having never turned round to see who it was that was speaking to him, and having therefore no idea that it was his own daughter, received in dignified silence the advances of a young person unknown to him. What course was now left to the unhappy Fanny? The old course—rush off the stage, and a swoon in the street. As soon as her back was turned, the Parson, forgetting to take away his hat with him, staggered out at the opposite side to continue his journey. He uttered as he went the following moral observation: 'No soul so lost to Nature, but must be lost eternally—my 'art is broken!'

The next moment, we were startled by a long and elaborate trampling of feet behind the scenes, and the villain Chartress ran panic-stricken across the stage, hotly pursued by 'good h'Adam Marle.' In the eloquent language of virtue, thus did Adam address him: 'Stay, ruffian, stay! Inquiring for Chartress at the bar of this inn, I found indeed that you were the very identical. You foul, venimous, treacherous, voluptuous liar, where is the un'appy Fanny? Where is the victim of your prey? Ha, 'oary-'edded ruffian, I have yer!' (*Collars Chartress*). 'But no! I will not *strike* yer; I will *drag* yer!' It was interesting to see Adam exemplify the peculiar distinction in the science of assault implied in his last words, by hauling Chartress round the stage. It was awful to observe that the Colonel lost his temper at the second round, murderously snapped a pistol in 'h'Adam's' face, and rushed off in hot homicidal triumph. We waited breathless for the fall of Marle. Nothing of the sort happened. He started, frowned, paused, laughed fiercely, exclaimed 'The villain 'as missed!' and followed in pursuit.

In the interim, Miss Fanny had been picked up in the street, for the fourth time, by a benevolent 'washerwoman' who happened to be passing by at the moment; had been conveyed to the said washerwoman's lodgings; and now appeared before us, despoiled, at last, of all the glories of the red polka, enveloped from head to foot in clouds of white muslin, and dying with frightful rapidity in an armchair. In the next and last scene, all that remained to represent the unhappy heroine was a coffin decently covered with a white sheet. With slow and funereal steps, the Curate, Miss Grace, 'h'Adam,' the Highwayman, and the 'venimous and voluptuous liar,' Chartress, approached to weep over it. The Curate had gone raving mad since we saw him last. His wig was set on wrong side foremost; the ends of his clerical cravat floated wildly, a yard long at least over his shoulders; his eyes rolled in frenzy; he swooned at the sight of the coffin; recovered convulsively; placed Marle's hand in the hand of Miss Grace (telling him that now one daughter was dead, nothing was left for him but to marry the other); and then fell flat on his back, with a thump that shook the stage and made the audience start unanimously. Marle—well-bred to the last—politely offered his arm to Grace; and pointing to the coffin, asked Chartress, reproachfully, whether that was not *his* work. The Colonel took off his opera-hat, raised his hands to his eyes, and doggedly answered, 'Indeed, it is!' The Tableau thus formed was completed by the Highwayman, the coffin, and the defunct Curate; and the curtain fell to slow music.

Such was the plot of this remarkable dramatic work, exactly as I took it down in the theatre, between the acts; noting also in my pocket-book such scraps of dialogue as I have presented to the reader, while they fell from the actors' lips. There were plenty of comic scenes in the play which I leave unmentioned; for their humour was of the dreariest, and their morality of the lowest order that can possibly be conceived. I can only say, as the result of my own experience at Redruth, that if the dramatic reforms which are now being attempted in the theatrical by-ways of the metropolis succeed, there would be no harm in extending the experiment as far as the locomotive stage of Cornwall. Good plays are good missionaries; and, like missionaries, let them travel to teach.

WILKIE COLLINS

XXVII

Lizzie Ann

ADELAIDE NEILSON, a gifted Victorian actress of uncommon beauty, was acclaimed both in London and the United States, especially as Juliet (and other Shakespearean heroines, the then neglected Isabella among them), and as Julia in Sheridan Knowles's inevitable *The Hunchback*. She died suddenly while on holiday in Paris in the summer of 1880.

Clement William Scott (1841–1904), for many years dramatic critic of the *Daily Telegraph*, admired her profoundly. In his book, *The Drama of Yesterday and To-day* (two volumes, 1899), he said: 'So many false stories have been written about her origin that I am glad to be able to tell the true one written, presumably, in the year of her death by a friend who knew her from childhood. A more romantic tale has seldom been told of any actress.' The romantic tale ('Spanish gentleman of title' and all) is here condensed.

LILIAN ADELAIDE NEILSON was born in 1848. Neither the place nor the date is known to a living soul excepting her mother.

Her surname was Browne; but some time after her birth her mother, an actress on what used to be known as the Northern Circuit, met at Leeds a Guiseley painter and paperhanger called

Bland. She married him. Her daughter, then nearly three, became known as Lizzie Ann Bland and went to live with her parents in the unromantic, unpretending town of Guiseley, at a house in Green Bottom. (It was demolished sixteen or seventeen years ago when the Midland railway line was cut from Leeds to Harrogate.) Lizzie Ann, a precocious child, attended the village school where she was something of a prodigy: it seemed reasonable that she came of no ordinary stock. Rumour says even yet that her father was a Spaniard of high birth, and that she was born at Saratoga. Mrs Bland said many times: 'I never told anyone of my daughter's father.'

Unexpectedly, the child herself discovered a clue. In the house at Green Bottom, Mrs Bland alone had the key to a certain drawer. She forgot to take the key with her when she left on a brief holiday, and Lizzie—with true womanly instinct—opened the drawer and found letters addressed to her mother from a Spanish gentleman of title; they alluded to 'the child'. Whether or not her mother was a gipsy, as some writers aver, I do not know. Maybe she was considered one because she travelled with an itinerant theatrical company, and maybe she had some Romany blood in her veins.

Lizzie Ann, before she was eleven, used to go from place to place to help her stepfather in his work. There is at present in Guiseley a gentleman who had a room in his house papered by Bland and his daughter, and who would not have the paper removed at any price, though after twenty years it is faded and tattered. Before she was twelve, Lizzie worked at Green Bottom Mill, Guiseley, as a 'filler.' Above mill life, she became a nursegirl, entering the service of Mr John Padgett, of Hawkhill House, when she was about twelve. Well-behaved, obliging, and clever at her domestic duties, she would read whenever possible, preferring Shakespeare or a volume from the Cumberland edition of stage plays. Going to her duties in the morning, she slept at home, and while at home she was frequently known to learn three or four pages of Shakespeare and to recite them as correctly as if she were reading from the book; she would sit in bed at night learning the lines. After she left the Padgetts, several plays were found in the nursery; it is now supposed that her mother must have had them by her, and Lizzie Ann made use of them.

What is more remarkable, until this time she had never seen a dramatic performance of polish or refinement. But she enjoyed the 'feasts'; the booths delighted her and she appeared never to be tired of their fantastic spectacles. Yet, though the drama absorbed her, she was one of the most diligent scholars (and anniversary reciters) at the Wesleyan Methodist Sunday School.

Lizzie Ann remained as a nurse-girl with the Padgetts for two years. Then when she was nearly fourteen, one evening in the autumn of 1861, she resolved to run away. ('I intend,' she had said often, 'to be *something*'.) Telling only the lady from whom I learnt this, she would hear of no compromise: she went out into the night.

After six years no tidings of Lizzie Ann Bland had reached Guiseley. Her stepfather had died; but her mother still lived there. At the end of that time London was acknowledging as the first actress of her day the beautiful Lilian Adelaide Neilson; she was announced to appear at the Theatre Royal in Leeds, and Mrs Bland, following a sudden intuition, found that the woman who occupied a suite at the Old White Horse Hotel in Bear Lane, attended by her own servants—was in fact her daughter. Three months later Adelaide Neilson returned to Guiseley, saw a few friends, and gave to her mother the interest on a newly-invested sum of three thousand pounds.

Two years after this, when she stayed for a week in Guiseley, she told her story to my informant. On the night she ran away, she had walked to Apperley Bridge, gone to Leeds by train, and slept with an aunt. Next morning, leaving the house as mysteriously as she had arrived, and with a single suit of clothes, she travelled to London where, having neither money nor friends, she passed the first night in Hyde Park. During a fortnight she worked as a seamstress, then she was engaged—the turning-point in her life— as a ballet girl at a London theatre. Philip Lee (a graduate of Brazenose College, Oxford) fell in love with her, offered to educate her, and placed her in a ladies' academy. 'I studied,' she said, 'eighteen hours in twenty-four.' When she was nearly seventeen her benefactor married her, a marriage that was kept a secret for three years.

Until her death she was solicitous for her mother, though she said that she could not bear to reflect upon her former life. Of her dramatic career I need say nothing; she made her début at the

Theatre Royal, Margate, and acted last in America. Of the details of her sad end you are well acquainted—how she was attacked by a pain in her side while driving in the Bois de Boulogne in Paris; how she was taken to the Châlet restaurant; how she suffered intense agony for twelve hours before her death. You remember also how her body was taken to the Morgue and subjected to brutal post-mortem examination, and how it was brought home to England for burial.* She is gone, and may she rest in peace!

Quoted by CLEMENT SCOTT

---

* *Editor's note:* In Brompton Cemetery.

XXVIII

Return of Post

IN THE year 1851 the actor-manager Charles Kean, then at the Princess's, purchased, for £300 each, from the dramatist, editor, and drama critic Douglas Jerrold, two three-act plays, *A Heart of Gold* and *St Cupid; or, Dorothy's Fortune*. (Though they agreed that *A Heart of Gold* should be acted first, *St Cupid*—owing to an unexpected turn of events—preceded it, in the spring of 1853.) Jerrold, in April 1852, had offered a third play, saying that he was urgently in need of money, so Kean (in spite of having two plays in hand) advanced £100 on account of another.

In 1853, and after *St Cupid* (which had been acted at Windsor before Queen Victoria) had appeared at the Princess's without commercial success, Kean asked Jerrold about the expected 'nautical drama' for which £100 had been advanced. Jerrold replied that he did not wish to write a 'nautical drama', which he held was an 'after-proposition', but another play. When Kean preferred to insist upon a nautical drama—for which he would pay another £200—or, alternatively, to cancel the agreement, Jerrold promptly returned £100 with a scrupulous 12 months' interest at five per cent. He added sarcastically: 'I might perhaps venture a slight murmur of disappointment that my first drama, written for your first season [*A Heart of Gold*], remains unacted in your third.' Kean insisted that it had been with Jerrold's agreement that *St Cupid* was acted first. By now politeness was fraying. But, after rather more than a fortnight, the correspondence continued. It is printed in *The Life and Theatrical Times of Charles Kean, F.S.A.* (1859) by John William Cole, Kean's secretary, who under the name of Calcraft had been previously an actor and also, for many years, a Dublin theatre manager. Macready mistrusted him, having once seen him arm-in-arm with Alfred Bunn.

                                          26 Circus Road, St John's Wood,
                                                             May 17, 1853

My dear Mr Kean.—Will you favour me by letting me know if it be your intention to produce my play of the *Heart of Gold* next season.

                                             Yours truly, Douglas Jerrold.

                                                                  3, Torrington Square,
                                                                       May 18th, 1853

My dear Mr Jerrold.—In all our business transactions I have never failed to consult your wishes, and am equally disposed to do so now. Tell me explicitly what you desire respecting the *Heart of Gold*, and it shall be carried out in every point, if practicable.

                                                  Yours truly, Charles Kean.

To this letter Mr Jerrold sent no reply.

[To Douglas Jerrold]   *August 24th, 1853*

Dear Sir.—As I infer, from your late correspondence with me, that you are anxious your play of the *Heart of Gold* should be produced without delay, I have determined, whatever may be the inconvenience to myself, to make it one of the earliest novelties of my next season.

As we close on Friday week, 2d September, it will be necessary that the drama should be read and the parts distributed before that date.

In the absence of Mr Wright, who leaves my theatre, I purpose giving the part of *Michaelmas* to Mr Harley; Mrs Walter Lacy will play *Molly Dindle*; Mr Ryder, the part of *John Dymond*; and the rest of the characters will be cast according to the ability of the company.

Perhaps you will so far oblige me, as to name the day (Saturday excepted), on which you will read the piece.

                                  I remain, yours faithfully, Charles Kean.

[To Charles Kean, Esq.]   *August 25th*

Dear Sir.—Probably I may be enabled to relieve you of my drama of the *Heart of Gold*. To the cast you propose *I cannot consent*. In the event of finding another theatre, are you disposed, the money being repaid, to return the drama to

Yours faithfully, D. Jerrold.

[To Douglas Jerrold]   *29th August 1853*

Dear Sir.—I will meet your wishes and immediately return the play of the *Heart of Gold* if you will refund the £300 I have paid you for it.

I do so under the conviction that no good can accrue to any party concerned in the production of my theatre, where a hostile and malicious feeling exists, on the part of the author, towards the person and management of the man to whom it is entrusted.*

As I quit London on the 3d September, perhaps you will be good enough to acquaint me with your determination respecting the re-purchase before that date.

Yours faithfully, Charles Kean.

[To Charles Kean]   *August 30th*

Dear Sir.—I do not return to London until the end of September; I will then, should I find my drama available elsewhere, of which I have little doubt, re-purchase it of you. Of course, you cannot forget that you applied to *me* to write the piece. I never sought *you*; the parts were written for Mrs Kean and yourself, and accepted with much laudation. After three seasons you propose a most damaging alteration of cast, and break your compact. Be it so.

And now, dear Sir, as to 'the hostile and malicious feeling' you attribute to me as regards your 'person and management,' I can believe that your habits may not enable you to perceive the ill manners and the injustice of such an unsupported imputation. Neither hostility nor malice exist in me towards you or your doings. You would probably think it very rude in me were I, because you have broken faith with me, to stigmatize you as a person vain, capricious, unstable in his agreements, with a festering anxiety to consider every man his mortal enemy, who is not prepared to acknowledge him the eighth wonder of the habitable world.

I feel almost certain that you would think this very rude in me. Therefore, be more chary of your imputations of malice and hostility towards

Yours faithfully, Douglas Jerrold.

---

* *Cole's note:* This is in reference to the repeated attacks made upon Kean in *Lloyd's Weekly Newspaper* and *Punch*.

[To Douglas Jerrold] *August 31st, 1853*

Dear Sir.—I wish to pass over that portion of your letter (received this morning) intended to be offensive, and confine myself to saying that, throughout our transactions, I have acted towards you with all the kindness, liberality, and consideration in my power, which I fear your unfortunate nature is not capable of appreciating.

Your personalities do not in the least surprise me, for you have taught me to expect them. Did I deserve the opprobrious epithets you have bestowed upon my character, I fear I should not be worthy of that 'respect from the respected' which I have throughout life endeavoured to gain, and which I have reason to believe I now enjoy.

You are quite right when you assert that *I* sought *you* in the first instance. No one has a higher estimate than myself of your talent, and the *Heart of Gold* was written in consequence of my expressed desire to possess a play from a man of your genius and celebrity. It is quite true that I have had that play by me for three seasons. It was not acted during the two first seasons, as you already know, from the unfortunate disagreement between me and * * *.

During the present season, you will remember, you were put aside *only* for YOURSELF. When you wrote the comedy of *St Cupid, you* sought *me*, because at the time you wanted money, which I at once advanced. And to suit *your* interest, quite as well as my *own*, it was determined *between us* that *St Cupid* should take the place of the *Heart of Gold* (which was then about to be presented) and be acted first. In our third compact, which you afterwards thought proper to break, *you* again sought *me*, because *again you* wanted money, which *I again* at once advanced. A year elapsed, and you had not written one line; you declined fulfilling your agreement with me; and the money I had last advanced, namely, £100 was returned to me with £5 interest.

To meet your evident desire that the *Heart of Gold* should be brought out without any further delay, I purposed making it the first novelty of the ensuing season, and the scenery was already in progress. I cannot understand the damaging alteration of cast of which you complain. I never contemplated withdrawing Mrs Kean from *Maud*; Mr Harley is cast in the character you expressly wrote for him; and when I mentioned Mrs W. Lacy, you appeared perfectly satisfied with her for the maid. The only alteration, then, is the substitution of Mr Ryder for myself as *John Dymond*, which, in theatrical parlance, is a rugged, heavy character, and an elderly one. Mr Ryder is a good actor, and certainly a favourite at the Princess's, while in other parts he seems acceptable to you. I cannot, then, see what serious damage you can imagine the cast sustains by the simple removal of an actor whose value you are ever endeavouring to depreciate. I never expressed my partiality for the part of *Dymond*, for I do not think it suited to me; but would very willingly have done my best with it to have satisfied the views and wishes of a popular and *friendly* author; although I see no reason why I should in the slightest degree inconvenience myself for one who studiously seeks occasions to indulge in unprovoked hostility towards

Yours faithfully, Charles Kean.

I quit London for the Continent on Saturday and shall be happy to hear from you respecting the re-purchase of your play, on my return in October.

[To Douglas Jerrold]   *Royal Princess's Theatre*
11th October, 1853

Dear Sir.—Having returned to London, I am anxious to ascertain if you are now prepared to carry out your own proposal of re-purchasing the *Heart of Gold*. Your answer will oblige

Yours faithfully, Charles Kean.

[To Charles Kean]   *26 Circus Road, St John's Wood*
October 12, 1853

Dear Sir.—My proposal to re-purchase the *Heart of Gold* was, as you will perceive, purely *provisional*. I have beset no manager with any communication on the matter, and, from the aspect of the British theatre in 1853, I see no likelihood of any very successful issue from the representation of the play elsewhere. I can only wish that the time bestowed upon it had been employed on any other composition, that would have borne, as it might, immediate results. Anyway, in the present condition of the London stage, I cannot give any further attention to a matter that has been productive only of annoyance and disappointment to

Yours faithfully, D. Jerrold.

[To Douglas Jerrold]   *Royal Princess's Theatre*
Oct. 13th, 1853

Dear Sir.—Your letter of yesterday's date has required me to refer to our correspondence in which you volunteer the proposal of re-purchasing your play of the *Heart of Gold*. In yours of the 20th of August last, you say, 'Possibly I may be enabled to relieve you of my drama. In the event of finding another theatre, are you disposed, the money being re-paid, to return the drama?' And again, on the 30th August, you write, 'I do not return to London until the end of September; I will then, should I *find* my drama available elsewhere, of which I have little doubt, re-purchase it of you.'

From these two communications, I naturally concluded you had some arrangement in immediate view. You are scarcely likely to *find* a purchaser, unless you *looked* for one; and if you have 'beset no manager' with any communication on the subject, I confess I do not see how any manager could know you had such an article to dispose of. There are two points in your letter I am unable to understand. First, how the aspect of the British theatre in 1853 can have changed during the short interval of seven weeks, which has elapsed since you made your first overture to me on the subject. And, second, whether your expression, 'I see no likelihood of any very successful issue from the play elsewhere,' is intended as a compliment to my particular theatre, or as an oblique condemnation of the insufficiency of *all theatres*. Having paid you £300 down on delivery of the play, in my humble judgment the 'immediate results,' as far as your interests are concerned, have assumed a tolerably substantial form. Mine, I regret to say, are for the present in rather a dim perspective, and the delay has been principally occasioned by your own proposal, which, I now understand, you *find yourself* utterly unable to carry out.

I am, dear Sir, yours truly,
Charles Kean.

[To Charles Kean]   *26 Circus Road, St John's Wood,*
Oct. 16th, 1853

Dear Sir.—I have little to add to my last. Should an opportunity present itself, promising a fair production of my drama elsewhere than at your theatre, I shall *most gladly* carry out my first provisional intention of re-purchasing the play.

Considering that you are the person who has originally broken faith in the matter, it is I who have the right of complaint, for procrastination and final disappointment. I have only to repeat that I did not seek you, and am heartily sorry that you ever addressed yourself to

Yours faithfully, D. Jerrold.

[To Douglas Jerrold]   *October 16th 1853*

Dear Sir.—My reply to yours of this date, shall be comprised in very few words and will, I sincerely hope, close our correspondence. Argument having failed, you seem disposed to retire on personalities. There I confess my inability to engage, and must decline to follow.

I most emphatically deny ever having 'broken faith' with you. This is a chimera of your own creation,—an imaginary disappointment,—which I think you will find it very difficult to substantiate beyond mere assertion. You say you are 'heartily sorry that I ever addressed myself to you.' The balance of regret ought to weigh heavily on my side; as, on looking over my books, I find I have paid you £600 for two plays (one as yet unacted); and that sum is considerably under the loss I sustained by *St Cupid*.

Yours faithfully, Charles Kean.

JOHN WILLIAM COLE

Editor's Note:

Kean finally staged *A Heart of Gold* on 9 October 1854, a homely piece with (according to the biased Cole) 'something inherently dreary and uncomfortable in the plot, incidents, and final development.' It had only eleven performances, to the intense anger of Jerrold, who had already been decrying Kean in *Punch* (for which he wrote drama criticism) and in *Lloyd's Weekly Newspaper*, which he edited. In *Lloyd's* on 15 October 1854, Jerrold had a special fling: 'With a certain graceful exception, there never was so much bad acting as in *A Heart of Gold*. Nevertheless—according to the various printed reports—the piece asserted its vitality, though drugged and stabbed, and hit about the head, as only some players *can* hit a play—hard and remorselessly.'

XXIX

The Dust Hole

THE PORTICO at the stage door of the Scala Theatre in Tottenham Street, London, was once the entrance to the Prince of Wales's where the teacup-and-saucer comedies of T.W. Robertson had their famous run during the eighteen-sixties. ('The stalls,' said Marie Wilton, writing in later life as Lady Bancroft, 'were light blue, with lace antimacassars over them; the first time such things had ever been seen in a theatre.') The Robertson plays staged there included *Society* (1865), with a scene at the Owls' Roost that might have recalled one of Sheridan Knowles's Bohemian clubs; *Ours* (1866), *Caste* (1867), *Play* (1868), *School* (1869), and *M.P.* (1870).

Between 1882 and 1886 the Prince of Wales's was empty; then for seventeen years it was a Salvation Army hostel. The new Scala Theatre was opened to the public in September 1905.

H. Barton Baker, in *The London Stage: Its History and Traditions* (1889), described the early years of the 'Dust Hole'.

SOMEWHERE in the latter decades of the last century a Signor Paschiali built a concert-room in Tottenham Street, Tottenham Court Road, which was afterwards purchased and enlarged by the directors of the 'Concerts of Antient Music,' whose entertainments were patronised by royalty. In 1802 the building came into the hands of a society of amateur actors called the Pic-Nics, who frequently provoked the satiric pencil of Gillray, and their success was great enough to bring down upon them the hostility of the legitimate theatre. In 1808 the Concert-room was converted into a circus which, however, enjoyed a very brief existence. After it had been closed for a time, Mr Paul, a gunsmith and silversmith in the Strand, whose wife fancied she had a call for the stage and would speedily become a second Vestris, bought the place and fitted it up as a theatre. The lady opened as Rosetta in *Love in a Village*. At the end of a few months the unfortunate husband was in the bankruptcy court, after which the assignees and some tradesmen attempted to carry on the theatre; the loss was so heavy that they soon relinquished their undertaking.

In the December of 1814 the property, which had begun its theatrical career so inauspiciously, though it had cost £4,000, was sold to Mr Harry Beverley for £315, and the scenery and other accessories were thrown in for another £300, while the rent was only £177 per annum and the taxes £35. After some considerable alterations, it was opened early in the following year under the name of the Regency Theatre of Varieties. It was essentially a minor, with a very mediocre company, though the manager, the father of William Beverley, the famous scenic artist, and his brother, Roxby Beverley, were both exceedingly clever actors who, had they chosen to remain in London, would have been in the foremost rank of comedians. Preferring to reign in the provinces to serving in a principal London theatre, they became the proprietors of a circuit in the North.

The Regency provided melodrama and farce as its simple fare. After six years' struggle the Beverleys retired in favour of Mr Brunton, but they returned for a season or two in 1826. Brunton, on assuming the management, rechristened the house the West London Theatre, and introduced a superior style of entertainment. His daughter, afterwards Mrs Yates, became the bright, particular star. Talk about driving a coach and four through an Act of Parliament, that feat was certainly accomplished by Brunton who, in spite of the Patent Theatres, played *She Stoops to Conquer*, *The School for Scandal*, *The Wonder*, and called them 'burlettas,' introducing a song or a few chords of music here and there to keep up the farce.

A little later, Planché describes the place as 'about as dark and dingy a den as ever sheltered the children of Thespis.' The stage was only twenty-one feet wide at the proscenium and thirty-six feet deep; at prices ranging from four shillings to one the auditorium would hold about £130. A picture representing the exterior of the theatre in 1826, shows that no alteration was ever made in the street frontage; there is the ugly squat portico and the blank wall beyond, just as it appears at the present day.

In 1826 the West London became the home of the French companies who visited London. There was a subscription season of forty nights; the plays, however, were given only once or twice a week, and only during winter and spring. It is suggestive to relate that when Mdlle. George was engaged, the prices were raised to two shillings and five; but the aristocracy, who at that time alone supported foreign companies, would not pay the price, and the great Parisian actress appeared to empty benches.

During 1829 three different people tried their fortunes at the West London—Tom Dibdin, Watkins Burroughs, and Mrs Waylett, now in the first rank of English cantatrices, rivalling Mrs Honey, and even the great Vestris herself. It is curious to mark how certain forms of art flourish and then disappear. During the early years of the century there was a positive glut of English songstresses, Miss Stephens, Miss Love, Mrs Honey, Mrs Waylett, Madame Vestris, all of whom for beauty of voice, exquisite method and expression, especially in what for lack of a better word I must call the serio-comic style, an expression horribly vulgarised by the music-hall 'artistes,' have no successors in the present day. These ladies, with the exception of the last, who frequently soared into a much higher region of art, were essentially ballad singers, and their favourite songs were brought into every piece they appeared in, with an utter disregard of the fitness of things which seems quite amazing to an age that prides itself upon its rigid correctness in theatrical details; as an instance, in a dramatic version of Beaumarchais' *Mariage de Figaro*, in which she played Susanna, Mrs Waylett sang 'The Soldier's Tear,' 'I'll be a Butterfly,' 'The Light Guitar,' 'My own Bluebell,' while, in a version of Boieldieu's *Jeanne de Paris*, she introduced, as the Princess of Navarre, 'I've Been Roaming,' 'The Merry Swiss Boy,' 'Oh, No, We Never Mention Her', and 'The Dashing White Sergeant.'

The fair manageress surrounded herself with a capital company, but, although she added melodrama to these more elegant pieces the public did not support her, and she soon gave place to other ambitious spirits . . .

In January, 1831, after being closed some little time for alterations and decorations, the theatre in Tottenham Street, as it had been called during the past two years, was once more rechristened the Queen's, and reopened under the management of Mrs Nisbett, who brought with her Mrs Glover, Mrs Humby, and a good stock company. If it had been possible to make the unlucky theatre pay, that feat should have been accomplished by one of the most beautiful women and exquisite comediennes of the time. Old playgoers still speak rapturously of that silvery laugh, to hear which alone was worth a visit to the theatre; of that wonderful verve and 'go' which, in the fullest sense of the word, created such parts as Constance in *The Love Chase* and Lady Gay Spanker in *London Assurance*. But although she and Mrs Glover played nightly in light pieces, Mrs Nisbett, in April, had to engage an extra attraction in the person of a French pantomime actress, Madame Celeste. She made her first appearance in London at the age of fifteen, as a dumb Arab boy in a piece called *The French Spy*, a part which, as she could not speak one word of English, was played throughout in dumb show; yet, by the beauty and grace of her dancing and action she made a decided hit.

No person could be much more unsuited for theatrical management than Mrs Nisbett, and on May 16th she retired. Yet she made another attempt in the following year, and engaged John Reeve. In 1833 the name of the house was changed to the Fitzroy; but not for long, as two years later it once more became the Queen's with Mrs Nisbett's name again at the head of the bill. The person who found the money, however, was the notorious Ephraim Bond, the moneylender, who kept a gambling-house in St James's Street, second only in importance to Crockford's (the Ephraim Sharpe of Disraeli's *Henrietta Temple*); he seems to have taken it for beautiful Mrs Honey. There was an admirable company, and the lightest of light pieces were performed, sometimes as many as six one-act trifles making up the bill.

During the Lent of 1837 and 1838—by which time Mrs Nisbett's name no longer figured as manageress, she being at Covent Garden with Macready—Madame Vestris and Charles

Mathews in consequence of some absurd regulations, being unable to play at their own theatre, the Olympic, brought their company to Tottenham Street when the theatre was again known as the Fitzroy.

In the October of 1839 the house, re-christened the Queen's, came into the hands of Mr C. J. James, a scenic artist, who, from that time until the final close of the theatre just recently, has never been dissociated from the management. For years the Queen's, or the Dust Hole, as it was irreverently designated among the actors, was one of the curiosities of London. Mr James began by reducing the prices to two shillings, one shilling, and sixpence, and this tariff was afterwards lowered to one shilling and sixpence, eightpence, and fourpence, with half price to boxes and pit. Melodrama of the most terrific description, bearing the most tremendous titles, constituted the bill of fare. Only fancy going to see *Footpad Joe, the Terror of Charing Cross; or, The Dog of the Abbey*; *The Death Wedding; or, The Witch of the Heath*; *The Inn of Death; or, The Dog Witness*. The great star of the latter was Mr Jack Matthews, who used to boast that he was the only 'Dog Hamlet.' At booths and fairs this gentleman played the Prince of Denmark with a large black dog at his heels, which used to 'bay the moon' at the sight of the Ghost and throttle the King in the last scene, reached in about half an hour. *The Skeleton of the Wave; or, The Ocean Spirit* was another favourite play at the Queen's, but what a feast of horror for one night was *The Demon Lord*; *The Poison Tree; or, The Law of Java*; and *The Spectre Bride and the Demon Nun*, and, to wind up on this particular night, *The Death Plank; or, The Dumb Sailor Boy*. These highly-seasoned dramas were, however, occasionally diversified by the engagement of Mrs Nisbett, Mrs Honey, and by Shakespearean productions. The style in which the plays were rendered may be imagined; no burlesque was ever half so extravagant; in one piece the villain was thrown into the corner fifteen times by the hero, and invariably consoled himself by the remark that he must dissemble, or that a 'time would come.' Anything so utterly stilted and unnatural as the acting it would be impossible to conceive at the present day; burlesque could not exaggerate it, as it was beyond the reach of exaggeration, even in the utterance of the simplest words. If a character asked for a piece of bread and cheese, or if he said 'How do you do?' he would raise and lower his eyebrows three times, and pause between each word, which was dragged up from the very pit of his stomach, and intoned as tragically as though he had requested a cup of poison.

The Queen's shared with the Bower Saloon in Stangate the reputation of being the lowest theatre in London; and then the neighbourhood! always impregnated with 'an ancient and a fish-like smell!' from fried fish, which was the staple commerce of the street. Such was the house that Miss Marie Wilton, in 1865, being at that time in search of a theatre, fixed upon as a home for elegant comedy.

H. BARTON BAKER

XXX

Pigmy Indignation

ONE OF anybody's favourite passages of invective must be the observations of Mr Pott (of the *Eatanswill Gazette*) on the *Eatanswill Independent*: 'Abhorred and despised by even the few who are cognisant of its miserable and disgraceful existence, stifled by the very filth it so profusely scatters, rendered deaf and blind by the exhalations of its own slime, the obscene journal, happily unconscious of its degraded state, is rapidly sinking beneath that treacherous mud which, while it seems to give it a firm standing with the low and debased classes of society, is nevertheless rising above its detested head and will speedily engulf it for ever.'

I think of that when reading the leading article ('Pigmy Indignation') with which Mr Wilfrid Wisgast, M.A., editor of a theatre journal called *The Players* ('The abstract and brief chronicles of the time'), lashed in his eighth issue a religious newspaper called *The Record*. Mr Wisgast, writing on 18 February 1860, enjoyed himself thoroughly; and some of the pomping folk must have regretted that he ceased to be editor in the early autumn.

Certainly Pott and Slurk (*Independent*) might have welcomed Mr Wisgast as a man and a brother, though I doubt whether they would have liked his habit of advertising, in his own paper, that he was 'prepared to write Entertainments, Lectures, Prologues for Elocution Classes, Pieces for Recitation, etc., on given topics; and to Revise, Edit, or Correct for the Press, Poetic, Dramatic, or other productions of Young Authors.'

PIGMY INDIGNATION

THE *Record* is displeased. Let society mourn in sackcloth and ashes; and let such grief be universally manifested as pervaded creation when the proclamation went forth that great PAN was dead. Something must be done to appease its wrath, or the world is lost. It has already commenced hurling its thunderbolts among the members of that profession to whose interest its pages are professedly devoted, and unless its anger be propitiated, the consequences may be alarming. It is mighty in its displeasure—let no one brave it. The torrents of its indignation, when provoked, fall like the mighty avalanche bearing down all before it. The thunderbolts are more terrible than those manufactured by old Vulcan and his Cyclops, and its ire is that of an incensed Jove. *Tantaene animis caelestibus irae!* * The theatre again, unfortunate in its tendency to give offence, has, with the very best intentions, provoked the displeasure of the *Record*. This time, too, it is not the public playhouse—which, from its position, must necessarily run counter to some people's feelings—but a private theatrical, acted in a drawing-room, limited in its influence to the domestic circle, and, therefore, one would have imagined beyond the reach of newspaper criticism. But the lynx eye of the *Record* has even penetrated the thick walls of Mr Ewart's house, and the world is made acquainted with what transpired there, and the just indignation of the *Record* thereat. The following paragraph will explain:

> A correspondent sends us a copy of the *Devizes Gazette*, containing a report of a theatrical performance at the house of Mr Ewart, M.P., Broadleaze. The piece performed was entitled *A Sheep in Wolf's Clothing*. The time represented was (we are told) the interesting period of 1685 when Judge Jeffreys went his sanguinary circuit. The dresses were as conformable as possible with the historical period of the play. Colonel Kirke, of Kirke's celebrated regiment, the 'Lambs', was represented by Colonel Daubeny; Lord Churchill by Mr Herbert Fisher; Jasper Carew, by Mr Cecil Fisher; and Kester by Mr Grant Meek. Ann Carew, the wife of Jasper Carew, was performed by Mrs Ewart; Keziah by Miss Louise Dowding; Dame Carew by Mrs Charles Smith; and Sybil, the child of the Carews, by Miss Edith Wood. As a commentary on this, we learn that Mr Herbert Fisher is a son of Canon Fisher, of Salisbury, and is private tutor to the Prince or Wales; and the Misses Wood and Dowding (both under fourteen) are

* 'Can heavenly spirits cherish resentment so dire!'

clergymen's daughters. Mrs Smith is the wife of a clergyman. It is deeply to be regretted that the near connexions of clergymen, should take part in such amusements. How can children, thus early initiated in a taste for stage entertainments, be expected to conduct themselves in after-life? And with what face can clergymen who countenance these things enforce the precept, 'Be not conformed to this world'?

Admirable *Record*! Thou art indeed a production worthy of the school of Mawworm. Clergymen's wives and daughters to take part in a theatrical performance! This surely must be the abomination that is to precede the end of this dispensation. The clerical profession is disgraced for ever, and the Church brought into universal contempt. One thing is clear. There must either be an end of this disgrace upon the Christian name, or of the *Record*. Both cannot go on. The world must take its choice. Let us not forget, however, that if the *Record* cease, the foundations of morality will be undermined, and we shall be left without a guardian of Christian virtue. What new crimes would follow such a catastrophe, we dare not imagine. No! live the *Record*, and perish the theatre.

Probably not one out of ten of our readers ever heard of the existence of this wondrous newspaper before, and many will not very likely care to hear of it again. To those who are in any way anxious to know something of its character, we may say—it is the organ of a renowned Dr Cantwell, of immortal memory, and devoted to the best interests of modern phariseeism. There is a word that Barnum has made familiar to us that would express its principles, but we may not utter it. It has for years been striving to bring about a state of universal gloom in society, and elevate the worship of melancholy into a fact. It is constantly lamenting over the wickedness of the world; yet if the world was not wicked it is clear that the *Record* would have nothing to fill its pages with. It is the expounder of the most narrow-minded cant that hypocrisy ever conceived, and the advocate of bigotry in its blackest form of intolerance. Sometimes it has a good word of faint damaging praise for its own small party; but the great mass of mankind it treats as outcasts, heretics, and scoundrels. It teaches that 'the present state of the human race, or at least of ninety-nine hundredths of it, is desperately wicked'; the inference being that the other hundredth—its own clique—is immaculate. The Poet Laureate is treated as a heretic, and a lady who called the love of a son for his mother one of the 'holiest affections of man's heart' is snubbed, and told that such feelings 'have in them the nature of sin.' Willis and Longfellow are politely excluded from the pale of Christianity, and treated as pantheistic infidels. The *Record* has for years been engaged in imputing base motives to some of the best of mankind; loading with abuse and calumny public benefactors, and venting its petty spite upon all whose minds are not narrowed down to its own diminutive dimensions. Anything like amusement has of course always been classed with the most heinous sins, and the theatre, in every shape and form, treated as a Satanic institution.

The authority, therefore, of this self-righteous and bombastic *Record* is not very great. Were its dictum of the slightest degree of importance, it would be interesting to inquire what is meant by the conduct in after life of 'children thus early initiated in a taste for stage entertainments'. Is not this a vile innuendo hurled against the most respectable families? Is it not a display of effrontery and ignorance combined, such as is rarely witnessed? We do not wish to push the consequence of this impudent *Record*'s reasoning to its legitimate bounds, because, poor unhappy wight, he is innocent of any knowledge of logic—his education having been shockingly neglected. Still, perhaps, he might have a perception keen enough to see that he is ascribing profligacy and dissipation in after-life to all who, in the days of their childhood, witness drawing-room theatricals or take a part in acting a charade. The *Record* professes great loyalty. Has it not cast a slur on the character of the highest family in these realms—private theatricals being tolerated at Windsor? But we will not reason further with this specimen of silly conceit and moping mawkishness. No one heeds its dictum, or it would merit something more than censure. As it is, however, after all, perhaps the highest compliment that can be passed upon anyone is the denunciation of the sapient *Record*. It is so accustomed to look at things through a distorted medium that whatever is straight appears to its defective vision warped.

WILFRID WISGAST

XXXI
The Young Soldene

EMILY SOLDENE (1840–1912) wrote *My Theatrical and Musical Recollections* (1897) in Australia whither she had retired after marriage. As a young singer, under the name of Miss FitzHenry, she began her career at the Oxford Music Hall, built by Charles Morton ('Father of the Halls') in what had been an old galleried inn-yard at the corner of Oxford Street and Tottenham Court Road. Burned down in 1868, it was rebuilt in 1869, again destroyed three years later, and again rebuilt. Soldene became leading actress (and director) of a light opera and *opéra bouffe* company, under Morton's management, at the Philharmonic, afterwards the Grand, in Upper Street, Islington, where she drew West End audiences and even the Prince of Wales himself. The great triumph was the operetta of *Geneviève of Brabant*. The Canterbury, in Lambeth, was the first organized music-hall.

AS A GIRL I was articled for two years to Mr Howard Glover, an accomplished musician and linguist, a cultured gentleman, musical critic of the *Morning Post*, and son of the celebrated actress, Mrs Glover. My master was very fond and proud of his mother, and often talked about her, and what a wonderful artistic life hers had been, though, from a domestic point, it was a failure.

Mrs Glover was a Betterton, her marriage was a not particularly fortunate one. Her husband used to draw and squander her salary, until it was arranged she should draw it herself in advance. She had rooms over Jeffery's, the music shop in Soho Square, on the site of which now stands the Roman Catholic Church of St Patrick. Among her most cherished belongings was a valuable oil-painting, a portrait of herself. When Mrs Glover went starring in the provinces, Mr Glover's favourite diversion was pawning his wife's picture, which Mrs Glover would redeem on her return. Mrs Glover had the privilege of supporting all her family; charming artist, lovely woman and loving mother, these responsibilities did not disturb her to any great extent. It seems that during her frequent absences the housekeeping was carried on by running accounts with the tradesmen, and that on one occasion, after a dreadful journey in the winter from Dublin, on looking over the bills, she, with a loud exclamation, threw them from her, and lifting her eyes and arms to heaven, broke forth with tragic violence: 'Oh, my God,' cried she, 'that I should cross that d—d Irish Channel to pay a thieving fishmonger twenty-four shillings for winkles!'

My terms with Mr Glover were £200 in cash and half my earnings during my articles. A careful and conscientious teacher, he not only attended to the musical part of the lesson, he cultivated my intellect, making me read, and recite, and comprehend, and understand the words of each study before beginning the notes. In 1864, I made my début at a morning concert at St James's Hall, at which Adelina Patti, Mme. Grisi, Mme. Albani, Sims Reeves, Mme. Guerrabella (now Miss Geneviève Ward), and most of the great foreign artists, in London for the season appeared. Mr Glover accompanied me; I stood in front of the piano close to his right hand, and, when I saw the audience, felt paralysed. The symphony (rather a long one) was played, but I, frozen rigid, could not force a sound from my lips. My master, leaning forward, whispered with suppressed rage, 'Go on.' I was afraid of him, the whisper struck me like a blow, and I went on. I sang a composition of Mr Glover's, 'The strain I heard in happier days.' My voice was good, I was a natural singer with sensibility. I made a good impression and got good notices, probably not entirely uninspired, and it was at the Crystal Palace, under the baton of M. August Manns, I earned my first five-pound note, singing

'Nobil Signor', from Meyerbeer's *Huguenots*, with great success.

I made decided progress, singing in public frequently, but always suffering exceedingly from nervousness; a nervousness distressing on the stage, but paralysing on the platform. Mr Glover said if I did not get into regular work I should never do justice to myself or to him. At this time the only form of musical entertainment outside the Royal Italian Opera, an intermittent season of English Opera at Covent Garden, and the big concerts at St James's Hall, were little musical burlettas and farces at the Haymarket. Mr Glover tried, but unsuccessfully, to place me at the Haymarket. Then he had what he considered a happy thought. I should go to Mr Charles Morton at the Oxford, get, if possible, an engagement, sing every night, and conquer my emotional enemy, instead of allowing it to conquer me.

At this period I had never been inside a music hall, had very lofty, indeed great ambitions, highly strung aspirations, great dreams of future glory and achievements. Going to sing at a music hall was indeed a come-down. It hurt my 'artistic pride.' But I swallowed my artistic pride, and armed with a letter from Mr Glover (written on *Morning Post* official paper), I presented myself under the *nom de théâtre* of Miss FitzHenry to Mr Morton. He was pleased to look upon me with favour, and Mr Jongmanns, the conductor, was instructed to hear me sing, and an appointment was made; I was to go to the Canterbury in Lambeth for that ordeal.

Going to the Canterbury was dreadful. I remember the shock I got when I went under the railway arch, down the dingy, dirty, narrow street, the greasy sidewalk, the muddy gutter, full of dirty babies, the commonplace-looking public-house. I felt I could not go in; but I did. The people were polite, and showed me upstairs; there was lots of sawdust. Soon I found myself in a long picture-gallery, at the other end of which a rehearsal was being held. The pictures delighted, but the smell of beer and stale tobacco smoke revolted me. I have since been told that on that day I carried my head very high, and by my manner conveyed the utmost scorn for the Canterbury and all its surroundings. 'Why, what's this, Ferdy?' asked Mr William Morton, as I appeared in the dim distance and proceeded to sail up the gallery. 'Dashed if I know,' said Ferdy (Mr Jongmanns), 'sent on by der governor; but it's all right if it can sing.'

I sang. Mr Jongmanns approved my vocal capabilities. I was engaged to the Oxford to sing 'a turn' of songs; also in the 'selections,' at a salary of—well never mind. I made my appearance, was a success, and within a year of signing my articles, began earning a regular salary. . . .

I went to the Oxford in the autumn of 1865, and 'Up the Alma's Heights,' a declamatory song, written by Capt. G. W. Colomb, was my first real hit. All the military men in London came to hear that. I soon got used to the people, the place, the management, and the manager, Charles Morton.

The Hall, a magnificent structure in the Italian style was beautifully decorated with frescoes, gilding and lots of light. Bars down the side were dressed with plenty of flowers, coloured glass, and any amount of bright, glittering, brass-bound barrels, and bottles. But, after all, the brightest, most glittering, and most attractive thing about the bars (of course, not counting the drinks) were the barmaids. Rows of little tables, at which people sat and smoked and drank, filled the auditorium, and in and out the tables circulated the peripatetic, faded, suggesting, inquiring, deferential waiter, and the brisk, alert, 'cigar', 'programme,' and 'book of the words' boy.

Of course there was a certain amount of 'gay' society, the 'Chappies' and 'Johnnies' of that period. And the 'daughters of joy' were not conspicuous by their absence. No doubt most good people think that excess of fortune and lots of drink may induce ossification of the heart and memory in these poor girls. They are wrong, and many a night have I, 'by request,' sung 'Home Sweet Home,' because 'I made 'em cry'. I daresay these were 'off nights,' there is the fact for what it is worth.

The chairman's table was a sacred place—sacred to a certain and profitable clique, and to win the applause of these quidnuncs was the direct aim of every one appearing on the stage. Winning it, one felt one's position assured. Then with the clique went the hammer of the chairman, a most stimulating and directing factor in giving 'a lead' to public opinion and applause. The Oxford was a great rendezvous for racing men. On the eve of, or after a big race, their busy hum was nearly as loud as the voices of the singers. Down would come the hammer of the chairman, 'Order, gentlemen, order!' To do the gentlemen justice, they did order, and much business was the result. So you see, music was not the only thing heard at the Oxford. Sometimes one got the current tip, and 'pulled it off.'

These were the halcyon days of Pony Moore, 'Moore and Burgess Minstrels' St James's Hall. Once a year Pony had a benefit. At night, after the show, Mrs Pony Moore, wearing diamonds worth a king's ransom, would 'receive.' Then came a ball and a supper. Such a supper, and such a company, all the prettiest women in London, and all the best men. Dukes, earls, marquises, and lords intrigued for invites. About 4.30 a.m., Pony, mounting the table, would make a speech welcoming his guests, and finish up by telling them he was a freeborn American, and what he had paid for the champagne. One night he handed me on to the table and begged me as a great favour that I would sing a song, 'Happy be thy Dreams.' I said I would. Then he sent for all his minstrels to come and take a lesson in ballad singing. When I'd finished, Pony addressed the crowd, 'Great God,' said he, 'if that gal 'ud only sing that song in New York, in Wood's "Muse-um", she'd knock 'em.' This was not very refined, but, all the same, Pony Moore's ball was one of the features of the London season, and everyone who by hook or by crook could, went.

Mr Glover, naturally anxious about my progress, would sometimes have a box at the Oxford, and sit out the 'selection'. He brought back all my nervousness, and I used to be dreadfully glad when he went out. The first time he came, Miss Russell [the soprano], was very anxious about his opinion, and the next night asked me, not 'What did he think of my singing?' but 'What did he think of my bust?'

So many people at this time thought me dreadfully dramatic and said I ought to study and go on the stage. One day, it was February 10th, 1868, I met Mr John Ryder by appointment, on the stage of the Queen's Theatre, to hear his opinion. He asked me, 'What could I do?' I said, 'Nothing.' He gave me the Portia speech, 'The quality of mercy, etc.,' to read. After I got through, he walked up and down for a minute or two, then stopped: 'You have tears in your voice,' he said, 'Are your tears near the surface? can you cry easily?' I could not tell him. 'Look at me,' said he, smiling, and reciting a few lines, the tears ran down his face as freely and as miserably as possible. Of course I was astonished. 'Come tomorrow, same time,' said he; 'we will have a serious lesson.' But to-morrow never came. That evening I sang the last 'turn' on the programme, and in the middle of the night the Oxford was burned. *I* sang the last song sung in it, and that song was, 'Launch the Lifeboat.'

EMILY SOLDENE

XXXII

Sword and Dagger

DURING his fifties, Clement Scott (1841–1904) put together in *The Wheel of Life* (new edition 1898) what he called 'a few fugitive recollections of a busy Bohemian life in London.' For example, 'It was once possible to see life in a far quieter and soberer fashion at the Holborn Casino which I well remember as a popular bath-house, as well as a dancing-room. . . . It was a quiet inoffensive place, innocent of noise or revelry. Sometimes a particularly pretty girl made a furore and held a kind of levée at the Holborn; all fashionable London claiming her hand in the dance, and treating her, in true chivalric fashion, as if she were a goddess or an empress. Who can have forgotten the days of Mabel Grey, who was originally a nursemaid in Camden Town, but came to be renowned as the most beautiful and extensively-photographed young woman in London—the success of Laura Bell, Skittles, Anonyma, Baby Jordan, and the rest of them?'

But here, away from chop-houses, old letters, Cromer ('Poppy-land'), and 'the Royal Dramatic College at Woking, which was such a dreadful failure in the days of Benjamin Webster, who heartily believed in it,' Scott is considering stage fights.

I HAVE been making enquiries from experienced actors notably from my dear old friend John S. Clarke, who knows the stage of

America and England during the last fifty odd years by heart, concerning the practice of actors in using unblunted and dangerous weapons in the exercise of their art. From all that I can learn, it is a miracle that there are not more accidents to be recorded. It is certain that the actors of the old school were not so foolhardy as those of the present day, for Edmund Kean, and doubtless Macready, partly protected themselves with basket-handled swords with which to fight the furious combats in *Richard the Third* and *Macbeth*. They would scarcely have risked their lives with the tempered weapons that modern realism insists upon. With Macready it would have been positively dangerous to risk an encounter with unblunted swords, for he roused himself to the passion of the scene by actually working himself into a fury behind the scenes. He would shake a ladder, stamp, sweat, rave, and do anything to simulate ungovernable frenzy, stopping short of the realism of Gustavus Brooke, who crammed his mouth full of chalk to make believe that he was foaming with rage, and tumbled off a chair on to the stage to simulate the position of a man who had just been thrown from his horse as Richard.

A good story is told of Macready and Phelps in the Macbeth and Macduff fight. Macready, as Macbeth, commenced the old game of groaning, cursing, and swearing at Macduff *sotto voce*. But he positively frightened Phelps, who, when he came off, expressed his disgust and horror, saying he was not accustomed to be abused in such an intemperate fashion. 'Oh, never mind that,' said a bystander, 'It's only Mac's way. Pay him back in his own coin, and give him a taste of your special Billingsgate.' Whereupon the very next night, directly Macbeth began swearing, Macduff swore more awful words still; when Macbeth cursed enough to make the blood boil and curdle, Macduff did the same, and the combined oaths were sufficient to take the poor prompter's hair off. But it is recorded that the fight never went better.

There is not so much danger in stage fights with foils, as they are always buttoned; but there is always the danger of the button falling off, when a clumsy thrust would kill a man as dead as a door nail. The peril is with dagger fights, unless what are called 'trick daggers' are used, that is to say, daggers mechanically made, whose blades sink into the shaft or handle when the blow is struck, and serious danger, also, in ordinary stage combats, when actors refuse to use blunted weapons. Conceive, for instance, the danger of the celebrated sword fight in the *Dead Heart* at the Lyceum, between Henry Irving and S. B. Bancroft! Both actors are short-sighted, and can see with difficulty without glasses, but here they were pounding away at one another night after night, saving their precious lives alone by careful practice and accurate timing. It is idle to say that experienced actors cannot go wrong in such matters. The facts of the stage prove the contrary. Allowance must always be made for excitability, and for the danger of 'losing one's head'. All actors cannot be 'calm, self-contained, and passionless', according to the mistaken Talma and Coquelin theory. The true artist does lose himself in the passion of the scene, and on the whole plays far better than the cool, calculating actor. I would not give a fig for an actor who can laugh, talk, and chaff two seconds before he goes on the stage for a serious scene, and allows his dressing-room to be full all the evening with silly chatterers.

Much more do I admire the artist who is brooding, talking to himself, and getting into the skin of the part behind the scenes, and who, if he were addressed before going on the stage on some irrelevant topic, would turn round like a fiend, as an old friend of mine once did, and said to the interrupter, 'D——n you, sir! How dare you address me? Don't you see I am going on the stage?' It is very much the same with me when I am watching a play, and compelled to get every detail of it into my head between the hours of eight and eleven thirty. During the progress of a play I hate to be interrupted or disturbed. If I am spoken to, I am like a bear with a sore head, and the empty chatter of the stalls between the acts drives me into a perfect frenzy. On these important occasions the inside of a box is a haven of rest and delight. At any rate, you can think there, undisturbed, and there is not much time, I can assure you, for thinking on the first night of a new play.

I am happy to say that I have only witnessed one painful and serious stage accident. That was the first night of *Michael Strogoff*, at the Adelphi, when Charles Warner nearly lost his life by clutching at the unblunted dagger worn by James Fernandez. It was a most painful scene. Five minutes before the curtain fell on the last act we saw that something had happened. The blood was falling from Charles Warner's hand in torrents, and the plucky actor was getting paler and paler under his 'make-up', and swaying to and fro in evident agony. But, like all nervous, excitable, and sensitive men, Charles Warner is a 'good plucked one'. When the curtain fell the actor fell also in a dead swoon, from pain and loss of blood. It was a miracle that the popular actor did not die that night. It was touch and go. But happily his life was spared, and the grim reminder of the accident is a stiff joint of the middle finger on the left hand. He has never been able to bend the knuckle since.

But now that we know that to inflict a deadly injury of the kind on your companion means homicide, what an awful complication occurs when the combatants are not friends in real life, but avowed enemies. Suppose they could be proved to be having a row, and wrangling and swearing at one another before they went on to the stage. It would in that event go very hard with the unfortunate actor who stabbed his companion, though it might have been pure accident all the same.

I remember Tom Robertson telling me a story of the kind that actually happened at Cremorne, or some public gardens of that pattern. Two acrobats who were sworn friends were accustomed to make a slight ascent from the ground outside the car of a balloon. When some hundreds of yards from the ground, the one swinging by the other's hands, they used to scramble back into the car. One night, just before the ascent, the acrobat who held the other by the hand discovered in a dark corner of the ground his friend kissing the elder acrobat's wife. Boiling with indignation, he did not say one word, but slunk silently away. The ascent was made as usual, and when a hundred yards from the ground, the elder acrobat, who had the life of the younger one literally in his hands, taunted him with his perfidy. 'You kissed my wife, did you? then down you go!' 'For God's sake, Jim, have mercy.' 'No! no! down you go!' He released his hands, and down went the younger acrobat with a full thud, stone dead amongst the appalled dancers. Verdict! Accidental Death! No one but the guilty woman knew the true secret of that awful tragedy in real life.

CLEMENT SCOTT

XXXIII

Dundreary

The English dramatist, Tom Taylor (1817–1880), did not dream when he wrote a poor melodrama called *Our American Cousin*, that it would make the name of a small-part actor, an Englishman, Edward Askew Sothern (1826–1881). Sothern had early success in Birmingham, then went to America, and after some tantalizing experiences, found himself, at the age of 32, cast for Lord Dundreary in Tom Taylor's play. Once intended for a 'comedian of the Yankee school' called Josiah Silsby, who happened to be in London during 1850–51, the script had found its way to America and the desk of Laura Keene.

Joseph Jefferson recommended *Our American Cousin* to Miss Keene after her business manager, turning over the play which had been left neglected, thought he saw certain merits in it. The parts of Asa Trenchard and Abel Murcott were considered to be its strength at the first green-room reading; but presently, in performance, Sothern, by a shrewd piece of extravagant playing, began to bring the almost overlooked dolt, Dundreary, to the top of the cast.

This was in 1858. By the time the play reached the Haymarket, London, in 1861, he had re-written much of the text. Dundreary, with his whiskers, his eye-glass, and his long frock-coat, became the centre of a fashion. T. Edgar Pemberton explained why in *Edward Askew Sothern: A Memoir* (1889).

Our American Cousin, by Tom Taylor, was produced at Laura Keene's theatre in New York. Much to his disgust, Sothern was cast for the subordinate character of Lord Dundreary, who was intended to be an old man, and who had only forty-seven lines to speak. At first he declined to play the part, but later, on condition that he should be permitted to re-write it on lines of his own, undertook it. Then he began putting into it everything he had seen that had struck him as wildly absurd. There was not, he used afterwards to declare, a single look, word, or act in Lord Dundreary that had not been suggested to him by people whom he had known since early boyhood. On the first night the part was by no means a success,—indeed, it was some two or three weeks before the public began to understand what an actor whose name had hitherto been identified with characters of a serious and even pathetic type, meant by this piece of mad eccentricity. But, once comprehended, Lord Dundreary's popularity was a thing assured, and very soon he made a not very interesting or brilliant play one of the greatest attractions that the American stage had ever known. Everything about the part—the famous make-up, the wig, the whiskers, and the eye-glass, the eccentric yet faultless costumes, the lisp and the stutter, the ingenious distortion of old aphorisms—was the outcome of Sothern's own original thought.

Only one thing—the quaint little hop (that odd 'impediment in the gait', which became as much part and parcel of his lordship as the impediment in his speech)—was the result of accident. At rehearsal one cold day, Sothern, ever restless, was endeavouring to keep himself warm by hopping about at the back of the stage, when Miss Keene sarcastically inquired if 'he was going to introduce that in Dundreary?' Among the bystanding actors and actresses this created a laugh, and Sothern, who at the time was out of temper with his part, replied in his gravest manner, 'Yes, Miss Keene; that's my view of the character.' Having so far committed himself, he felt bound to go on with it, and finding as the rehearsal progressed that the whole company, including the scene-shifters, were convulsed with laughter, he made capital at night out of a modified hop.

Months grew into years while Lord Dundreary reigned supreme upon the American stage, and English playgoers were almost wearying of waiting, when it was modestly enough announced that on November 11, 1861, Mr Sothern, 'formerly of the Theatre Royal, Birmingham, and from the principal American theatres,' would make his first appearance at the Haymarket, in a character which he had already played for upwards of eight hundred times. In theatrical circles the experiment was, oddly enough, considered to be most dangerous, and it was only because the Haymarket was sadly in need of an attraction that Sothern got a chance of appearing on its historic boards. Lord Dundreary, it was said, had become popular in New York because the American theatre-goers of those days revelled in a gross and insulting caricature of an English nobleman; in London the performance would, no doubt, be condemned as entirely wanting in humour, taste, and judgment. That Sothern himself was uncertain about it the following incident will prove. During the rehearsal of the play one of the oldest members of the Haymarket company came upon the stage while Sothern was running over his famous letter scene. He turned and said, 'My dear madam, don't come on here till you get your cue. In fact, on the night of the performance, you will have twenty minutes to wait during the scene.'

'Why,' said the lady satirically, 'do you expect so much applause?'

'Yes,' replied Sothern; 'I know how long this scene always plays.'

'Ah!' answered the actress, 'but suppose the audience should not take your view of the matter?'

'In that case,' said Sothern, 'you won't have to bother yourself, for I and the piece will have been condemned a good hour before your services will be required.'

All the actors and actresses of the Haymarket company, including Buckstone, who played Asa Trenchard (a part that never suited him), Chippendale, Rogers, Clark, Braid, Mrs. Charles Young, Miss M. Oliver, Miss H. Lindley, and Miss Henrade, predicted the certain failure of the piece and its principal performer; but Sothern attacked his work boldly, and although the piece did not make an immediate success, the humour and originality of his acting were universally acknowledged.

It was indeed some time before *Our American Cousin* (which is, in truth, but a poor play) drew remunerative audiences. In despair of its ever doing so, Buckstone had actually put up notices announcing that it would be immediately replaced by *She*

Stoops to Conquer, when Charles Mathews, who had seen and well knew how to appreciate Sothern's admirable acting, strongly advised him to keep it in the bill, declaring that Lord Dundreary had only to become known to be phenomenally popular. How right in his judgment Mathews was the sequel proved. The fame of his lordship spread far and near, the success of the performance became as great as it was then unprecedented, and for four hundred consecutive nights the Haymarket was crowded.

Lord Dundreary became the rage not only of London but of England. Dundreary was upon every lip. Men cultivated Dundreary whiskers and affected Dundreary coats; indeed, at that time, Sothern was such a good friend to the tailors that, if he would have accepted them, he might have been furnished, without any mention of payment, with clothes sufficient for a dozen lifetimes. His dressing-room at the Haymarket was crowded with parcels sent by energetic haberdashers, who knew that if by wearing it upon the stage, he would set the fashion for a certain make of necktie, or a particular pattern of shirt-cuff, or collar, their fortunes would be half made; and hatters and bootmakers followed in the haberdashers' wake. Dundreary photographs were seen everywhere; 'Dundrearyisms,' as they came to be called, were the fashionable *mots* of the day; and little books (generally very badly done) dealing with the imaginary doings of Dundreary under every possible condition, and in every quarter of the globe, were in their thousands sold at the street corners. Concerning Dundreary quite three parts of England went more than half mad, and not to know all about him and his deliciously quaint sayings and doings was to argue yourself unknown.

Take for example, his Lordship's remark when Asa Trenchard asked him if he had 'got any brains?' 'He wants to find out if I've got any brains, and then he'll scalp me; that's the idea!' Or again, when Dundreary, after copious potations of brandy-and-soda, is alone in his bedroom and says, 'Everything seems wobbling about. I know as well as possible there are only two candles there, and yet I can't help seeing four. I wonder, if I was to put those two fellows out, *what would become of the other two?*' And then, when Asa comes in and suggests they shall 'have the liqueurs up and make a night of it,' Dundreary replies, '*Make* a night of it. Why, it *is* night! It's just twelve o'clock.'

The letter from Sam (the immortal Sam who never had a

'uel'), which used to be the great success of the evening, and which, delivered as it was, used to make people absolutely sore with laughing, must be given, with the stage directions, in part:

(Before opening letter, reads 'N.B.' outside it): 'N.B.—If you don't get this letter, write and let me know.' That fella's an ass, whoever he is!

(Opens letter, taking care he holds it upside down.) I don't know any fella in America except Sam; of course I know Sam, because Sam's my brother. Every fella knows his own brother. Sam and I used to be boys when we were lads, both of us. We were always together. People used to say 'Birds of a feather'—what is it birds of a feather do?—oh 'Birds of a feather gather no moss!' That's ridiculous, that is. The idea of a lot of birds picking up moss! Oh no: it's the early bird that knows its own father. That's worse than the other. No bird can know its own father. If he told the truth, he'd say he was even in a fog about his own mother. *I've* got it—it's the wise child that gets the worms! Oh, that's worse than any of them! No parent would allow the child to get a lot of worms like that! Besides, the whole proverb's nonsense from beginning to end. Birds of a feather flock together: yes, that's it! As if a whole flock of birds would have only one feather! They'd all catch cold. Besides, there's only one of those birds could have that feather, and that fella would fly all on one side! That's one of those things no fella can find out. Besides, fancy any bird being such a d——d fool as to go into a corner and flock all by himself! Ah, that's one of those things no fella can find out. (*Looks at letter*) Whoever it's from he's written it upside-down. Oh no, I've got it upside down! I knew some fella was upside down. (*Laughs*). Yes, this is from Sam; I always know Sam's handwriting when I see his name on the other side. 'America.' Well, I'm glad he's sent me his address! 'My dear brother'. Sam always calls me brother, because neither of us have got any sisters.

'I am afraid that my last letter miscarried, as I was in such a hurry for the post that I forgot to put any direction on the envelope.' Then I suppose that's the reason I never got it; but who could have got it? The only fella that could have got that letter is some fella without a name. And how on earth, could he get it? The postman couldn't go about asking every fella he met if he'd got no name!

Sam's an ass! 'I find out now' (I wonder what he's found out now?) 'that I was changed at my birth.' Now, what d——d nonsense that is! Why didn't he find it out before? 'My old nurse turns out to be my mother.' What rubbish! Then, if that's true, all I can say is, Sam's not my brother, and if he's not my brother, who the devil am I? . . .

Oh, here's a P.S. 'By the bye, what do you think of the following riddle? If fourteen dogs with three legs each catch forty-eight rabbits with seventy-six legs in twenty-five minutes, how many legs must twenty-four rabbits have to get away from ninety-three dogs with two legs in half-an-hour?'

Here's another P.S. 'You will be glad to know that I have purchased a large estate somewhere or other on the banks of the Mississippi. Send me the purchase money. The enclosed pill-box contains a sample of the soil.'

Though in all the public announcements of *Our American Cousin* the play was stated to be the sole work of Tom Taylor, in a manuscript copy of it which is now before me, it is clearly set down that 'the character of Lord Dundreary was written and created by Mr Sothern' . . . Through infinite painstaking, he became the established theatrical hero of the day. Every saying and every action of the apparently semi-idiotic creature was the result of careful observation and study; even the preposterous counting of the fingers was a transcript from what had been seen. 'You remember,' said Sothern, 'that in one act I have a by-play on my fingers in which I count from one to ten, and then, reversing, begin with the right thumb and count ten, nine, eight, seven, six, and five are eleven. This has frequently been denounced by critics as utterly out of place in the character, but I took the incident from actual life, having seen a notoriously clever man on the English turf, as quick as lightning in calculating odds, completely puzzled by this ridiculous problem.'

How *Our American Cousin* was revived, and re-revived on the Haymarket boards, and how, even when he was attracting large audiences with other plays, Sothern found it expedient to appear in little after-pieces in which Dundreary figured, is a matter of stage history. One of these farces (it was the joint work of Sothern and H. J. Byron, and in it all Tom Taylor's characters were absurdly burlesqued) was entitled *Dundreary Married and Settled*; another *Dundreary a Father*. The one was as ephemeral as the other, and, amusing as both were, neither added much to the fame of Sothern or the popularity of Dundreary.

In due course Dundreary tried his fortune in Paris, but there he did not make a success. French audiences failed to see the humour of the creation, and his lordship was slightingly alluded to by critics as '*un sort de snob*'! It is interesting to note that Henry Irving, Edward Saker, and John T. Raymond were members of the company. Irving played the drunken lawyer's clerk.

In England—both in London and in the country—the popularity of Lord Dundreary seemed to be inexhaustible, and, in spite of the great successes that Sothern made in other pieces, *Our American Cousin* was constantly reproduced at the Haymarket, and in America, I believe, never lost its charm.

With Sothern this quaintly conceived and marvellously elaborated conception died. It is true that his clever and handsome son—poor Lytton Sothern—whose early death still leaves an unhealed sore in the memories of those who knew and cared for him, played the part with some degree of success; but though the imitation was almost exact, an indescribable something was wanting, and one could not but feel that a claimant had arisen for a title that was extinct.

T. EDGAR PEMBERTON

XXXIV

Criticism

JOHN WILLIAM COLE, in *The Life and Theatrical Times of Charles Kean, F.S.A.* (1859), had a few words on criticism, a matter about which both he and the subject of his book felt keenly. In these days he might have added to his vogue-words the luckless hack, 'convincing'.

STRANGE eccentricities are sometimes indulged in by professional chroniclers who undertake to instruct the world on the passing events of the day. Criticisms have been written beforehand, in anticipation of the performance of a play only announced, but suddenly changed because of the illness of a principal performer; the writer, not intending to be present, but having made up his mind as to who he should praise and who condemn. On the following morning the public have been enlightened with an elaborate disquisition on what never took place.

On the 5th October, 1805, a revival of Farquhar's comedy of *The Constant Couple* was announced for that evening at Drury Lane, but postponed on account of the illness of Elliston. A Sunday paper, however, contained the following account:

> Last night Farquhar's sprightly comedy of *The Constant Couple* was most laboriously and successfully murdered at this theatre. Elliston tamed down the gaiety of Sir Harry Wildair with a felicity which they

who admire such doings can never sufficiently extol. The gay knight was, by the care of his misrepresentative, reduced to a figure of as little fantastic vivacity as could be shown by Tom Errand in Beau Clincher's clothes. Beau Clincher himself was quite lost in Jack Bannister; it was Bannister, not the Clincher of Farquhar, that the performance suggested to the audience. Miss Mellon was not an unpleasing representative of Angelica; but criticism has not language severe enough to mark, as it deserves, the impertinence of Barrymore's presuming to put himself forward in the part of Colonel Standard. We were less offended, though it was impossible to be much pleased, with Dowton's attempt to enact Alderman Struggler. But the acting was altogether very sorry.

The maligned actors brought an action against the authorities of the paper, who compromised, and got off cheaply, by paying £50 to the theatrical fund.

During the summer of 1857, a morning paper published a studied criticism on the first performance of Madame Bosio and Mario at the Italian Opera House, Lyceum, in *La Traviata*, telling how the theatre was crowded from floor to ceiling, how the great singers were applauded, how they were called for at the end of each act, and how they were crowned with acclamations and bouquets at the close. There were also many flourishes on *andante* movements, ascending scales, *fioriture,* and other musical obscurities, known only to the chosen few who are learned in the Eleusinian mysteries of the opera. The music was a fiction, for the piece had been unexpectedly withdrawn, and another substituted. On the next day an editorial apology announced the summary discharge of the inventive reporter.

In the *Theatrical Inquisitor* for October 1812 (a periodical in continuation of the *Monthly Mirror*), we find the following extract, headed 'Newspaper Criticism', taken from the pages of the identical journal's predecessor:

> Oct. 3rd,—We were supremely gratified on Tuesday evening, a Covent Garden Theatre, during the representation of the opera of the *Cabinet*, to hear that Mr Sinclair had attended to our critical advice, and that his adoption of it was eminently serviceable to his professional character. In executing the *polacca*, he very prudently abstained from any wild flourishes, but kept strictly to the law of melody, by which he gained upon the public ear so strongly, and so deservedly, that he was encored three times, by the unanimous desire of the whole audience; and we trust, after so decided a victory upon the part of true melody over

the vagaries of science, that he will never more be fantastical. Unadulterated nature is modest and simple, and, like the pure beauty, is ever most efficient in attraction when she is unbedizened by the frippery of art. A meretricious female resorts to finery in the hope of acquiring a substitute for the lost loveliness of virtue; but the most cunning labour of her toilette is not propitious to the mind of her desire.

On this foggy jargon the *Inquisitor* comments thus:

'To this exquisitely laboured piece of criticism, there is but one solitary objection—the opera of the *Cabinet* was indeed underlined at the bottom of the Monday play-bills for the following night; but in those of Tuesday it was changed to the *English Fleet* which was accordingly represented on the Tuesday evening—the very evening on which the reporter of the veracious journal to which we allude heard Mr Sinclair thrice encored in the *polacca*. This is exercising the power of second sight with a vengeance.'

When Bouffé was last in London, in 1851, it so happened that the writer of these pages had never seen him. Watching the announcement of one of his most popular characters, he repaired to the St James's theatre, full of expectation. But the great luminary was suffering a temporary eclipse, and unable to shine. Instead of flourishing on the boards, he lay writhing in bed, under the gentle discipline of two physicians. There was a total change of performance, but, of course, no Bouffé. The next day a paper of extensive circulation stated that he had appeared on the previous evening with unwonted brilliancy, and had sent the audience home in a state of rapturous delight. Particular points were noticed with particular praise. The reader was sorely puzzled, and began to doubt if he had been there; long habit having induced him to place implicit reliance on anything he saw in such responsible columns. 'Can such things be?' thought he, 'and am I only a myth, a fabulous existence, a embodied chimera, a sort of physical dream?'

When newspapers are thus committed, through the carelessness of their subordinates, if the mistake inclines to the side of panegyric, it may be passed over with a smile, though injurious to the credit of the journal in question, and tending to lower the character of criticism in general; but when an opposite course is adopted, when certain individuals are selected for specific censure, and slashed right and left with a mortal tomahawk, he matter becomes too serious for pleasantry and gives rise to painful reflections.

As a general rule, criticism which inclines to extreme censure rather than to praise, attracts by far the greater share of attention. There is more nerve and more excitement in vituperation than in eulogy. Few like to confess the fact; but there is a latent pleasure in seeing a hole picked in your neighbour's coat, especially if you have any suspicion that the said neighbour sets up for a better or wiser man than yourself. No one brooks assumed superiority with complaisance, and it is meat and drink to find our betters assailed with ourselves. A tale of scandal is propagated much more quickly than a deed of benevolence. Unpleasant tidings travel fast, and an ill-natured article in a newspaper or magazine is sure to be communicated by some anxious friend.

Among other peculiar features of dramatic criticism may be remarked a vice of recent growth—the affectation of interlarding foreign words and idioms to such an extent that the whole composition becomes an ill-assorted hybrid, neither French nor English, but an unnatural jumble of both, in the midst of which the honest vernacular loses all sense of identity, and wonders at its own transformation, and how it has got mixed up in such a fantastical masquerade. Acting a part is now called *interpreting a rôle*; songs are not sung, but *rendered*; a play is no longer simply got up, but *mounted*; the dresses and decorations are mystified into the *mise en scène*, and the whole affair is called the *ensemble*. But these are transparent obscurities compared with the *idiosyncratics, aesthetics, syncretics, synthetics, architectonics, esoterics, idealisms, transcendentalisms*, and a legion of other incomprehensible *modernisms*, which, as Junius says of Sir William Draper's figures of speech, 'dance through' some of these articles 'in all the mazes of metaphorical confusion.'

There seems to have been always a conventional style exclusively appropriated to criticism. Sterne, more than eighty years ago, gives an amusing imitation of the mode in his day, winding up this: 'Grant me patience! Of all the cants which are canted in this canting world, though the cant of hypocrisy may be the worst, the cant of criticism is the most tormenting.'

JOHN WILLIAM COLE

XXXV

Period Piece

THE following *pièce d'occasion* (published in *The Players*, but after Mr Wisgast's day) was written for a special performance at Covent Garden in May 1861, in aid of the Royal Dramatic College, a scheme that dwindled away into the mists. The programme, in which the second act of *Hamlet* (with Fechter) appeared to be a mere incident, ended after half-past one in the morning. In the middle of it, Mrs Stirling, as Anne Bracegirdle's ghost, and Fanny Stirling, her daughter, as Miss Thalia, spoke the past-and-present duologue provided for them by Tom Taylor.

ANNE BRACEGIRDLE'S Ghost rises through a trap. She wears the costume of 1693.

> Well! here I am at last! A poor old ghost
> In this new o'ergrown London feels quite lost!
> Ghosts or no ghosts, change is the thing for ladies,
> And I was fairly sick to death of Hades.
> I watched old Cerberus into his lair—
> Coaxed Charon—Rogue! He can't resist a *fair*;
> Slipped, unobserved, past the out-picket Fury,
> And here I am once more, in dear old Drury!
> How sweet is the familiar must and damps!
> The orange-peel—and (*sniffing*) but I miss the lamps!
>   *Looking round hesitatingly.*

And yet I don't know. Have I made a blunder?
Can my Old Drury be so changed, I wonder?
The stage I trod in sixteen ninety-three,
With Barry, Mountford, Betterton, and Leigh,
Was, sure, not half so wide—these wings seem taller;
The House, I vow, was a good two-thirds smaller.
Alas! If thus the upper world run round,
Methinks we ghosts were better underground,
Reviving plays, we used to say was mad,
Reviving actresses is just as bad—
(*Going, pauses*) And yet 'tis hard to quit the battlefield
Where truncheon-like my fan I used to wield,
To guide the alternate charge of smiles and sighs,
And aim the fire of two resistless eyes!
Vain joys! vain battles—what if won or lost,
To me, a bygone public favourite's ghost!

Becoming conscious of the audience.

What's that? Have I not drank of Lethe's stream?
Those sounds! Those smiles!—Is't real or a dream?
That merry buzz! As sure as my name's Nancy,
'Tis my old British public, and no fancy!
The sight, the sound, revives my ancient vein—
Bracegirdle's ghost Bracegirdle's self again!
Is't tragedy or comedy you want,
Melting Almeria, flashing Millamant?
With Rowe's blank verse, say, shall I drown the pit,
Or bring the boxes down with Congreve's wit?
High comedy or low—great folks or small—
Parts and spectators too—have at ye all!

Enter MISS THALIA, 1861

Miss T. (*astonished at the Ghost's energy*) I say, old lady!
Mrs B.   Old, well?
Miss T.   What's this spouting?
(*Aside*) who can have given the old guy an outing?
Tip us your fist!
Mrs B.   My fist! Her language pardon.
Shades of Old Drury!
Miss T.   This is Covent Garden!

Mrs B. This Covent Garden! How my fingers itch
  To cuff the manager.
Miss T.   Who? Guy?
Mrs B.   No, Rich—
  I hated the curmudgeon's stingy ways.
Miss T. He's gone—we've no Rich manager nowadays.
  And now make yourself scarce, my dear old soul—
  I want the stage just to go through my rôle.
Mrs B. Your rôle?
Miss T.   My part!
Mrs B.   Why not say 'part' instead?
                      (*Contemptuously.*)
  Methought the stage could hardly be your bread.
Miss T. (*saucily*) My bread—I hope 'twill be my bread and butter.
Mrs B. Thou forward chit! Is that the tone to utter
  The point and pathos of stage wit and poet?
Miss T. Pathos and point indeed—not if I know it.
  I am Miss Thalia—eighteen sixty-one—
  For point and pathos give me slang and pun.
Mrs B. Don't you act Shakespeare then?
Miss T.   Oh, the old swell's
  Still to be seen, I've heard, at Sadler's Wells.
  In Oxford Street, too, they say Hamlet draws—
  But that dear Frenchman, Fechter, is the cause.
Mrs B. A Frenchman acting Hamlet! 'Woe is me
  To have seen what I *have* seen—see what I see!'
Miss T. But who are you?
Mrs B.   I'm Anne Bracegirdle's ghost.
Miss T. I never heard of her.
Mrs B.   I was the toast
  Of London when '*twas* London—in the day
  When men were witty—manners light and gay.
Miss T. Oh! I daresay—'toast' were you?
Mrs B.   Of the town.
Miss T. And as a toast, were you done very brown?
Mrs B. (*disgusted*). Oh! vile!
Miss T.   You don't like puns? 'Tis these burlesques;
  Words are so tortured on our authors' desks
  With double meanings our por tongue they gall,

Till soon no meaning 'twill convey at all.
Mrs B. I'll back to Hades. Oh, degenerate age,
  The drama's dead!
Miss T. (*stopping her*) Then ghosts should keep the stage.
Mrs B. Unhand me!
Miss T.   To resist if you presume,
  I'll send for that strong medium, Mr Hume,
  He'll shut you up in a table or a chair,
  Sofa or chest of drawers—or Lord knows where.
Mrs B. Shut me up? Why?
Miss T.   To make a show and flout of you
  As long as e'er he can get one rap out of you.
Mrs B. Why should I stay? My day's gone by, I see;
  Where chits like you act, there's no room for me.
Miss T. Is Miss Thalia fallen so far below
  Her grandma of a hundred years ago?
Mrs B. In all—in art and heart—
Miss T.   No, grandma, stop—
  'Tis a bad workman speaks ill of the shop.
  Worse artists we *may* be than in the days
  When you with Betterton divided praise,
  But not less kind, less helpful to each other,
  Less mindful of poor sister, stricken brother.
  Witness the cause that brings me here to-night,
  And makes the Garden, as we see it, bright!
Mrs B. Why, 'tis a play, sure—
Miss T.   Play, and earnest too;
  They mix as in the world they always do.
  We play to aid the New Dramatic College—
Mrs B. Like that Ned Alleyn founded once at Dulwich?
  Be warned by that—let the bees taste the honey—
  See Actors get what's raised with Actors' money.
           Loud applause.
Miss T. You'll help?
Mrs B.   To rear the roof, where from the stage
  The outworn player may betake his age;
  To teach, where hard-wrought parents cannot spare
  The means to give their young a teacher's care;
  And where our aid comes all too late to save,
  Give our poor comrades that last boon, a grave.

Will I *not* help? . . .
I hate your slang and puns, your off-hand mien,
Your hat, your boots, *all* but your crinoline—
That's something like the hoop that stately rose
When women dressed, whereas they now wear clothes;
I scorn your stage, detest your style of art,
But you're the old Thalia still at heart,
Feeling true griefs through all your mimic task,
And capable of tears beneath your mask.
If Pharisaic zealots turn aside
From the poor player—shunn'd, abused, decried—
Let kindlier Christians, to their faith more true,
In this good cause their efforts join with you.
Here on the boards your helpful part is played,
And there (*to audience*) kind British hearts your labours aid.

('Sleep, Gentle Lady,' sung by the Vocal Association of Two Hundred Voices.)

TOM TAYLOR

Editor's note: The Dramatic College scheme provided for the erection, on a site at Woking in Surrey, of a number of small cottages for stage pensioners, with a central hall for committee meetings and annual banquets. Though the plan succeeded for a few years, funds dwindled, pensioners died and their cottages were left empty, and at length land and buildings had to be sold for a very small sum.

XXXVI

Sweethearting

JULIAN CHARLES YOUNG, Rector of Ilmington in Warwickshire, was on the Committee that organized the Shakespeare Tercentenary Festival at Stratford-upon-Avon in April and May 1864. He recorded in his journal (published in 1871 as a pendant to a memoir of his father) the reactions of his servants to a performance of *Othello* (William Creswick as Othello, James Bennett as Iago) in the timber Grand Pavilion behind the houses of Old Town. Its site is marked now by tall poplars.

LAST week I had my house full to repletion, it being the week of the Shakespeare Tercentenary at Stratford-upon-Avon. When my visitors had left me, as some return to my servants for their zeal and attention, I sent them in one night, and treated them to the theatre—a place they had none of them ever been in before. The play was *Othello*.

The next day I asked my butler, one of the most respectable and trustworthy of men, but staid and demure withal, how he had liked what he had seen, and all I could elicit from him, and this in the most cautious and deliberate manner, was the following tribute to the merits of the actors. 'Well—Sir—thank you, Sir, for the treat. The performers—performed—the performance—which thay had to perform—excellent well—especially the female performers—in the performance.'

I then went to the stables and asked my coachman, an honest, simple creature, but not over-burdened with imagination, how he had been impressed with what he had seen. Grinning from ear to ear with pleasurable reminiscences, he replied, with infinitely more alacrity than his predecessor—'Twas really beautiful, Sir. I like it onaccountable!'

The cheerful face clouded over as I asked him what it was about.

'I don't ezactly know, Sir.'

'Do you mean to say that you saw the play of *Othello*, and can't tell me what it was about?'

'Well, Sir, if you'll believe me, I don't rightly know the meaning on't; but it was very pretty—that it were.' (Then, after a moment's reflection, as if he had recalled the thread of the tragic tale)—'Oh! I know, Sir, now; I know. It ran upon *sweethearting*. Aye that it did—and there were two gennelmen, one was in white, and the other was in black; and, what was more, both of these gents was sweet on the same gal!'

This reminds me that, when I was living in Lyneham, in Wiltshire, I sent a favourite old gardener of mine and his wife to the theatre at Bristol, whose answers to my questions were much of the same character as those I have just mentioned.

'Well, Robert, what did you see last night?'

(No answer, but a look of bewilderment and annoyance at the question.) 'Well, Sir' (after a pause), 'I see what you sent me to see.'

'And what was that?'

'Why the play, in course.'

'Was it a tragedy or a comedy?'

'I don't know what you mane. I can't say no more than I have said, nor no fairer! All I know is, there was a precious lot on 'em on the theayter stage; and there they was, *in and out, and out and in again*!'

Somewhat discomfited by such a meagre account, I turned to his wife, and asked her if she had seen more than one piece.

'Ah dear! yes, Sir; we had the pantrynine [pantomime]; and what I liked best in it was, where this fool fellar stooped down and grinned at we through his legs.'

JULIAN CHARLES YOUNG

XXXVII

A French Juliet

IN 1891, Henry Morley (1822–1894), who was Professor of Literature at University College, London, collected his drama criticism under the title, *The Journal of a London Playgoer, 1851–1866*. This included a review of Stella Colas, the French actress who played Juliet in English at the Princess's Theatre. Instructed by John Ryder (who had also trained Adelaide Neilson), Colas sharply divided the critics, some of whom—like Clement Scott—immensely admired the Potion Scene, while others, such as Morley and G. H. Lewes, loathed it. Walter Montgomery was the 1863 Romeo. John Nelson, who succeeded to the part in 1864, and at Stratford-upon-Avon where Colas acted for a night in the Pavilion erected for the Tercentenary Festival, 'looked well, albeit a little too stout'.

That was the opinion of Robert E. Hunter in his record of the Tercentenary celebration, *Shakespeare and Stratford-upon-Avon* (1864). Of Colas he said simply: 'As I have so strong an aversion from hearing the sublime and beautiful language of Shakespeare read with a foreign and broken accent, I cannot say anything of the performance myself.'

I BELIEVE that on the whole a theatre audience shows better taste than an opera audience; probably because it has a more real understanding of what it has come out to enjoy. Real as far as it goes. But what are we to say to palliate the success of Mdlle. Stella Colas in *Romeo and Juliet* at the Princess's [1864]? Let me be fair both to the lady and the public. The lady has returned to us not quite so bad as she was; and the public applauds her not quite so much as it did. I saw her again on the first night of her reappearance, and compelled myself to sit out—as on her original first night I could not—all the five acts of Shakespeare murder. There was nothing like the frantic enthusiasm of the first reception. If the management had not dealt liberally in the morning with Covent Garden, and supplied the lady in the evening with the consequent apple-basket full of bouquets, her reception might have seemed to her a cool one. Yet her English was more intelligible, and she had got rid of some of the worst absurdities of action; the upward gesture of snipping with scissors, for example, that accompanied Juliet's suggestion concerning Romeo, that Night, when he died, might 'take him and cut him out in little stars', a line that, to a dressy, second-rate French ingénue, inevitably suggested millinery, and Night as the editor of *La Belle Assemblée*. But although not so bad as it was, this Juliet is still abominable; for not only it is not what it ought to be, but it is precisely all that it ought not to be.

Juliet is an innocent Italian child, enjoying with an exquisitely simple honesty the first passion of love. Artless, guileless, pouring out all the beauty of a most pure girlhood in the newly-awakened poetry of an ungrudging, unsuspecting love, hers is the very last character to be represented to us by the stage-artifices and ghastly grimness of a French ingénue in her stage-innocence, the most self-conscious of all forms into which the front of womanhood has ever been recast. Mdlle. Colas cannot even seem to forget herself. When Juliet, after her first entry, has only to stand at her mother's chair, hearing much, answering little, Mdlle. Colas perks her head, grins, twists, ambles from one side of the chair to the other, and looks obtrusively conscious of every part of herself from the tip of her nose to the tips of her toes. In the balcony scene her coquetry with Romeo is abominable; and the way in which, for example, she speaks of their swift contract as

> '*Too like the lightning, which doth cease to be
> Ere one can say—it lightens,*'

jumping up to deliver the last two words dramatically with big eyes and a pretty surprised stare, is enough to make one gnash one's teeth till they break. Her great point with the audience is in the soliloquy before the taking of the sleeping potion. It is done with a great deal of misdirected force, ending in a shriek and recoil of horror at 'Stay, Tybalt, stay!' I am quite sure that no Juliet whom Shakespeare in his time had the advising of ever recoiled with such a shriek from the imagined ghost that sought the Romeo who, being thus suggested, was in the next instant yet more intensely present to her disordered vision. Mdlle. Colas spends so much force upon the shrieking at and cowering by the bedside from Tybalt's ghost, that she can only add as an insignificant tag to that claptrap stage-effect the line in which a greater actress would have found the true climax, 'Romeo, I come! this do I drink to thee.' Juliet drinks the potion with her mind full not of Tybalt, but of Romeo. Ghosts do not themselves stab, poison, or strangle, and overpowering sense of peril to Romeo certainly is not the thought indicated in these lines:

> 'O look! methinks I see my cousin's ghost
> Seeking out Romeo, that did spit his body
> Upon a rapier's point. Stay, Tybalt, stay!
> Romeo, I come! this do I drink to thee.'

Every word of that last line, which Mdlle. Colas shuffles through as an anti-climax after her great shrieking effect, is emphatic; so emphatic, that it is the dramatic balance to the whole preceding part of the soliloquy. At sight of the potion that was to lay herself in imaged death, there coursed with a thrill through her girl's blood the gruesome images that it suggested, till to her disordered mind the image of Tybalt seeking Romeo turned her thought to the search for Romeo, on which she also was, by that dread way, bent. Instead of screaming the 'Stay, Tybalt, stay', Juliet more probably whispers it with abhorrent voice and hands, yet less indicative of supernatural dread than of returning thought of Romeo, whom not Tybalt, but Juliet, must be the first to find. Her eye meanwhile wanders distraught in search, until she sees the marriage-bed and Romeo there present alone to her mind's eye. Her cry of 'Romeo' then pours out her heart's love towards him. Each word in the 'I come' is emphatic—it is I, not Tybalt; but the sense of this should be most lightly indicated, for always in this play the thought of Tybalt hardly lives at all when Juliet's mind fills with the thought of Romeo. Towards the imaged Romeo, towards the marriage-bed, she hurries, fluttering with love. Every one also of the next words, 'This do I drink to thee', has its poetic force. The 'this'—the phial in her hand, which, apart from Romeo, had suggested all those ghastly dreads in the lines beginning 'What if this mixture'—now that the image of Romeo is present to her, brings joy, not dread, 'This do I drink to thee.' She drinks as from a festive bridal-cup, and as she is bending in endearment over the bridal-bed the form of death changes her face and fixes it. So she then falls, and lies upon the bed in her long swoon.

A really good actress might, no doubt, find other and better methods of interpreting the lines; my only purpose is to show that in every good interpretation the last line must inevitably be the great one, for it is, as it were, the clenching of all that had gone before. When Mdlle. Colas makes a great scream at the ghost of Tybalt, and flies and crouches as if she would take refuge under the bed, then huddles anyhow over the last line, takes the poison, and gets into bed as best she can, she may bring great applause from an audience at the Princess's, but she is not acting Shakespeare. Neither do I think anything in the rest of the play really well done, except the Nurse of Mrs Marston. Mr Nelson is but a heavy Romeo. The part of Friar Lawrence is, with conventional stage-gestures, actually ranted! The gentleman who plays Capulet deliberately speaks the part as if it were a heavy-father in broad farce. Mr Vining is out of his element, and gives but a low-comedy suggestion of that light-hearted gentleman, the airy, graceful, quick-witted, and quick-blooded Mercutio, of whom in our time Mr Charles Kemble has been the only sufficient representative. There is nobody now on the stage able to play the part.

HENRY MORLEY

XXXVIII

An Italian Lear

Joseph Knight (1829–1907), a familiar, scholarly, long-bearded figure in the first-night stalls, was dramatic critic of *The Athenaeum* from 1867. In this review, reprinted from *Theatrical Notes* (1893), he discussed the Lear of the Italian tragedian, Ernesto Fortunato Giovanni Rossi (1827–1896), whose Shakespearean work was less approved in England and America than elsewhere. Rossi acted Lear at Drury Lane in May 1876.

Signor Rossi's successive performances reveal two facts; the first, that he is one of the most accomplished actors that have of late years appeared before the public; the second, that it is useless to expect from him any fresh light upon the creation of Shakespeare. So far, indeed, foreign art has done as little as foreign criticism to furnish the student with new views concerning the masterpieces of Shakespearean tragedy. Signor Salvini's *Othello* proved that southern theories concerning acting might, in the case of a character essentially southern, bring to light aspects which had previously been unobserved or unexpressed. Here ends the gain our stage has seen. The Hamlet of Signor Salvini and the Hamlet and the Lear of Signor Rossi, so far from possessing any gift of illumination, scarcely reveal the germ of what can be called an idea of the characters. Such intellectual subtleties as have exercised the wits of English critics have not even presented themselves, and the artist who has come over to enact these parts is surprised to hear of their existence. Taking up the theory that Lear is a study of madness commencing to declare itself when the King yields his dominion to his children, attaining its height at the moment when he stands upon the heath, amid the elemental confusion, and passing away with passing life, Signor Rossi has presented this view again and again before admiring audiences in Italy and France. Quite dumbfounded is he to learn that something more is expected in England. We who have accustomed ourselves to find in every word of Lear some touching revelation of character and suffering, are not prepared to accept a representation in which breadth of view alone is aimed at, and all subtle gradations of shade are swallowed up in masses of colour. Like Signor Salvini, Signor Rossi has not only never seen those patient analyses of character which English criticism has framed; he has never, it is obvious, studied in Shakespeare the personages he presents. A slovenly, feeble, inaccurate and misleading version of a portion of a play has supplied him with the outline of an individuality which he presents, but which is as unlike the creation of Shakespeare as the Aeneas of Cotton or of Scarron is to that of Virgil.

Thus, though the powers of the actor are remarkable, and are such as especially commend themselves to the more highly-trained portion of his audience, the result to the student, at least, is blank disappointment. In place of the hearty, impetuous, rash, and choleric King, impatient of contradiction, pitiless in his revenge upon slight wrong, and yet burning with a desire to be loved by all around him, we find at the outset a capricious and half-irresponsible being, whose uncertain walk and impatient movements tell of fading intellect. This misapprehension continues, and is accentuated until, at the end, when we wait to see the bowed and whitened head sink to the ground in desolation and heartbreak, we find in its place a study of the physical agonies of dissolution. There is scarcely a glimpse of that dignity which is a principal characteristic of Lear, and which makes him even in the very whirlwind of his madness recollect his state, and enjoy the consternation of those who dare not face his frown

Ay, every inch a King!
When I do stare, see how the subject quakes.

It has, with some show of reason, been doubted whether Lear is a fit subject for histrionic illustration. Shakespeare, however, who intended the character for the stage, was a tolerable judge in such matters, and the avowal that no actor can greatly impress us in Lear involves only a condemnation of the state of our stage. There is much of Lear that is easier to present than corresponding portions of Othello, Hamlet, or Macbeth, though it may be admitted that the talent which would give adequate exposition to the entire character is not easy to find.

A single instance of the kind of errors which constantly occur in the Italian version will serve to show how difficult it is to deduce from it a rational conception of Lear. Small as appears the change, which consists only in the omission of a preposition, its effect is completely misleading. From the moment Lear sees Edgar on the heath, disguised as Tom, he conceives a remarkable regard for him. Vainly Gloucester seeks to lure the King to shelter. He says:—

> First let me talk with this philosopher.—
> What is the cause of thunder?

And again:—

> I'll talk a word with this same learned Theban.

When, accordingly, Gloucester bids Edgar go into the hovel:—

> In, fellow, there, into the hovel! keep thee warm!

Lear follows him, saying:—

> Come, let's in all.

These last words are translated into Italian, 'Zitti andiamo tutti!'—'Let us all go'. Acting on this, Signor Rossi, instead of attempting feebly to follow Edgar, turns in the very direction in which Gloucester strives vainly to entice him. Quite useless is it to multiply instances of faults of omission and commission. From the Shakespearean standpoint, Signor Rossi's *Lear* is an admirable piece of acting, informed by no soul.

JOSEPH KNIGHT

XXXIX

Writing the Play

WILLIAM GORMAN WILLS (1828–1891) was an Irish dramatist, poet, and painter who wrote various useful romantic plays (*Charles I*, for example) for the Lyceum where Henry Irving glorified such a speech as the farewell to Queen Henrietta Maria (vaguely we think of another King's farewell to another Queen):

> Oh, my loved solace on my thorny road,
> Sweet clue in all my labyrinth of sorrow,
> What shall I leave to thee?
> To thee I do consign my memory!
> Oh, banish not my name from off thy lips
> Because it pains awhile in naming it.
> Harsh grief does pass in time into far music.
> Red-eyed Regret, that waiteth on thy steps,
> Will daily grow a gentle, dear companion,
> And hold sweet converse with thee of thy dead.
> I fear me I may sometimes fade from thee,
> That when thy heart expelleth grey-stoled grief
> I live no longer in thy memory:
> Oh, keep my place in it for ever green,
> All hung with the immortelles of thy love;
> That sweet abiding in thy inner thought
> I long for more than sculptured monument
> Or proudest record 'mong the tombs of Kings.

'All hung with the immortelles of thy love' is a rich Victorian line.

The Revd. Freeman Wills, part author of *The Only Way*, Martin Harvey's favourite melodrama, described his brother's working methods in *W. G. Wills: Dramatist and Painter* (1898).

His method of working when left to himself was as unmethodical as could be. Like Pope, he wrote on backs of envelopes or any scrap of paper handy. These, fastened together, would be flung into a wicker basket, and sorted out and arranged, like a puzzle, when a play was to be completed. Or he would write here and there in sketch-books, beginning at both ends, and then in the middle, and interspersing his notes among studies of limbs or leaves. As a result, he naturally suffered much from the disorder of his materials and mislaying of manuscript. A friend of his tells how he unearthed once, from an old box that served the purpose of a dustbin, three acts and part of a fourth of a play called *Merry and Wise*, since his death completed under another name. When shown to the author he was greatly delighted at the find, and exclaimed, 'My dear fellow, you have done me the greatest service in the world. This is one of the best plays I ever wrote, and I thought I had lost it years ago.'

He went to work at five in the morning, like Victor Hugo, and he smoked all day, like Tennyson. After twelve in the day he would seldom do any writing, but would adjourn to his studio and paint till dusk. He never began at the beginning. He liked to get the most difficult scenes done first. He rarely corrected his work, and would never, if left to himself, rewrite any portion of it, as Mr Herman, his collaborator in *Claudian*, insisted on his doing. His best work was done at the first intention, and with great rapidity; but his most slovenly work would also pass without revision. He had not that practical knowledge of the stage which Herman possessed in such a superlative degree, and his stage directions were few and far between. He imagined the action of his characters, and left it to the imagination of the actors. He disliked realism, and saw everything through the veil of poetry. He was impatient of being asked to make alterations, and he took no pains to see his work was properly interpreted. It was gall and wormwood to him to have to go over the same ground twice, and he washed his hands of his work as soon as he could. If he were much pressed to finish, when he did not feel the inclination, he laid a play aside, or else wrote it badly. His good work was done by inspiration, not by mechanical labour and pen-polishing, although he brooded over his subject and realised his characters in his own mind until they surrounded him as creatures of flesh and blood; then they began to speak and act. He had a contempt for the help obtained by much reading, and all the materials he set to work with were a pencil and paper.

I think it was a result of the discomfort in which he lived that, from the time he had to work on his plays many hours of the day, he took to writing almost entirely in bed. This custom naturally spoiled his athletic powers, and helped to age him prematurely. But if he lost one kind of activity he gained the activity of thought which results from freedom from bodily tension. Except when he was making a clean copy of a play, I can hardly picture him to myself writing at a desk or table, and when he did it suggested an idea of discomfort, and was so unlike his habit that one felt distressed for him.

One consequence was that he soon found the convenience of having an amanuensis, to whom he dictated as fast as the pen in longhand could conveniently follow his thoughts. A man named Russell first acted in this capacity; but afterwards a young dramatic aspirant became his secretary, and as my brother had learned from Westland Marston, so the youth learned from my brother the dramatic art and imbibed some of the characteristic feeling of his mind. The younger playwright was always ready to volunteer an opinion, and dispute the ground which he took up inch by inch. If my brother was made very savage by objections and criticisms, he has told me that it roused him to strong writing. A shade of mortification on his scribe's face when he was doing exceedingly well would make him secretly triumph, and dictate with increasing vigour and success. If the face of his amanuensis, on the contrary, cleared, he became depressed, and felt he was doing but indifferently well. This is too characteristic to omit; but I ought in fairness to say that this dramatic apprentice was my brother's very sincere friend.

One of my brother's idiosyncrasies as a dramatist was the help which he received from music. It seemed to lend wings to his thought. He had a large musical-box which played a number of operatic airs, and he used to wind it up and write to its strains. In course of time, however, from being made the receptacle of hair-brushes and combs, and other odds and ends, it became disabled, and when it fell into my possession, all its teeth were gone, but it now grinds out, as of old, *Trovatore* and *Lucia*.

If the habit of writing in bed was the result, as I think, of the outside discomfort of the studio, it was, on the other hand, curious how he could abstract himself from a crowd, and actually found a flood of human beings about him helpful to composition. He would take a note-book to South Kensington Museum, or sit on the pier at Brighton, completely undisturbed by promenaders, or the public entertainers of the motley scene on the front, bodily present, but mentally caught up into a world of imagination. When alone he grew restless, and could not settle down to his work. He wanted company, but such as would not disturb the surface of reflection, or break up its pictures into wavering fragments by trivial interruptions. He liked to be let alone—not left alone.

There was one other very congenial medium, not for writing, but for thinking out his plays, and that was a warm bath. He found this close to the studio in Fulham Road, and he was a constant patron of it; indeed, it was there that he purchased his large musical-box, having experienced the pleasing effect of its accompaniment to his thoughts while luxuriously enjoying the plash of the water. From the fact that, in his absence of mind, he habitually smeared his face and bald head over with paint and charcoal, legends arose which might discredit this, but his habits were quite those of the present generation with regard to the tub.

FREEMAN WILLS

XL

Down Along

CORNWALL, in the theatre, has always been comically the home of melodrama—what Hardy, in another context, called 'the dire duresse that vexed the land of Lyonesse'. After a fairly modern specimen—though not, I think, that about murder in a tin mine—I found myself writing my own play from which I take a few stage directions:

'In silence the Crone places on the table numerous mackerel, a saffron cake, and a keg or two of marinated pilchards. An Idiot Boy enters, laughs feverishly, performs the Furry Dance on a tin whistle, and goes out again. There is a sustained shriek of seagulls. Some coarse-looking wreckers rush by the door. Thunder and lightning. Somewhere off-stage, Trelawny dies.'

'A Madwoman, carrying a chopper, glances in, hums for a moment in a manner wistful and sinister, and leaves again.'

'Sustained hooting. Enter a sea-mist.'

Edward Dutton Cook (1829–1883), who here reviews a redoubtable melodrama ('Soon it is made evident that Anne Trevanion had been buried alive'), wrote for the *Pall Mall Gazette* (1867–1875) and *The World* (1875–1883). The extract is from *Nights at the Play*, published in the year of his death, and the subject is J. B. Buckstone's *The Dream at Sea*, staged first at the Adelphi in 1833, and revived early in 1875 at the same theatre. The end of Black Ralph may remind us of the death of Bois-Guilbert in *Ivanhoe*: 'unscathed by the lance of the enemy, he had died a victim to the violence of his own contending passions.'

GEOFFROY, the French critic, has defined melodrama to be 'an opera in prose, which is not sung, but merely spoken, and in which music discharges the duty of a valet-de-chambre, her office being simply to announce the actors to the audience.' The production of melodrama in England seems to have been due, however, rather to accident than to design, and without any very clear conception of the nature and constitution of the matter in question. It is true that Holcroft's *Tale of Mystery*, an adaptation from the French supplied with music by Dr Busby, and produced at Covent Garden in 1802, has been usually accounted the first work of the class ever performed in this country; but plays with musical accompaniments had long before been familiar to our minor theatres as a means of evading the restrictions imposed upon them to the advantage of the patent houses. The regular spoken drama could be exhibited only at Drury Lane, Covent Garden, and the Haymarket during the summer months; but it was somehow established that 'burlettas' could be presented upon any stage licensed by the magistrates for entertainment of music and dancing. No care was taken, however, to define in what a burletta really consisted; it was soon manifest that its etymological connection with the word burlesque was not by any means to be insisted upon; and presently under the pretext of performing burlettas every kind of theatrical entertainment was produced— from *Macbeth* down to *Tom and Jerry*. And especially was the term employed to cover productions which could only properly be described as melodramas.

At the Adelphi Theatre, indeed, which, from the first opening of its doors in 1802 down to the present time, has always been famed for its performances of this character, the managers, sometimes in their endeavour to combine accuracy of description with regard for legality, resorted to rather complicated announcements. Thus Mr Fitzball's *Pilot*—an adaptation to the stage of Fenimore Cooper's novel—was described in the playbills of the time as 'a nautical melodramatic burletta.' But usually, until the abolition of the privileges enjoyed by the patent theatres rendered further employment of the term altogether needless, 'burletta' was the general title applied to every play performed at a minor house; and it was, accordingly, as a burletta that Mr Buckstone's *Dream at Sea* forty years ago made its first appearance upon the stage.

Upon its recent revival at the Adelphi Theatre, however, with a view to the gratification of the playgoers of today, the *Dream at Sea* is properly described as a melodrama; and indeed it is a melodrama of a very uncompromising kind. Whether the disinterment of the work was altogether an expedient proceeding is a question perhaps concerning the manager of the theatre than any one else; but, at least it may be stated that the performance of the *Dream at Sea* is of interest chiefly to theatrical antiquaries. There is something possibly in the nature of melodramas that compels them to grow old with greater rapidity than plays of a more sober character; the time arrives when situations cease to thrill and effects no longer startle as once they did, and over the whole work there descends like a pall or a wet blanket a sense of its infirmity and decay. In some way it would seem as though the spectators had been behind the scenes of these old-fashioned productions, noting the clumsiness of their artifices, the poverty of their cunning, and the thinness of their disguises. And then modern burlesque has made serious havoc of bygone melodrama. There is lack of faith in the audience, who will no longer connive at their own delusion and excitement; while the players are dispirited by the futility of their attempts to conjure with contrivances long since exploded and found out.

Nevertheless the story serving as the foundation of the *Dream at Sea* is not deficient in certain romantic and dramatic qualities. A sailor lover, one Launce Linwood, dreams while at sea—the dream being simply narrated, not exhibited, in the form of a vision—that his mistress, Anne Trevanion, has been in peril of her life. He hastens home—the scene of the story being laid upon the coast of Cornwall—to learn that Anne Trevanion has really been murdered. In her lover's absence it seems Anne has been compelled by her father—one of those imperious parents who have always abounded in the theatre—to accept the suit of his nephew Richard Penderell. A ball has been given in celebration of the forthcoming marriage; Sir Roger de Coverley has been danced, and the healths of the affianced couple have been formally toasted. But one Black Ralph, a wrecker, has intruded upon the festivities in quest of plunder, with the excuse that he aims at providing his family with bread. Suddenly encountering Anne Trevanion, Black Ralph has felled her to the ground. He effects his escape, and seeing that while attacking her he had chanced to wear the cloak of her lover, suspicion falls upon Launce Linwood, who is indeed formally accused of the murder, to which it is supposed he has been prompted by jealousy. Anne Trevanion is buried in the village church on the cliffs; but soon it is made evident that she had been buried alive. Launce Linwood, animated by a desire to contemplate once more the face of his beloved, digs up the body; when lo! she sits up in her coffin, and finally addresses her lover by his Christian name. Of course when this incident is reached, the end of the story is in sight. The true lovers are made happy, and Black Ralph saves trouble by perishing of an exceptional kind of remorse. He frankly avows that in the way of his business as a wrecker, he has knocked many a man on the head without suffering any inconvenience afterwards from that summary mode of dealing with his fellow-creatures; the murder of Anne Trevanion, however—for he believes himself guilty of no less a crime—is something more than even his robust conscience can digest and dispose of, and consequently he expires.

These serious events are intermingled with comic incidents, which have lost somehow the power of moving laughter in any great degree. The usual soubrette is present throughout the play—linked to its interest by the fact that she is the foster-sister of the heroine—and is furnished with a lover, the muffin man of her native village. A third comic character is an overseer and tax-collector, who meets with many misadventures, and incurs much derision from the other *dramatis personae*, but whose humour, generally considered, is certainly of a cheerless kind. The players spare no exertions to give life to the drama, and the Launce Linwood of Mr Fernandez, the Biddy Nutts of Miss Hudspeth, and the Tommy Tinkle of Mr Fawn—a spirited low comedian from the Surrey Theatre—meet with considerable applause. But, on the whole, the *Dream at Sea* must be said to be but an inferior production, feebly written, constructed with little art, and interesting only to those playgoers who care to make acquaintance with a work which enjoyed great favour forty years ago.

DUTTON COOK

XLI
Stratford, 1879

ON THE drenched evening of 23 April 1879, after a day's steady rain, the first Shakespeare Memorial Theatre on the Bancroft meadow at Stratford-upon-Avon opened with *Much Ado About Nothing*. Though, during a life of barely forty-seven years, it became as much of a stock joke as the Albert Memorial, this complicated structure in bright red brick, 'modern Gothic' with plum-cake turrets and a striped sugar-stick tower, probably drew as much affection as any theatre had known. In 1879 metropolitan critics laughed at what seemed to be a wild adventure in the backwoods. Charles Edward Flower, the Stratford man who had presented the site and who headed the subscribers' list, giving much of the £20,000 needed for the theatre, spoke out firmly at a ceremonial Birthday luncheon in the Town Hall: 'They say we are a set of respectable Nobodies. Rather let criticism be given to those great social and literary Somebodies who have done nothing. We shall be ready to go on quietly and patiently with our work, knowing that we do so in a true spirit of love and reverence.'

The principal players in *Much Ado About Nothing* that night were Helen Faucit, who acted for only one performance (Ellen Wallis succeeded her as Beatrice) and Barry Sullivan, the robust tragedian, Birmingham-born, who would appear also as Hamlet and Jaques. The veteran John Ryder spoke the first Shakespearean lines heard in the Memorial Theatre, Leonato's 'I learn in this letter that Don Pedro of Arragon comes this night to Messina.'

Mrs Charles Calvert,* who would play Gertrude in *Hamlet*,

* *Sixty-Eight Years on the Stage*, 1911.

had been surprised, on her arrival at Stratford, when the station-master said to a porter, 'Here, Shakespeare, take charge of this lady's luggage.' ('It came upon me like a shock.') Two days later, just before the Birthday luncheon, Charles Flower, calling for Mrs Calvert, who had spent the morning with his invalid wife, said: 'You'll scarcely believe it, but this is what has kept me. As Miss Faucit is here for only one night, I ventured to have the green-room fitted up for her as a dressing-room, and my wife sent across a few things to make it look pretty. Barry Sullivan after the rehearsal happened to look in and see it. He said, "What's all this?" "Miss Faucit's dressing-room, sir." "Oh then, take my compliments to Mr Flower, and say that unless *my* dressing-room is arranged the same way, I don't appear to-night." And so I had to remain to give orders about some furniture, and you, my dear [to his wife], must send across silver candlesticks, vases of flowers, and a lace pincushion for Mr Barry Sullivan.'

Sir Theodore Martin wrote in his biography, *Helena Faucit, Lady Martin* (1900):

WE AVAILED ourselves of the Easter holidays to escape from the pressure of social engagements in London to our retreat in Wales, where she could give that fresh study to Beatrice, and to the play of which Beatrice is the heroine, which she always gave to every Shakespearean part before appearing in it, however often she had acted it before. [On 21 April] we travelled to Stratford. Next day we visited the Shakespeare House, where the lady custodians presented my wife with a bouquet of Shakespeare's flowers, which are cultivated in the garden of the house. She also visited Anne Hathaway's cottage at Shottery, and spent from 7 to 11 in the evening rehearsing at the theatre. Next day (23 April) she writes:

> The town quite *en fête* to-day—flags flying, bands playing. Went to the theatre for a short time to go over some of the worst bits. Then to the church. Charmed with the monument. Can see so much of the *man* behind it. The profile also tells so much. The profile, especially on the

left, speaks of the grandeur, the full face of the humour and sweetness. There was no seeing it, until we were admitted within the altar rail. The bust looks like a living friend, whom one would wish *never* to part with. There is no thought of death or separation about it.

Alas! the day is wet—as bad as two years back [the Stonelaying *], only not so cold. Everybody has gone to the luncheon at the Town Hall. Poor people! Determined to be gay even in the pouring rain. Cannons firing. In the high up, far, far away planet or orb of light, where Shakespeare must be, can a reflex, a faint murmur, reach him of the little doing in his birthplace today in reverence for and honour of his memory? If it can, his kindly heart would be pleased—would find no fault—would take the will for the deed. Let us try and do likewise. I will not mind how I am put out, or what I have to put up with to-night, in Beatrice . . . Lord Leigh brought me a lovely bouquet all of white flowers from Lady Leigh.

He did more than that. Indeed, but for him there would have been no Beatrice at the theatre that night. It was raining in torrents, and every vehicle in the place was forestalled to carry people to the theatre. We were in despair; but when told how matters stood, Lord Leigh, who could not wait for the play, most kindly said he would somehow find his way home to Stoneleigh Abbey, and accordingly placed his carriage at my wife's disposal for the evening—a courteous solution of what for a time seemed to be an insuperable difficulty.

This was my wife's last performance of Beatrice. She says of it [in *On Some of Shakespeare's Female Characters*, 1885]: 'Every turn of playful humour, every flash of wit, every burst of strong feeling told; and it is a great pleasure to me to think that on that spot and on that occasion I made my last essay to present a living portraiture of the Lady Beatrice.'

THEODORE MARTIN

[Next day, though the Birmingham newspapers praised Helen Faucit, Benedick had little luck. According to one paper, 'Mr

---

* April 23, 1877. At the luncheon, when rain soaked through the tent, and the company had to eat under umbrellas, Tom Taylor (said Helen Faucit in her diary) 'gave a long speech upon the uses the building of which they had just laid the first stone might be put to, and among others (Oh, Spirit of our great Shakespeare!) the amusement of amateur actors'.

Sullivan played the part in a manner that, no doubt, would have been highly acceptable to an East End London audience.' The *Daily Telegraph* was similarly rude about his Hamlet: 'He enacted Hamlet in a fashion accepted by such as disbelieve entirely in the address to the Players: He was vigorously applauded by the citizens of Stratford and their wives and daughters, but when the dramatic school is founded, there will probably be a rule to suppress such fanciful readings as "I know a hawk from a heron—pshaw!"' Even so, Sullivan had the goodwill to reappear in a three weeks' Festival during 1880. His ghost has probably been satisfied with a tribute from Bernard Shaw who wrote: 'I never saw great acting until I saw him.']

XLII

One Night Only

THERE have been single-night West End runs in our time. One was in 1953, when a dramatist who had adapted a play from the French took a taxi to the theatre next morning to find that, externally, at least, all traces of his work ('the unfortunate events of the previous evening') had vanished. Bad luck indeed; but the fate of *Oonagh* (1866), as described by Clement Scott in *The Drama of Yesterday and To-day* (1899) must be hard to match.

Écarté, a comedy in four acts by Lord Newry, was staged at the old Globe Theatre (Newcastle Street, Strand) on 3 December, 1870.

IT IS A very rare occurrence for a play to be acted for 'one night only'. This was however the unhappy fate of the maiden effort years ago of an able young man, always an enthusiast in the cause of the drama, a very brilliant amateur actor, and who has since proved himself to be an expert and clever dramatist. His first dramatic child was, alas! stillborn, or got strangled at its birth: and it gave rise on a Saturday night to one of the most remarkable scenes I have ever witnessed.

The play was called *Écarté*, and it was written, I think, in the interests of the star—Miss 'Nita Nicotina'—who began life in a tobacconist's shop in the Strand, and was the idol of the smart young clerks at Somerset House, many of whom were my intimate friends. They took me behind the scenes of the tobacconist's shop to flirt with the beautiful girl long before she dreamed of going on the stage, in order to gain notoriety as an actress.

A Mr Fairclough, an Australian tragedian, who afterwards played Hamlet, was engaged to support the fair and ambitious star. In the course of the play, which might in other circumstances have been a very good one, there was a picnic scene; and the enthusiast, anxious to be liberal as well as artistic and realistic at the same time, provided a sumptuous repast from Fortnum and Mason in Piccadilly. So good were the Périgord pies, the truffles, the seductive chickens, and the etceteras—particularly the champagne, 'which flowed like water' as the reporters say—that the action of the comedy was considerably delayed, and tried the patience of the Saturday night audience, which has always one eye on the stage and the other on the clock, since to go home unrefreshed must ever be a serious personal inconvenience.

At any rate there have been more first-night 'rows' on Saturday than on any other night of the week. It seemed as if that stage picnic in *Écarté* would never end. The laughter, the jokes, the repartees of the picnic party were no doubt very amusing to the artists, but they were irritatingly inaudible to the audience. Besides, was it not adding insult to injury when the poor occupants of the pit and gallery seats saw their chances of a stirrup-cup on a Saturday night disappearing altogether, while those on the stage were tasting the dainties they could not touch, and drinking the Pommery that would never delight their parched throats?

Unfortunately, unlimited champagne does not agree with the sober art of acting. It is apt to obfuscate the intelligence, and make the actor or actress, as the phrase used to be, 'thick in the clear.' That fate befell poor 'Nita Nicotina,' a remarkably handsome woman, but I fear an indifferent actress. She forgot her words, and in endeavouring to recover them, gave a ghastly and silly grin. This tickled the 'gods' immensely, who in those days used to chaff much more than they do at present. They didn't wait until the end of the play to applaud or 'boo' as they do now, but accompanied the dialogue with a running fire of chaff. Once that spirit had set in seriously, the play was usually doomed. Nothing could stand against it. No human effort could pull the play out of the fire of failure.

The dimmed star got worse and worse. She managed to save

herself through a scene or two, and at last appeared hopelessly dazed and demoralised, in boots of different colour, one green, one red. Whereupon there was a wild yell of derisive laughter, which evidently annoyed the fair actress, who came forward to the footlights and said, in a well-wadded voice, 'Now you stupid fools, when you have done laughing and making idiots of yourselves, I will go on with this (hiccup) beastly play.' This of course was a somewhat serious affront to the poor author.

From that moment the game of *Écarté* was played out. She had trumped her partner's best card. I wrote an account of the play and the scene for the *Observer* that was to appear on Sunday morning, but that settled it. *Écarté* was never acted again, and on Monday the theatre was closed.

Years before, there had occurred a silent and impressive scene of destruction at Her Majesty's Theatre. This was a case when a play was acted for one night only. No, I am wrong, it was not even acted for one night. The real play was never finished, and never will be finished until the crack of doom. Many of us saw the beginning of *Oonagh*, a few of us witnessed its collapse; but how it ought to have ended no human being save the luckless author ever knew. Edmund Falconer, a most excellent Irish comedian, was the most long-winded author that the stage has ever known. His verbiage was excessive and monotonous. He was also about the unluckiest speculator of his time; all his enterprises failed him. Accordingly on November 19, 1866, he took Her Majesty's Theatre—the worst possible place in the world—in order to produce there another Irish play called *Oonagh, or The Lovers of Lisnamona*, founded on two novels, Maria Edgeworth's celebrated story, and Carlton's *Fardourougha the Miser*. Falconer, who was devoted to weird characters, played the Miser, and Fanny Addison, the sister of Carlotta, both daughters of a very excellent old actor, was Oonagh, the heroine.

On this occasion there was no actual disturbance, no one shouted or screamed, but I expect very many enjoyed a peaceful slumber. On! on! on! went the interminable story. Eleven struck. Twelve struck. One a.m. struck. On went the relentless *Oonagh*. The audience adopted the American system. It made no sign, no protest, but gradually, one by one, the most devoted subsided. 'They folded their tents like the Arabs, and silently stole away.' It must have been close on two o'clock in the morning when only a chosen band of critics and Bohemians were left. Among them, as far as I can remember, were dear old Palgrave Simpson, Herman Merivale, Jack Clayton, Lewis Wingfield, a distinguished amateur and the friend of everybody in all the arts, a man of extraordinary versatility, who acted, wrote novels and essays as well as very good and entertaining criticisms in the *Globe* (signed 'Whyte Tighe'), painted huge pictures which never could be exhibited anywhere, and acted as war correspondent for the *Daily Telegraph* at the siege of Paris; Joe Knight, or 'good night' (as he is ever called, because he never goes to bed until cockcrow), and your humble servant.

But no empty house, or chiming of morning clocks or early cock-crows, disturbed the verbosity of the actors, who were heard delivering prosy platitudes, 'all in a row,' at uncanonical hours on Sunday morning. At last the stage carpenters took the law into their own hands: it was a terrible position; they thought of their anxious wives and families at home. There was only one way of stopping this tornado of talk, and the stage hands adopted it. They pulled the carpet deliberately from under the feet of the author and his companions, and down they all went prone on the floor. Then the curtain was rung down. *Oonagh* was played no more. And I suppose it is about the only drama on record that was never finished.

CLEMENT SCOTT

XLIII

An Actor Calls on Tennyson

THE SCENE, described so gravely in *An Actor's Notebooks* (1912), is a Victorian luncheon party in Surrey during January 1885. Frank Archer (Arnold), the narrator (1845–1917), was a serious and capable actor, in his fortieth year. Interested—though he had no influence—in finding a management for Tennyson's *Becket*, which at the time Irving could not afford to undertake, Archer was invited to luncheon at Aldworth House in Surrey. Tennyson then had no intention of dealing with the play. 'If, however, Mr Archer likes to come over to Aldworth some afternoon, we shall be very glad to welcome him, but *not* on business.' In the eighteen-eighties it was a royal command. 'It was not easy for me,' said Archer, 'to realise that I was to meet our great poet face to face'.

On the morning of January 12 Archer found a little open 'pony car' waiting at Haslemere Station. In company with the composer, C. (later Sir Charles) Villiers Stanford, he was driven for three miles into the Surrey hills. On arrival at Aldworth the visitors learned first that Lady Tennyson was indisposed, and then bowed to the poet himself.

A TALL figure, dark, almost swarthy, with a slight stoop and fine eyes, a noble head, with the longish, thin, and straggling hair that can be seen in many of his portraits. The great poet stood before us.

He advanced and shook hands, and we fell into commonplaces and the weather. 'I hope, Lord Tennyson, your health is good', I remarked. 'Pretty well', he replied 'for an old fellow of seventy-six.' He continued, with a little amused conceit in his manners, 'I am an older man, you know, than Gladstone.' Then the conversation was about the great statesman, and his love for felling trees, and about the scenery in the neighbourhood of Aldworth, which the poet was very proud of. His daughter-in-law remarked that it only wanted water to make it perfect, with which he quite agreed. He spoke of the lovely effects of storm visible from those hills sometimes, and added that the largest rainbows he had any experience of he had seen from Aldworth.

During our chat Professor Jowett, the great Greek scholar and Master of Balliol, was announced. A fresh, plump, somewhat florid-looking old gentlemen, to whom I was duly introduced. 'Cherubic', the word that has been used to describe his appearance, was certainly very apt. . . . Francis Turner Palgrave also appeared. He succeeded Principal Shairp as Professor of Poetry at Oxford, but is more generally known, I suppose, by his 'Golden Treasury' series. He had been an intimate friend of Tennyson's for many years.

Luncheon was announced, and we went in; the poet's son and his daughter-in-law taking each end of the table. On Hallam Tennyson's left he sat himself, and I was asked to take the place next to him; the place on my left being occupied by Professor Jowett. We were scarcely seated when I was somewhat embarrassed and surprised by Tennyson turning to me suddenly, and saying 'What's your business?' adding in a grimly humorous way, 'I don't mean what's your business here.' I was certainly unprepared for his query, and it was evident to me that, though he had heard my name, he had not realised who or what I was. 'I am an actor', I replied; 'that is, I am an actor by profession.' 'Are you a critic?' he asked. I said, 'No; no further than any man is who judges of another's work, and says what he thinks.'

There can be little doubt that Tennyson was suspicious and chary in his intercourse with strangers, and he had been so misrepresented, not to say tormented also, by all sorts of people, that one could not help sympathising with him. 'True privacy,' as Lecky remarked, 'became impossible to him.' One or two things at luncheon proved amusing. He passed me an ivory pepper-mill, then, I suppose, something of a novelty, with the query, 'Have you seen this dodge?'

After an interval he said to me, 'How did you come here?' I told him I came up in one of the little sugar-basin-on-wheels sort of cars peculiar to Surrey. 'Why do you call it a sugar-basin?' he asked again in his peculiarly grim way: 'Because it contained so much that was sweet?' This must have been repartee of exceptional politeness. We talked of plays and players. He remembered with delight Macready's Macbeth, though he did not care for his Hamlet. Charles Kemble's Mercutio he admired greatly. He was impressed by his innate and perfect gentlemanliness. Something afterwards evidently recalled *Romeo and Juliet*, for he said he could never make out the meaning of Mercutio's verse, 'an old hare hoar, and an old hare hoar,' etc., etc. Could I explain it? 'I suppose,' I said, 'that the generally accepted idea is right. Either that it is a snatch of some old ballad, or a coarse jingle improvised by Mercutio.' In speaking of *Coriolanus*—there had been talk at the table of the great length of some of Shakespeare's plays—he believed he could play Coriolanus, particularly the passionate scenes. 'But could you,' I said, 'manage the long level passages where a certain restraint and suppression are essential?' He was in doubt how far he would be effective in these. He felt he had the spirit and theory of acting, 'though in practice,' he added, 'my voice would most likely break down in my attempt.' . . . We talked of *Julius Caesar* and the character of Brutus. 'I think, in some respects,' he remarked, 'Brutus is the noblest thing that Shakespeare ever did.' In an allusion to *Hamlet*, he said he believed that if it were produced to-day as an original drama, it would not have much chance of success.

[The conversation turned to Tennyson's old friend, the late Tom Taylor.]

Our talk of his old friend was the occasion for his reverting with some irritation to an attack made upon him in *Punch*. And here I was very much surprised to find how extremely thin-skinned the poet was. That a man of the greatness and in the position of the Laureate should have been sensitive to such things seemed absurd, and such querulousness as he showed it was hard to understand. Truly, as a clever author says, 'the forces which turn fire-mist into stars are not more inscrutable than is human character'. . . .

I asked him if he often went to the theatre. 'Rarely now,' he replied. He thought the last thing he saw was the Rip Van Winkle of Jefferson which he liked extremely. His son corrected him, and said that this was not the last occasion, the last being, I think, a visit to the Lyceum. He inquired of me who 'this Mr Barrett' was. I told him, but did not feel called upon to let him know that I had been in communication with him [i.e. Barrett]. Wilson Barrett at this time was playing Hamlet in London; and evidently Tennyson had heard or read of it, for he remarked, 'I can't understand "a little more than kin, and less than kinn'd" at all.' Chattering on other matters, he told us a story with evident amusement of a letter he had once received from the landlord of some hotel, making a big claim for expenses incurred by his son. Tennyson wrote and told him that his two little boys were at present at school!

When luncheon was over, he said, 'I am going to have a nap, but I shall see you again.' Hallam Tennyson, Villiers Stanford, Palgrave, and myself then went up into his study, some of us to smoke. Jowett did not join us here. His son took me aside, and we chatted about *Becket*. His father was not averse to having it produced, but not immediately. He spoke of *The Promise of May* which had been acted and had resulted in a fiasco. He was of opinion that it had not been judiciously treated. My own view on reading the play was that no acting, stage-management, or alteration could have made it successful with the general public. That it was ever put upon the stage was unfortunate, as it did not in any way increase the Laureate's reputation: particularly as on the first night of its production [at the Globe Theatre, November 11, 1882] an unpleasant disturbance took place in the theatre. . . .

Tennyson now came into the room: 'Ah, I can smell a cigar through the smoke!' he exclaimed. (He was himself an inveterate pipe-smoker.) As I was the culprit, I asked him if he objected to it. 'Not in the least,' he answered; but he declined my offer of a cigar. 'I have tried to sleep, but I can't,' he remarked; 'I never can when I know anybody is waiting for me.' Some one spoke of the splendid light he had in his study, owing to the large windows, and to the sweeping, extensive view into the lovely hollow before the house. 'Yes,' he said, 'the view is very fine. The Duke of Argyll once looked from those windows, and said it gave him the feeling of being up in a balloon.'

Now I had to leave by the four o'clock train in order to reach London in time for my duties at the theatre, and I realised that the opportunity for further talk with the poet was somewhat limited. I offered him what I supposed to be his place—a seat on the sofa or divan by the fire—but he begged me not to disturb myself and took a chair at a small table by my side. Stanford and Palgrave were sitting on the opposite side of the fireplace, but we remained tête-à-tête the whole time. I took the seat to be Tennyson's, because I noticed a book on astronomy or some kindred subject, opened and turned downwards on it, evidently in course of reading. We fell into conversation about *Becket*. He seemed to think it might make a good acting play * and I spoke warmly in admiration of much of it. I remember asking if it had given him serious labour. He said, 'I really don't remember'; but his son had previously led me to suppose that it had done so. I had recently re-read *Harold*, and was able to pay a very honest and hearty tribute to it, mentioning particularly the last scenes in which Stigand, Edith, and Aldwyth are engaged. My commendation was evidently very gratifying to him. On one or two other occasions, after we had talked upon other subjects, he suddenly came out with 'I'm glad you like my *Harold*!' He said that Irving too was pleased with it, and told him that he would produce it. His difficulty was that he could not find an actor for the part of William.

Speaking of Irving as an actor, he continued: 'I did not like him much in *The Cup*, though it was beautifully produced. His Philip in *Queen Mary* I thought very good. I think Irving is only very good in the villains.' He distinctly showed that he was hurt at Irving's neglect in not answering his letters. . . .

He fell into some delightful conversation about Sir Walter Scott. As both author and man he much admired him. He mentioned the fine things in *Old Mortality*—Andrew Fairservice he recalled. He thought very highly of Scott's characterisation. 'I don't admire him much as a poet', he said, 'except "Flodden".' My wife and I had been re-reading *The Heart of Midlothian*, and I alluded to that exquisite touch where Jeannie thought the plaid would please the Duke of Argyll. Tennyson queried, in his peculiarly brusque manner, 'Is your wife Scotch?'

* *Editor's note:* Tennyson did not know how to contrive a drama ('The mechanical details necessary for the modern stage'), and he left it to his actors to make something of the carefully burnished verse.

'Oh, no,' I said, 'but she can, I hope, appreciate the beauty of a Scotch story.'

From fiction we returned to the drama. Speaking of dramatic construction, he said: 'Good acting plays don't read well to me always,' which I tried to explain by telling him what was so often between the lines—that which was, in fact, supplied by the actor. 'Yes,' he said, 'but the old dramatist supplied literary work *and* good plot.' I reminded him that after all we could not boast of many great plays in every way. Often, I remarked, the literary qualities of a play were slight, but if it showed real heart, and elements that, when interpreted, touched the people worthily, it was not to be thought poorly of. 'I have a low opinion generally of the popular taste,' he said.

Talking of adaptation, I praised the skill of Tom Taylor, especially mentioning that capital little play from Madame de Girardin's *Une Femme qui deteste son Mari*, called *A Sheep in Wolf's Clothing*. He did not know it. He told me, however, that he thought at one time of writing a play on the subject of 'Monmouth'. The conversation veered round to French plays. 'Shakespeare's honest coarseness,' he said, 'we can endure, but in some of the modern French plays the very pivot and central idea is immoral.' I spoke to him of Westland Marston. 'I know his name well,' he replied, 'but not his work.' I alluded to the beauty and skill of two of his plays, *Marie de Méranie* and *Strathmore*, mentioning at the same time what an admirer the dramatist was of his poetry. There was in *The National Magazine*, in the year 1857, an interesting critique by Marston on the poetry of Tennyson. The name of Marston possibly suggested his Elizabethan namesake, for he expressed warm admiration for some of the work of Marlowe and Webster. In reverting to criticism—our talk, it will be noticed, was very disjointed—he alluded to two distinct views that had been taken of Rosamund in *Becket*—one opinion was that it was all that was bad, the other in praise of its great beauty. He confessed he liked his own Rosamund.

The poet told me that he still believed in *The Promise of May*, which he had re-read since its appearance on the stage. My impression is that he did not see it acted himself, but I am not sure of this. At any rate, he had not a high opinion of modern criticism. Once in the course of our conversation, he repeated some lines from his own poetry, with the phrase, 'To quote myself,' but, somewhat after the manner of the prim man in *Pickwick*, I did not catch what it was, and have forgotten the subject it was applied to. Our talk had so engrossed us that I had not regarded the time, and found on looking at my watch that I must move at once if I was to catch my train for London.

He rose and hurried downstairs. In spite of my remonstrances, he would put on his hat—the broad-brimmed felt so well known in the pictures of him—and come outside, where the pony carriage was waiting, to see me off, though there was a cold north wind blowing, with driving sleet. He shook me warmly by the hand, and said how pleased he should be if I could at some time come down to Aldworth and spend a few days with him. 'Thank you, Lord Tennyson, for your kindness,' I replied, 'I fear I should be only too liable to abuse it.' 'What do you say?' he asked. 'You would be abusive? I couldn't stand that.' I corrected him, and said if we did quarrel and fight it out on the lawn, I had no doubt he could hold his own. He laughed, and I jumped into the carriage. Then he and his friends—who had joined him— waved their hats as we drove away. I say 'we', as I found I had for companion Dr Dabbs, Lady Tennyson's adviser from the Isle of Wight. His name, I remember, had been a source of some amusement to us at luncheon. He was very pleasant. . . .

Thus ended my visit to Lord Tennyson. I never saw him again. After his cordial invitation I was often tempted to take advantage of it, but circumstances were too strong for me. One last small incident I may mention. A day or two after my visit I sent the poet a copy of Westland Marston's works. I was gratified to get a line from him in his own handwriting, which, if there be any truth in the adage, must be 'the soul of wit':

Aldworth, Haslemere, Surrey
January 18, 1885.

Dear Mr Archer.—Accept my thanks for your kind present of Marston's plays and
     Believe me,
      Yours very truly,
       TENNYSON

FRANK ARCHER

XLIV
'Careless, Immoral Authors'

CLEMENT SCOTT ended *The Drama of Yesterday and To-day* (1899) with a word on the Censorship. He would be a sadly startled ghost in the theatre of the nineteen-sixties.

THE SECOND Examiner of Stage Plays, George Colman the younger, who died in 1836, had peculiar views as to profanity or irreverence as expressed in dramatic dialogue. He considered the application of the phrase 'My angel' to a beautiful woman or an adored wife to be 'profane', and cut out the unholy words accordingly. When he was asked why he cut out 'angel' as applied to a woman, he replied, 'Because it is a woman, I grant, but it is a celestial woman. It is an allusion to the scriptural angels, which are celestial bodies.'

The words 'Oh, Lud!' or 'Oh, La!' he deemed irreverent and out they went, in defiance of the old dramatists. When asked why he cut out 'Damme!' which he had used so often in his own plays, he replied, 'At that time I was a careless, immoral author. I am now the Examiner of Plays. I did my business as an author at that time, and I do my business as an Examiner now.'

But, for all that, George Colman the younger was keen about his fees, and on one occasion was very anxious to licence an oratorio. It was decided by the authorities that the Bible did not require the Lord Chamberlain's licence.

William Bodham Donne [the fifth Examiner, who succeeded John Mitchell Kemble in 1857] was a learned antiquary and scholar to whom clung some of the traditions of the prudish George Colman school. One day, so it is said, they found his children in his study prone on the floor, all studying plays for licence.

'Father, father!' shouts one, 'Here is "God" again.'
'Cut out "God," my dear, and substitute "Heaven."'

A crucifix was prohibited on the stage in a play called *The Actress of Padua*, licensed for production at the Haymarket in 1855; but at the same theatre, in *A Man's Shadow*, produced by Beerbohm Tree in 1889, a crucifix was permitted in a French Law Court over the judge's head, as realistically represented.

Camille, one of the early versions of *La Dame aux Camélias*, by the younger Dumas, was refused a licence for Drury Lane on March 23, 1855. When John Oxenford wrote *Daddy Hardacre* * for Robson at the Olympic in 1857, he was instructed to alter 'O God!' to 'O Heaven!', and to omit 'O Lord!' everywhere. In a play called *The Amazon's Oath*, October 25, 1858, the words, 'and as no more worthy to be called your son', were ordered to be omitted, as contained in the Biblical version of the story of the prodigal son.

Phèdre has been played in this country both by Rachel and Sarah Bernhardt without offence as a great classic; but, during the Censorship of Charles Kemble's son, a licence was refused for a play called *Myrrha*, in which Madame Ristori had to express the Greek mythological love of the heroine for her father—in fact, *Phèdre* and *The Cenci* reversed.

CLEMENT SCOTT

---

* *Editor's note: Daddy Hardacre* was by John Palgrave Simpson (from *La Fille de l'Avare*). In the following year, 1858, Frederick Robson appeared in *The Porter's Knot*, adapted by John Oxenford from *Les Crochets de Père Martin*.

LAST WORDS

So we come back to South Cornwall in the eighteen-seventies, and to the legendary pomping folk. It is a carpet-bag phrase for all between Mr Irving (once Johnnie Brodribb of Halsetown)—a name that, though it may be blazing in London, means little by Gillan Creek—and nearer home, indeed in the very midst, a covey of unprincipled and stubborn girls, set to destroy themselves and their neighbours. Had not William Prynne, the Puritan, written long before: 'Every Lord's Day at night the devils did use to meet in hell, and there did recreate and exhilarate themselves with stage plays'? And now: 'Doan' 'ee do it!' said an old man when he heard that my mother and two of her sisters, 'they James girls' from Boden, were to appear in a missionary tableau. Hope abandoned, the pomping folk must lie with the deadly worm, 'a-wruggling' in the dust.

That was ninety years ago. The village, in its lost world, had not yet recognized what a writer for the pomping folk called once, and briefly, 'the humours and tricks of that old bald cheater, Time'.

J. C. T.